MW00813287

THE ARCHITECT'S GUIDE TO

Small Firm
Management

THE ARCHITECT'S GUIDE TO
Small Firm Management

RENA M. KLEIN, FAIA

 THE AMERICAN INSTITUTE OF ARCHITECTS

WILEY

John Wiley & Sons, Inc.

This book is printed on acid-free paper. ∞

Copyright © 2010 by John Wiley & Sons, Inc. All rights reserved

Published by John Wiley & Sons, Inc., Hoboken, New Jersey
Published simultaneously in Canada

No part of this publication may be reproduced, stored in a retrieval system, or transmitted in any form or by any means, electronic, mechanical, photocopying, recording, scanning, or otherwise, except as permitted under Section 107 or 108 of the 1976 United States Copyright Act, without either the prior written permission of the Publisher, or authorization through payment of the appropriate per-copy fee to the Copyright Clearance Center, 222 Rosewood Drive, Danvers, MA 01923, (978) 750-8400, fax (978) 646-8600, or on the web at www.copyright.com. Requests to the Publisher for permission should be addressed to the Permissions Department, John Wiley & Sons, Inc., 111 River Street, Hoboken, NJ 07030, (201) 748-6011, fax (201) 748-6008.

Limit of Liability/Disclaimer of Warranty: While the publisher and the author have used their best efforts in preparing this book, they make no representations or warranties with respect to the accuracy or completeness of the contents of this book and specifically disclaim any implied warranties of merchantability or fitness for a particular purpose. No warranty may be created or extended by sales representatives or written sales materials. The advice and strategies contained herein may not be suitable for your situation. You should consult with a professional where appropriate. Neither the publisher nor the author shall be liable for any loss of profit or any other commercial damages, including but not limited to special, incidental, consequential, or other damages.

For general information about our other products and services, please contact our Customer Care Department within the United States at (800) 762-2974, outside the United States at (317) 572-3993 or fax (317) 572-4002.

Wiley also publishes its books in a variety of electronic formats. Some content that appears in print may not be available in electronic books. For more information about Wiley products, visit our web site at www.wiley.com.

Library of Congress Cataloging-in-Publication Data:

Klein, Rena M.
　The architect's guide to small firm management / by Rena M. Klein.
　　　p. cm.
　Includes index.
　ISBN 978-0-470-46648-3 (cloth : alk. paper)
　1. Architectural practice–United States–Management.　I. Title.
　NA1996.K55　2010
　720.68–dc22　　　　　　　　　　　　　　　　　　2009041799

Printed in the United States of America

V10010234_051319

CONTENTS

ACKNOWLEDGMENTS

I am deeply grateful to all those who assisted and supported me in writing this book. I am indebted in particular to those who offered their insights as peer reviewers of the text and illustrations: Colette Wallace, Assoc. AIA, Robert Smith, AIA, Alan Ford, AIA, and Richard Hobbs, FAIA. Their comments improved the contents and meaning of this book beyond measure.

I would also like to thank the many practitioners who were interviewed and observed in the course of this book's creation. I am grateful for knowledge gained through working with my consulting clients and with various groups of colleagues in the AIA. In addition, I would like to acknowledge the contributions of the wider community of architectural practice. In many ways, this book was co-created by all the architects and designers with whom I've had conversations and shared stories over the years, especially my fellow small firm practitioners.

This book would not have been possible without the encouragement and mentoring of Barbara Nadel, FAIA, who taught me a great deal about writing. I also appreciate the help given by Linda Reeder, AIA, significant in the initial phases of this work. The opportunity to write for AIA national's online knowledge resource and to work with Richard Hayes, PhD, AIA, was also meaningful in the development of this book.

I would also like to thank John Czarnecki, Assoc. AIA, Sadie Abuhoff, Kerstin Nasdeo, Nancy Cintron, and all others at John Wiley & Sons Publishing who contributed to this project. I appreciate their professionalism and assistance throughout this entire effort.

I would be remiss if I did not express my heartfelt appreciation for the ongoing personal and professional support given to me by Marga Rose Hancock, Hon. AIA. And, I am now and will always be full of gratitude for the love and support of my partner, Sheila Fox, in this project and in countless other ways. Thank you all.

INTRODUCTION

I know what it's like to run a small design firm. I've been there in the trenches, running my architectural firm in Seattle for over 20 years. I understand the excitement and the satisfaction that can be had from serving clients and the community through excellent design solutions. I also understand the frustration that can result from low compensation, long hours, rushing from deadline to deadline, and coping with endless work load fluctuations.

In 1994, after running my firm for 12 years, I decided to go to graduate school to study management. I was not feeling content in my practice and I wanted to understand how the architectural workplace could be improved, and how small firm practitioners, including myself, might become more satisfied in our work. And on a more practical note, I wanted to acquire the tools to make running my firm less stressful and more profitable.

After my graduation, I was inspired to share my newly acquired knowledge with other small firm practitioners. I began to teach through the AIA, at local, regional, and national venues. I also began to deepen my knowledge through an emerging consulting practice, helping leaders of other small firms gain more satisfaction and profitability at their firms. Since 2003, my primary professional focus has been consulting with owners of small design firms, writing about design firm practice, and teaching about management to both practitioners and students of architecture and design.

Call me naïve, but when I started my graduate education, I was amazed to discover that there was actually a discipline of management, with a history, a theoretical basis, and a body of knowledge. I also discovered the discipline of organizational design and development. I began to understand that it was possible to design organizations with the same basic processes that we use to design buildings. I realized that my design colleagues could benefit greatly by learning that the same holistic thinking required to design a building could be applied to developing and managing a firm.

Underlying all business challenges for design firms is the reality that we operate within a milieu of unpredictability. The day-to-day demands caused by this unpredictable environment can make it difficult for firm owners to reach their professional goals, such as acquiring more interesting projects, or growing their firms. The intention of this book is to help entrepreneurial architects and designers develop their firms into flourishing and stable businesses that are also reflective of their values and personal definitions of success.

Definitions of "small firm" vary in our thinking and in the literature on the subject. For the purposes of this book, a small firm is defined loosely as a firm with less than twenty people. A word about the case studies included in this book. The reader will notice that there are two kinds of case studies cited: those that are anonymous (fictitious initials are used); and those that are attributed to particular practitioners and used with their permission. Of the stories that are anonymous, most are composite or typical experiences and are not based on material from a specific practitioner, despite any accidental resemblance that may occur.

This book also includes stories of very small firms, of couples who own a design firm together, and of solo practitioners. These types of firms are numerous, but their stories are seldom told and the knowledge they acquire often is not widely circulated. Gathering and spreading some of the wisdom of small firm practitioners is another purpose of this book.

While there are many books on practice management that outline the proper ways to manage a design firm, most approach the subject in a reductionist manner and many completely ignore the experience of small firm practitioners. Topics are separated into functional silos such as operations, marketing, human resource, or finance. This can be helpful for specific business problems and there are chapters in this book that focus on individual business competencies such as finance and leadership.

However, this book approaches small firm practice as a whole system experience. All of the functional silos merge when small firm owners do everything from writing proposals to sweeping the floor. Decisions are more likely to be made through conversation and intuition than through the use of analytical tools and best practices. Like a complex design problem, everything in a small firm is closely connected and the effects of any action can ripple quickly through the entire system.

Some of the material in this book is quite theoretical. But as stated by social psychology pioneer Kurt Lewin, a name well known in management history, "There's nothing as practical as a good theory." I think most architects and designers would agree. Along with theory, there are also many tools, examples, and case studies in the book intended to increase the reader skill in managing and strategically developing a successful design firm. I bring my years of experience as an entrepreneurial architect, my academic studies and research, my work as a consultant, and my common-sense approach to the writing of this book. My hope is that reading this book will assist my fellow small firm architects and designers in meeting the challenge of "making chaos work for you."

THE ARCHITECT'S GUIDE TO

Small Firm
Management

PART I

MANAGING IN AN UNPREDICTABLE ENVIRONMENT

CHAPTER 1

BRINGING ORDER OUT OF CHAOS

Managing a small design firm can be like running a three-ring circus. Anything can happen at any time. The action is unrelenting, demanding, and unpredictable. To keep it all in motion, many small firm owners work evenings and weekends on a regular basis. It is not unusual for these firm principals to spend their days "fire-fighting," or scrambling to take advantage of a sudden opportunity.

Take the case of BB Architects. The principal there usually works 60 to 70 hours a week. Often he is in his office until eight or nine at night, he regularly works on weekends, and when he does go home, he takes work with him. He would like to spend more time with his friends and family, but the demands of his six-person practice seem to make that nearly impossible. For example, last week one of his project architects was out sick, and there was no one else but the principal to do the necessary work. At the same time—in addition to the usual work load—a great job opportunity arose which required that a quick proposal be written. This week, a project in construction is demanding immediate attention, the bookkeeper quit, and a major deadline looms. The principal likes his work and is stimulated by the pressure and variety, but feels vaguely like he's on a treadmill, never advancing, even falling a little more behind each day. Often he's just tired, and wonders how long he can go on this way.

Many principals in firms with fewer than 20 on staff will describe their work life this way. The work can be incessant and often challenging. Yet, most small firm principals are stimulated by the pressure and enjoy the autonomy, the control, and the opportunity for design expression. Nevertheless, there is often an underlying feeling of dissatisfaction and apprehension, working hard, but never sure what the future will bring. Constantly coping with day-to-day demands of projects, contractors, clients, and staff, while also running a business, can take its toll.

PROFIT AND SATISFACTION

Like the design of a custom home, the development of a small design practice presents the opportunity to create a firm that truly reflects the tendencies and proclivities of its owners. The organization doesn't have to be conventional or rigid, but it could be if that was the nature of its leadership. Big firms are like big buildings—they need to be more formal and have well-defined structure to make them function. There's less opportunity for personal choice and personal expression. Small firms are often able to maximize flexibility and creativity as long as they don't get bogged down in a chaotic atmosphere, lacking organizational structures that foster effectiveness.

It seems almost self-evident that the skills firm leaders apply to their work as design professionals can be used to plan the development of their firms. The discipline of organizational design was derived from an understanding that it is possible to design organizations with processes similar to those used to design the built environment. Designing a firm means considering financial goals, purpose, size, optimal structure, and the best possible integration between the social systems and the technical systems of production.

Like all design processes, organizational design requires that design criteria be established. The personality, competencies, interests, proclivities, and aversions of the principals will be the primary source of these design criteria in small firms. External factors such as location, markets, and availability of skilled staff may also play a significant role, perhaps as design constraints. Of the criteria determined by the principals, the most important of these is how success and satisfaction in their work is defined. How important is financial success? How much money is enough? How important is name recognition and design awards? Does success include "doing good" for the local community? Does it include having a happy and cared for staff? How important is fun?

Naturally, satisfaction varies among design professionals and usually includes fair compensation, although that is often near the bottom of the list. Anecdotal evidence shows that many small design firm leaders derive the most satisfaction from working effectively with clients, consultants, and staff to deliver excellent projects. Most enjoy their freedom and the control of their work environment. Few enjoy the business aspects of running their firm and many are challenged by the frequent unexpected occurrences and never-ending demands. Figure 1.1 illustrates the interrelationship between profit and satisfaction in small design firm practice.

Again, based on anecdotal evidence, it is fair to say that in most architecture schools, students are led to believe their careers will reside in Quadrant 4—highly satisfied, but poorly compensated. Not to imply that this is always bad. There are noble organizations and design professionals who manifest this way of working

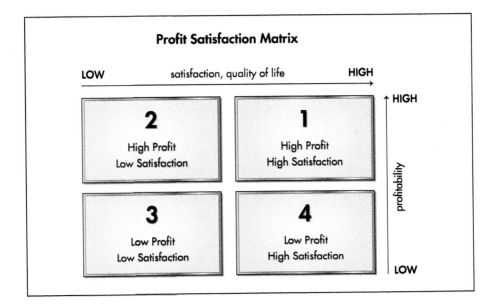

Figure 1.1   Small firm owners experience varying levels of profitability and satisfaction.

without complaint, deriving significant satisfaction without the need for big paychecks. Nevertheless, there are many small design firm owners who undervalue themselves in the marketplace because of this low-pay expectation.

Unfortunately, there are also many design professionals who reside in Quadrant 3, not enjoying their work and not making much money either. This situation is usually a symptom of poor management and perhaps, lack of self-aware leadership—principals (and solo practitioners) who do not "walk their talk." And, since much of the work architects and designers must do is tedious and routine, it is easy to understand how the work can become unsatisfying. Clearly practicing in Quadrant 3 is not sustainable and action plans for change should be considered.

Quadrant 2 isn't much better. Leaders of firms in this quadrant are making good money but are still dissatisfied. Often these are skilled practitioners who are bored with work that once was interesting but now has become quite ordinary. These firm owners often create successful but somehow limited practices. Another common manifestation of Quadrant 2 are practitioners who lack a work-life balance. Many practitioners give up quality of life in order to make more money. This is as equally unsustainable as Quadrant 3, although it may be harder to recognize.

Most design professionals hope to reside in Quadrant 1—highly satisfied and well compensated. Many accomplish this by staying true to their interests, talents, and passions while acquiring knowledge that is highly valued in the marketplace. Firms that stay grounded in their values and vision as they grow, and create a culture of learning, have a better chance of succeeding in both satisfaction and compensation.

Organizational design is the means through which small firm leaders can chart a course to Quadrant 1. While the core competencies and dispositions of firm leaders are clearly the primary design criteria, the business model of a design firm is also significant. Being intentional about a business model, and understanding its staffing and managerial implications, is an essential aspect of bringing order out of chaos in small design firm practice.

DESIGN FIRM BUSINESS MODELS

In general, a business model is a plan that articulates what business is being conducted and how the business will make money. Well-known consultant David Meister[1] has identified three business models that are common in professional service firms. Each of these business models can yield growth and profitability, assuming that they are staffed and managed appropriately.

Design Firm Business Models

Efficiency
- We can do it better, faster, cheaper.
- We do projects that are not complex and have many repeatable elements.
- We employ more junior and technical staff.

Experienced
- We know what we are doing.
- We can do unique, complex projects by applying our accrued knowledge.
- We employ a mixed and balanced staff.

Expertise
- We have special knowledge or talent.
- We serve as expert consultants or are design stars.
- We employ mostly highly experienced staff.

Efficiency-Based Firms

The first of these models is known as "Efficiency," illustrated in Figure 1.2. It describes firms that are focused on fast and less expensive project delivery. These firms often specialize in one project type or a narrow range of services and tend to serve clients that are looking for standard solutions and quick turnarounds. For example, a small architectural firm that serves residential developers might operate effectively within this efficiency model.

Because efficiency firms do projects with a significant amount of routine work, they can be staffed with a large percentage of junior or technical workers. With

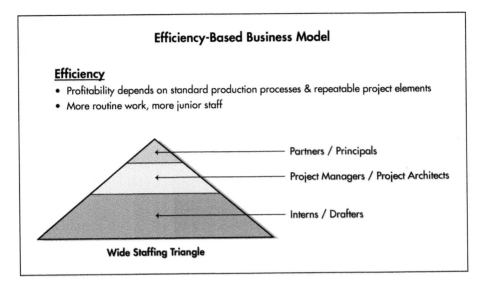

Figure 1.2 Efficiency-based firms rely on repeatable processes.

repeatable elements and standard processes, project delivery can be streamlined. Principals at the top acquire jobs and a small number of well-paid senior staff can organize the work and deal with the nonroutine aspects of the jobs. Profitability is dependent on volume and productivity and is relatively easy to obtain once systems are in place. Because there is more routing work and junior staff, the management style in efficiency firms is likely to be more directive and control based. Sustainable success in these firms requires continuous improvement of work processes and staying current with technology and trends.

CASE STUDY OF AN EFFICIENCY-BASED PRACTICE: SCHACHNE ARCHITECTS & BUILDERS

Stan and Donna Schachne of Schachne Architects & Builders in South Florida run a design-build firm specializing in residential remodeling, new homes, and light commercial projects. They are typical of a large number of small firms that base their practice on the efficiency model. Although the projects often are not routine, they are similar enough that it is possible to apply routine processes to their delivery.

For example, the Schachnes have developed a project delivery process that is repeatable with each new client. Based on the efficiency their process offers, the Schachnes can be unambiguous with their clients about what to expect. This process is clearly outlined on their website for potential clients to review before calling for an initial consultation.

Educated as an interior designer, Donna is integrally involved during all phases of the design. "She works well with our clients, especially the women, and provides a high level of customized service," according to Stan, a licensed architect and AIA member. The couple typically works together on the schematic design for a project. Once the design concept and budget are approved by the client, Stan and Donna continue to collaborate on interior specifications and preparation of the construction documents. In keeping with the need for an efficiency practice to stay current with project delivery technology, the firm converted to Autodesk® Revit® in 2008 by hiring an expert user to teach Stan. Now, all the efficacy of 3-D modeling can be applied to the delivery of relatively noncomplex residential projects.

Soon after starting their business as a traditional design firm, Stan and Donna recognized the opportunity to offer general contracting services along with design. As explained by Stan: "It seems that in the South Florida market, people just aren't into design. The residential market is mostly developer driven. We found that to design a small addition, we couldn't charge more than a few thousand dollars, yet the construction cost might be over $200,000. So I thought, 'Why can't I be the contractor?'" The construction part of the business now earns most of the firm's revenue.

As a result, Stan and Donna will often offer their design services as a loss leader, allowing them to demonstrate their competence and gain client trust before a large financial commitment is required. They see their design skills and their integrated approach as a competitive advantage in their market. Through the use of trusted subcontractors under Stan's management, the firm is able to predict and control construction costs, and deliver a high-quality product to their clients. According to Stan, "We prefer doing small jobs because we find that we make more money. Small jobs are easier to control and involve less risk."

Schachne Architects & Builders are a successful efficiency-based firm because they have specialized in noncomplex projects and have honed their project delivery processes to be effective and repeatable. They stay current with technology and trends which enables them to make money through high productivity (many small jobs) rather than high margins.

Experience-Based Firms

When asked, most small firm leaders will describe their firms as operating within the second business model, experienced-based, and most are right, to a greater

Experienced-Based Business Model

Experienced

- Profitability depends on well-managed projects and skillful use of staff resources
- Mixture of tasks and staffing levels

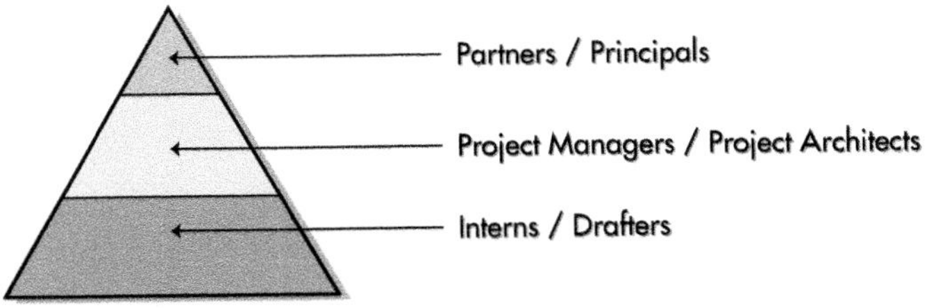

Partners / Principals

Project Managers / Project Architects

Interns / Drafters

Balanced Staffing Triangle

Figure 1.3   Experience-based firms rely on skillful use of staff resources.

or lesser extent. In contrast with efficiency-based firms who have deep experience but engage in routine projects, true experience-based firms are practiced at solving nonroutine and complex design problems. Their "experience" may be in a certain project type, such as public schools or museums, but their core competence is the ability to successfully organize and deliver significant and complicated projects. Experience-based firms, illustrated in Figure 1.3, are also adept at creating and acquiring new knowledge while solving complex problems.

Experience-based firms need a staff that is balanced in terms of professional capabilities. The management challenge for this type of firm is to match the project task to the "pay grade." Much of a design fee can be wasted if highly paid staff members perform work that could be done by someone less experienced with a lower salary. Studies show that up to half of the tasks that managers (or principals) do could be performed equally well by someone who is paid less. Once the up-front work of mentoring and transferring knowledge is complete, time is freed for the senior staff to do the tasks that only they can do, and opportunity for growth and learning is given to others. This is known as "delegating down" and is often an effective strategy to improve profitability for experience-based firms.

Profitability in these kinds of firms depends on proper staffing, excellence in people and project management, and staying current with trends in design and building science. Experience-based firms are usually both design and service oriented.

CASE STUDY OF AN EXPERIENCE-BASED PRACTICE: XCHANGE ARCHITECTS

Although Derrick Choi's small firm is a startup, it can still be described as an experience-based practice. Educated at Columbia University and Harvard Graduate School of Design, Derrick began his career in a large firm where he soon became involved in airport projects. He went on to become a project manager for aviation design consultants before opening his practice in Brookline, Massachusetts, in 2008. While still at the beginning of his career, Derrick has had significant experience and involvement in complex design projects.

As described on the website of his firm, XChange Architects, Derrick Choi, AIA, LEED-AP, "brings nearly a decade of experience in infrastructure and transportation planning, design and construction. He has been involved in the planning and design of over 20 airports and in 6 countries . . . he is familiar with both managing complex projects of various scales and with navigating through the public and private process." This capacity to manage complex projects is the hallmark of an experience-based firm. While many such firms have a project type focus, such as transportation and infrastructure, these firms have the capacity to apply their experience to a wide range of complex problems.

Like many leaders of experience-based firms, Derrick developed numerous personal contacts during his employment with other organizations. These contacts have generated major assignments for his fledgling firm. Working internationally and in the United States, Derrick continues to be involved in the design and management of complex infrastructure developments, as well as smaller-scale, urban design and architecture projects in the Boston area.

At the time of this writing, XChange Architects is a firm of one. Nevertheless, Derrick is supported by a number of "collaborators," as he calls them, and also has in place strategic alliances with other firms. This enables a flexible and nimble approach to staffing production capacity. Leveraging his experience to create his firm, Derrick is positioned to broaden his knowledge and build a larger firm, or perhaps take the route of deepening/narrowing his knowledge to become a small expertise-based firm.

Expertise-Based Firms

Expertise-based firms, illustrated in Figure 1.4, have service offerings that rest upon deep knowledge and/or exceptional talent. These firms include those headed by

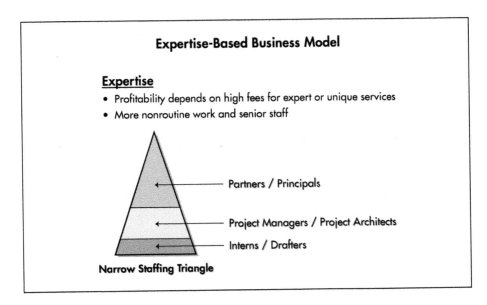

Figure 1.4 Expertise-based firms rely on the principals' deep and specialized knowledge.

"starchitects" with their unique style and abilities. More commonly, expertise firms are specialists in a narrow band of professional knowledge, such as acoustic design or commercial kitchen design.

Expertise-based firms tend to be top-heavy, with a high percentage of very experienced and skilled partners or principals. Often these firms are focused on cutting-edge and innovative applications of their knowledge. Since most of the work is nonroutine and complex, management style is likely to be supportive and democratic. Few middle level and junior staff are needed to complete the work. One- or two-person firms can be very successful using this model since profitability often depends on high hourly rates for services.

CASE STUDY OF AN EXPERTISE-BASED PRACTICE: STUDIO PACIFICA

Karen Braitmayer, FAIA, of Studio Pacifica in Seattle, Washington, provides an exemplary model of an expertise practice. As a lifelong wheelchair user and a licensed architect, she has leveraged her professional training and personal experience into an expertise that serves both her clients and the general public. Karen recounts how she naturally became an informal expert on accessibility early in her career but was reluctant, as a young architect, to define herself solely in this way. By 1993, when she started her firm, she had forged a meaningful identity as a disabled person and had become part of an emerging community. Before long Karen was a passionate advocate for accessibility and universal design.

As an activist and dedicated design professional, Karen became involved in numerous volunteer activities relating to accessibility codes and public policy. These include the Washington State Legislative Building Accessibility Advisory Committee, WSBCC Barrier-Free Technical Advisory Group, and many other advisory committees including those established to give input into the design of public projects, such as Sea-Tac Airport and Safeco Field. According to her website, "[Karen] continues to be a key resource for federal, state and local government officials, architects and disability rights advocates across the country. Since 1989 she has participated in the development of codes and standards to ensure that the State Accessibility Code reflects the needs of the citizens of Washington."

These volunteer activities, while not intended as marketing, have helped Karen grow her practice. She has had the opportunity to meet others who share her passion and has been able to gain expanded knowledge and considerable influence. These activities, along with speaking engagements, involvement with professional organizations, and her personal experience have helped to establish Karen as an undisputed expert in her field. This results in inquiries that she describes as "coming from out of nowhere— referred from someone who knows someone who served on a committee with me."

Like all design professionals who maintain expertise-based firms, Karen works hard at staying "ahead of the curve" in terms of her professional knowledge. She says that her consulting work forces her to stay involved in the development of construction documents and the application of codes, some of which she has helped to write. Karen is in touch with a large community of friends and colleagues in accessibility and universal design with whom she can discuss any issue that arises. And, with humility, she says, "I take every educational offering about accessibility that I can get myself to. People sometimes wonder at seeing me there, thinking the information would be too basic for me, but I find that there is always something new to learn."

As a business model, expertise-based firms are likely to operate within a niche and hold specialized knowledge within this narrow arena. Karen believes that a specialization "helps firms stand out in a crowd" and is a good strategy for any type of firm. In contrast with experience-based firms, which are usually generalists capable of handling any complex project, expertise-based firms are usually specialists that handle complex, yet narrow problems.

ANY PROJECT THAT COMES THROUGH THE DOOR

Some small design firm leaders will have a difficult time recognizing their firm in any of the three models presented thus far. They have built their firms on accepting all comers and often prosper from the generalized knowledge they have acquired. The downside of this strategy is that it may limit the depth of professional knowledge acquired over time, leading to fewer opportunities for complex projects. Firms that accept "any project that comes through the door" can become unfocused and spread thin.

Naturally, the core competencies, personal connections, and interests of firm leaders will attract certain clients and projects even if there is no intentionality. At some point in the firm's life, especially if growth is a goal, a more intentional approach to the firm's business model will be required. Figure 1.5 illustrates how the business models are formed by the interrelationship between a firm's level of specialization and its capacity to deliver complex projects.

While Figure 1.5 may imply that business models are static, nothing could be further from the truth. They often change as a firm matures and moves through its lifecycle, beginning with an entrepreneurial period. Firms may begin their lives as efficiency-based firms, gaining market share by offering lower cost services. Over time they may grow to be highly experienced and capable of delivering complex projects, or even develop a deep expertise that is highly valued. Conversely, firms might begin as innovators, experts in new technology or approach, like the early adopters of sustainable design in the 1960s and 1970s. Over time they may find

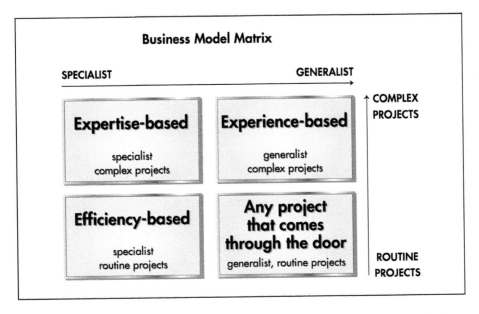

Figure 1.5 Business models for design firms relate to the level of project complexity and specialized knowledge required.

that others share their expertise and unless they stay ahead of the curve, firms such as these may become experience-based or even efficiency-based.

Once a firm's business model is understood, firm growth and/or sustainable stability become more possible. However, many small firm owners with clear vision and understanding of their business model still fail to create adequate levels of satisfaction and profitability. They become stuck in operational cycles and personal dynamics that seem to self-sabotage efforts to succeed. Until these underlying patterns are understood, goals and visions may be difficult to actualize.

One tool or group of tools for understanding underlying patterns and existing organizational interrelationships is known as "systems thinking." Systems thinking prevents looking at a problem in isolation and requires consideration of the whole context a problem inhabits. Systems thinking teaches that a symptomatic problem is likely to have a complex multitude of origins; not simply sourced from linear cause and effect. Systems thinking also enables organizational patterns to be diagrammed in a way that illustrates the interrelationships between the multiple causative factors of current situations. Since the 1980s, diagrams have been developed, known as systems archetypes,[2] that illustrate common patterns of organizational behavior.

SMALL FIRM ARCHETYPES

By applying systems thinking, it is possible to diagram common organizational patterns that frequently lead to difficult circumstances in design firms. Three systems archetypes relevant to small firms are presented here. Many small firm leaders may recognize their own firms in the diagrams of the situations described. In the following chapters, each one of these will be explored individually for strategies that neutralize and reverse the destructive patterns. The first is called "Everyone Is Dissatisfied," illustrating a situation where both the partners and the staff feel overworked and underappreciated (Figure 1.6). The second archetype, "Administrative Breakdown," illustrates what can happen when there is underinvestment in administrative processes that causes them to remain ineffective and unimproved over time (Figure 1.7).

The third archetype is titled "Unintentional Enmity" and was adapted from a systems archetype developed by Jennifer Kemeny.[3] This archetype illustrates a situation where partners become inadvertent adversaries, despite the obvious benefits they each receive from their partnership. According to Kemeny, this archetype applies to "teams working across functions, joint-ventures between organizations, union-management battles, suppliers and manufacturers, family disputes, and even civil wars."[4] Clearly, this archetype can also apply to partners running a small design firm together (Figure 1.8).

Archetype One: Everyone Is Dissatisfied

This archetype, illustrated in Figure 1.6, describes a situation where firm leaders are feeling stretched, pressured, and unsatisfied. Although the leaders are often unaware of it, in these firms it is likely that the staff is feeling similarly. Other symptoms

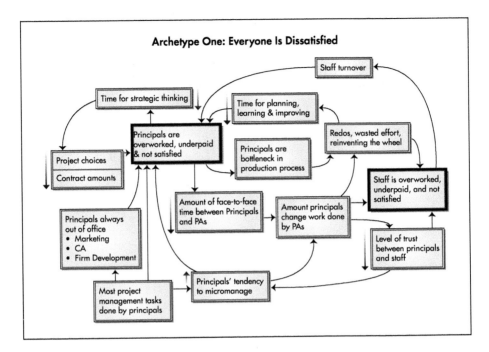

Figure 1.6 Vicious cycles can cause both principals and staff to feel overworked and underpaid.

of this situation may be a low level of trust between staff and leadership, no time for firm development, and an atmosphere of "fire-fighting."

As shown in Figure 1.6, several vicious circles are in play in this situation. When principals are overstretched and often out of the office, they are likely to be less available to project architects (PAs). When they are less available to PAs, principals can become bottlenecks in the production process causing an increase of waste, the need for redos, and lots of "reinventing the wheel." This may result in deadline-generated crises or other perceived emergencies leading to less time for strategic thinking, less time for process improvement, and ultimately, even more demands on the principals. It may also result in an increase in the principals' tendency to micromanage, a decrease in trust between principal and staff, and an increase in dissatisfaction among the staff. Increased dissatisfaction among the staff may lead to increased turnover, which, in turn, increases demands on the principals. These patterns may continue year after year, punctuated by events such as the bitter loss of a key employee or illness due to overwork and stress. Firms that are stuck in this pattern have a difficult time growing, no matter how clear the vision of the firm may be. Sometimes the level of dissatisfaction is not overt or easily perceived, but lies beneath the surface awaiting triggers for eruption or sudden unexpected change. The ways out of this system mostly reside in the realm of project management and self-aware leadership. Archetype One is revisited in Chapter 5: Lifecycle of a Small Firm in the section titled "Getting to the Next Level."

Archetype Two: Administrative Breakdown

Many small firm leaders underestimate the impact of administrative effectiveness on the success of their firms. It's easy to give firm development attention to marketing or to acquiring new design or technical capability. However, the ability to translate firm capacity into steady cash flow and the ability to have a stable and productive work environment often depends on the effectiveness of administrative functions.

In small firms, administrative functions include reception, marketing support, bookkeeping, benefits administration, project management support, executive support to principals, and general office management. The accompanying sidebar list of tasks is impressive and it is certainly not complete. Considering the importance of the tasks, many small firm leaders underinvest in administrative technology and personnel. While drawing technology is continually upgraded, administrative software is often left unchanged and can become severely out of date. When additional professional staff is hired, administrative staff is often expected to handle more work in the same amount of time, frequently with software that requires constant work-arounds and manual posting.

Administrative Functions

- Reception
  - Phone
  - Email
  - Walk-ins
  - Greeting guests/clients
- Marketing Support
  - Proposal preparation
  - Tracking proposals
  - Tracking contacts and follow-ups
- Bookkeeping
  - Invoicing
  - Accounts payables
  - Payroll
  - Project tracking
  - Financial reports
- Benefits Administration
  - Healthcare
  - Paid time off
  - Vacation schedule
- Project Management Support
  - Project startup support
  - Project budget tracking
  - Utilization rate tracking
- Executive Support to Principals
  - Appointments
  - Miscellaneous clerical
- General Office Management
  - Office equipment and technology
  - Supplies

Because administrative work is usually not billable, and represents a significant percentage of overhead expense in a small firm, it is understandable that investment might be delayed. While there may be some short-term benefit to that strategy, Figure 1.7 shows what can happen in the long term when administrative processes break down.

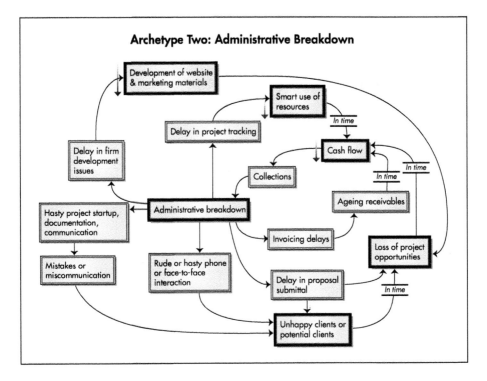

Figure 1.7 Breakdown of administrative functions can impact cash flow, project acquisition, and client service.

Archetype Two shows that when administrative processes are ineffective there are three significant effects over time: a drop in cash flow due to late invoicing and project tracking; unhappy clients or potential clients due to mistakes or an atmosphere of fire-fighting; and loss of potential projects due to delays in submitting proposals or lack of marketing development. It's clear to see that firm development and firm growth can be significantly inhibited by a breakdown in administrative processes.

Figure 1.7 also illustrates that administrative work must be done and, as a result, if there is not adequate administrative support, the firm partners will end up doing some or most of these tasks. The partners' time will be counted in overhead at a higher rate than an administrator's hours and may also represent a significant loss in time spent on billable work, project acquisition, or firm development. It is easy to see that having capable and adequate administrative support is crucial to profitability and overall firm success.

The general ratio of professional staff to administrative support in design firms is about five to one, according to the Society for Design Administration (SDA). This refers to full-time equivalencies so administrative hours will include some of the partners' time, the professional staffs' time, and the time of external consultants. This means that once a firm grows to six or seven, a full-time administrator will likely be needed. Firms that are ten to twelve will probably need two full-time administrators and firms from fifteen to twenty will probably need two administrators plus some external support, such as a payroll service or a marketing consultant. Small firms of all sizes will benefit from the use of performance management software, a topic fully discussed in Chapter Three. Also see Chapter Three for an analysis of how the situation depicted in Archetype Two can be reversed.

Archetype Three: Unintentional Enmity

The third archetype of small firm practice centers on firm leadership. Often com-posed of two or three partners, the relationship between the partners can have a significant effect on both profitability and career contentment. This archetype, shown in Figure 1.8, is about partners who have much to benefit from their asso-ciation and are committed to the success of their partnership. Even though loyal to the partnership, each partner continues to act in ways that promote their indi-vidual style, competencies, and interests. Without intention to harm, these actions

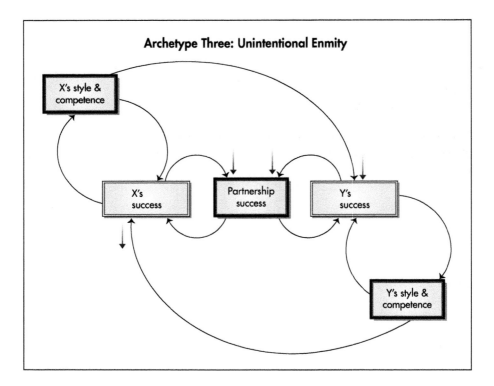

Figure 1.8 Partners with ample motivation to get along still might unintentionally sabotage each other.

somehow obstruct the success of the other partner and ultimately diminish the success of the partnership.

In partnerships of two firm owners, this dynamic is especially destructive when it plays out in the form of interpersonal relationships. Take the case of BC and DW, partners in a firm of 15. With differing professional experience and personality styles, BC and DW have built a successful generalist firm, emphasizing their ability to do projects of all sizes. They each benefit significantly from the strengths of the other, each attracting clients from differing market sectors and each highly capable of delivering projects, although with differing styles.

The same personality differences that benefit the partnership also make it extremely difficult for them to work together productively. BC is introverted, yet expressive of his emotions, occasionally having impulsive outbursts. He tends toward a directive tone with the staff and could not be described as warm. Nevertheless, BC is introspective, willing to pursue personal growth and willing to engage in difficult conversations. BC explains that his outbursts are meaningless and they help him concentrate.

DW, on the other hand, is extroverted and personable. He manages through being well-liked and is highly supportive to the staff. However open he may seem, DW is very emotionally withholding. He abhors confrontation and tends to bury his feelings while building resentment inside. DW believes that endless conversations are counterproductive and it's best just to go on and let events determine the course of things.

Each partner is very disturbed by the behavior of the other and feels that it diminishes their ability to be effective. Each is building a case against the other, noting examples that validate their stance and are becoming more competitive and hostile each day. Despite the fact that they benefit substantially from their partnership, it is likely to be short-lived. This is an example of the "Unintentional Enmity" archetype in action. The nature of partnerships in small firms and how this situation might be reversed or prevented is discussed in Chapter 4, Leadership Matters.

ENDNOTES

1. David Meister, *Managing Professional Service Firms*, Free Press Paperbacks, NY, 1993.
2. Daniel H. Kim, *Systems Thinking Tools*, Pegasus Communications Inc., Cambridge, MA, 1994.
3. Jennifer Kemeny, "Accidental Adversaries," *The Fifth Discipline Fieldbook*, Senge, Kleiner, Roberts, Ross, and Smith, eds., Doubleday, NY, 1994, p. 145.
4. Ibid.

CHAPTER 2

WHOLE FIRM SYSTEM

The archetypes introduced in Chapter 1 sometimes result in an organizational paralysis that can prevent firm leaders from reaching their goals. These situations are usually not the result of personal failure, although the weaknesses of firm principals can contribute. The situations illustrated in the archetypes are almost always the result of a complex system of variable factors. Not the least of these is the changeable environment in which small firms operate. The day-to-day demands make it hard to take time to plan for the future and, even when firm owners do plan, there are no guarantees.

Take the case of DD Architects. The firm principal thought that her firm could leverage its experience with public projects to acquire work as a consulting architect with the local transit agency. The jobs were bread and butter, station renovations and the like, but there was some promise of future new development and it was steady well-paying work. The principal thought work like this would provide base revenue that would allow her firm to grow and pursue more interesting, higher-profile jobs. She worked hard on the proposal and the relationship building necessary to win this work and finally was awarded a substantial contract. Based on the projected revenue, she hired additional staff and arranged to lease larger office space.

However, the work failed to materialize. Politics and funding problems continued to delay the start. She knows the projects could happen any time, but also knows they may never happen. She doesn't want to reduce her staff, she likes the people she has hired, but she is beginning to have trouble keeping them busy. And she is not sure what to do about the new space. She despairs that even though she planned carefully and took strategic action, the outcome was still not predictable.

Situations like this are not unusual. They happen in small design firms everyday and for most firm leaders, the questions persist. How can constantly shifting workloads and unexpected circumstances be managed? How can the demands of the marketplace be met while still creating a satisfying workplace? How can professional goals be set and achieved in this environment of unrelenting change?

Unfortunately, the answers to these questions do not lie in the usual realm of problem and solution. Problem solving only works when the cause of the problem is straightforward and the results are predictable. However, linear cause and effect is not common in the milieu of design practice. Usually, whatever result is seen, whether it is a principal chronically working overtime or an unanticipated cash flow crisis, the cause is usually a complex web of interlocking factors. Like a complicated design problem, everything is connected.

LINEAR THINKING AND SYSTEMS THINKING

Consider the difference between linear thinking and systems thinking, first introduced in Chapter 1. At the top of Figure 2.1 is a diagram of linear thinking. This is logical, step-by-step thinking, supported by science and Newtonian physics. "Every action has an equal and opposite reaction," A causes B causes C, every time, predictably, with a predictable outcome. Machines work this way, and much of modern culture is built on the results of this kind of reductionist thinking. However, during the twentieth century, science itself changed, discovering that on the subatomic and submolecular level things are not so straightforward. And, on the macro, large-scale level, increased complexity has forced scientists, business leaders, and politicians

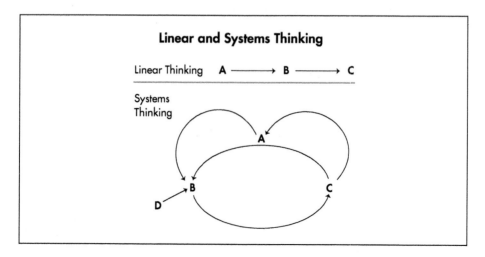

Figure 2.1   Understanding complex and interconnected issues requires systems thinking.

to look at the world with a more systemic approach. A causes B causes C is no longer a working model because things are just too complex.

Applying systems thinking, shown in the lower half of Figure 2.1, allows diagrams of complex situations to be created. A influences B, which influences C, which in turn, influences A. C might also influence B, and there might be an outside influence D that affects B as well. Systems diagrams are useful tools for illustrating complex relationships and understanding their likely outcomes. It also allows for the identification of points of leverage that could move the system in a preferred direction.

This is important because of the ever changing and often complex environment in which small firms operate. Small firm owners often complain that their days are filled with "fighting fires," one alarm sounding after another. In this environment, it is difficult to step back and assess the big picture, but that is exactly what is required. Stepping back may allow a glimpse into how to fight fires more effectively, or even better, put fire-prevention measures in place.

An example from practice can illustrate this concept. It is not unusual for project architects (PA) to complain about last-minute design changes made by the principal in charge of their project. These changes often cause rework and deadline crunches since many drawings may be affected by one design change. This situation could be caused by inadequate one-to-one communication between the principal and the PA during the course of the project, by the principal's need to micromanage, or perhaps, by the PA's lack of experience. Maybe it's a combination of all three. Yet if this situation happens over and over again, it too has results—reduced trust between principal and PA, reduced productivity, and possibly reduced quality of work. This situation is diagrammed in Figure 2.2.

Diagramming a practice situation in this way can help firm leaders understand what is actually happening and what possible actions could move the situation in a positive direction. In the situation diagrammed in Figure 2.2, such actions might include:

- Preventing miscommunication by increasing one-on-one time between principal and PA; plan for regular and frequent contact—daily if possible.
- Providing training needed by PA through mentoring, coaching, or classes.
- Examining the principal's need to micromanage; is it always really necessary to be involved in every little thing?
- Debriefing at project close-out involving all who worked on a project inhouse—valuable for lessons learned, knowledge capture, and building trust between firm members.

This kind of thinking can help firm leaders get to the underlying causes of problems that they are experiencing in their firms. It recognizes and works with the complexity and unpredictability of the work environment by noticing recurring patterns. This notion of recurring patterns is basic to chaos theory and its application to business organizations.

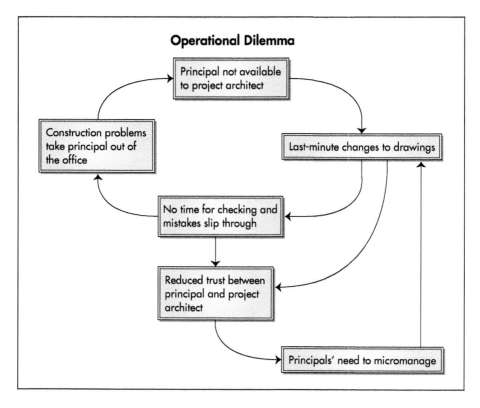

Figure 2.2   Systems diagrams can be used to understand recurring operational situations.

RECOGNIZING PATTERNS

Chaotic systems, as observed in nature, are defined as unpredictable, acting in nonlinear and complex ways, and as systems in which small influences can create huge unexpected effects. According to Chaos Theory, the direction of a chaotic system cannot be known until the system has been observed over time. Over time there is an inexplicable tendency toward order and repetition. Patterns will emerge from even the most irregular circumstances.

As explained by organizational planner T.J. Cartwright, "Chaos is order without predictability."[1] In other words, given certain circumstances, certain things will always happen; but you can never predict exactly when those causative circumstances will occur. Hurricanes are an example of this kind of phenomenon. The lesson here for design firm leaders is that observing short-term results will provide very little insight about what will happen next. Only by observing and noticing patterns over time is it possible to predict likely outcomes.

Noticing patterns over time will give firm leaders an improved sense of what is going on in their firm and what to do about it. This is always preferable to reacting to a single circumstance, no matter how significant it may seem. For instance, looking

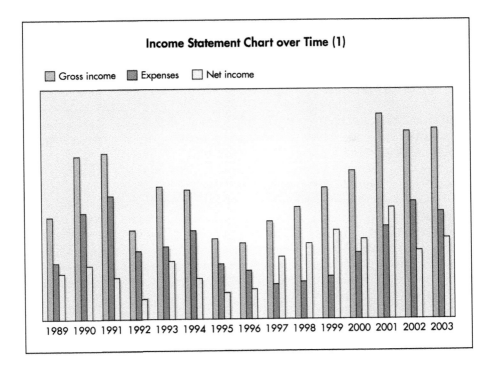

Figure 2.3   Simple charts can reveal important trends.

at a firm's income statements over time is a more effective way to understand financial trends than planning based on one very good, or very bad, year.

Project management software that is integrated with accounting software can assist in tracking patterns over time, especially project-related performance, staff utilization trends, and overall financial results. Once firm leaders understand the operational and economic patterns that are recurring at their firms, smart strategic decisions can be made.

Even without project management and accounting software, it is possible to create simple spreadsheets and charts that can be updated easily and checked frequently. Although it may be time consuming, investing in data collection and reporting tools that show performance trends over time is a vital step in making sense of the chaos. Figure 2.3 illustrates an example of a simple and easily constructed tool.

Tracking Trends

Figure 2.3 shows the relative gross revenue, total expenses, and net income of a small firm over a 10-year period. Notice the years between 1989 and 1995. In many of these years the net income decreased relative to the year before, even though the gross revenue went up or stayed steady. This indicates that the total expenses were increasing at a greater rate than the gross revenue.

When this pattern occurs it indicates that having a greater volume of work may not be a guarantee of more net income. Firm leaders work hard to acquire projects with a larger scope and budgets, but fail to put in place the operational capacity to handle the increased workload. For example, as firm owners acquire more work, they may hire new staff that needs training and/or does not work efficiently for a variety of other reasons. Another scenario may be an overload in terms of capacity utilization resulting in reduced productivity. An underlying cause of this situation could be an inexperienced firm leader who is unable to manage the larger workforce and bigger projects effectively. It's most likely all of the above.

Generating a year-to-year income chart is a relatively simple process using spreadsheet software. Seeing a pattern such as this should be a wake-up call to firm leaders that something is not quite right. It could be poor productivity as mentioned above, or it may be that the larger jobs were not priced correctly and the revenue is just not there to support the work required to deliver the project. Whatever the cause, the results illustrated in Figure 2.3 show that the time between 1989 and 1995 may have resulted in some years when firm employees were compensated better than firm owners. Seeing a pattern like this can leave firm leaders wondering, "Why am I doing this?"

The important lesson here is that simple quantitative models and tools can yield substantial information about trends over time. Without examining trends over time, it easy to think, "Oh this is just a bad year when I had a lot of expenses, it will get better next year," but that rarely happens all on its own. If patterns are watched over time, it will help unearth the underlying circumstances that make things turn out the same way over and over again.

In the case of the firm illustrated in Figure 2.3, the firm owner pursued education in management and help from skilled consultants. As shown in the chart from 1996 forward, the firm owner became more financially successful. This is indicated by stable expenses and a net income that increased in parallel with gross revenue.

Symptomatic and Fundamental Solutions

Earlier in this chapter, the dilemma facing the principal of DD Architects was intro-duced. Although the firm principal implemented a sound strategy for firm growth, circumstances beyond her control left her in a difficult situation. Her circumstance provides a valuable lesson about planning in unpredictable business environments.

It is common wisdom that building a firm on only one major client is risky, and perhaps the owner of DD architects was too quick to make changes to her firm. Perhaps if she had acted more incrementally—lining up contract workers who didn't need office space, for instance, she would have fared better. Yet by taking the risk, she has gained increased capacity in her firm and is now more capable of acquiring projects from diverse sources. Now the principal's challenge is to market her firm more broadly and leverage her significant investment in growing the firm. Figure 2.4 illustrates the situation of DD Architects.

This diagram is of a situation where the unintended consequences of symp-tomatic solutions make it more difficult to implement fundamental solutions to the

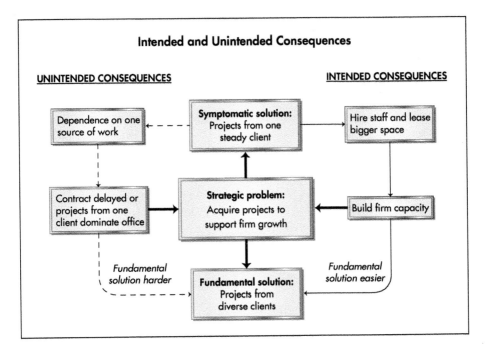

Intended and Unintended Consequences

UNINTENDED CONSEQUENCES

INTENDED CONSEQUENCES

Dependence on one source of work

Symptomatic solution: Projects from one steady client

Hire staff and lease bigger space

Contract delayed or projects from one client dominate office

Strategic problem: Acquire projects to support firm growth

Build firm capacity

Fundamental solution harder

Fundamental solution: Projects from diverse clients

Fundamental solution easier

Figure 2.4 Sometimes the consequences of symptomatic solutions can make it harder to implement fundamental solutions.

presenting problem.[2] In the case of DD Architects, the symptomatic solution was to court one client with the potential of steady well-paid work. While not a bad idea, the strategy failed to recognize the unpredictability of the system. A more fundamental solution would be to target a diverse group of clients to provide a more secure stream of work for an expanded firm.

As illustrated on the right side of Figure 2.4, the positive consequences of hiring and expanding the firm are that it builds capacity and makes it more capable of taking on projects from diverse clients. On the left side of the diagram the unintended consequences are shown—becoming too dependent on one source of projects that may or may not actually manifest. The resources dedicated to acquiring this one client and the steady work if it does come through, may actually make it more difficult to implement the fundamental solution of acquiring projects from many diverse clients.

By diagramming the situation, the principal of DD Architects might see that it is critical to plan her marketing efforts to include more than one targeted client. For instance, pursuing the same type of work with a number of different public agencies might have been more effective in assuring that some of the work would actually come through.

The principal of DD Architects might also learn that making decisions based on a "sure thing" may be unwise in a relentlessly changeable environment. Complex systems in nature always include redundancy and are therefore naturally resilient when one road to success is blocked.

Often patterns such as these become discernable with simple questions: "Have we seen this before?" or "What feels familiar here?" For example, the principal of DD Architects would be well advised to reflect on whether risk-taking has been a frequent strategy in the management of her firm, and whether that approach has led to success. If a situation brings forth the thought, "Wow, this has happened over and over again," firm leaders need to look into it more carefully. This is probably an area of high leverage, where a small change may elicit a large beneficial effect.

By understanding the recurring patterns of practice, firm leaders can begin to bring "order out of chaos." Instead of trying to control and stabilize, order comes from creating systems that allow you to keep track of what's going on over time, so you can work more effectively with the rhythms already present in the organization and in the environment in which it operates.

Summary

Order Out of Chaos

- Patterns emerge over time in chaotic systems.
- Ask, "Have we seen this before?"
- Examine processes: What are the usual outcomes? Are the processes working over time?
- Set up data collection systems that are tailored to notice patterns and trends.

These ideas are summarized in the sidebar *Order Out of Chaos*. Patterns emerge over time so data collection and compilation systems must be tailored to reveal trends. Remember that which gets counted quantitatively is what gets noticed, so think carefully about what needs to be tracked. Are the hours, costs, and profitability of each project being tracked? How do the actual job costs relate to the fee being charged? How many new job inquiries come in over a given period of time? In general, what is being tracked and is it really useful?

Asking "have we seen this before?" can guide firm leaders to easy fixes that can have a significant effect, sometimes known as "low-hanging fruit." Examining processes is similar; different results will not come from repeating a flawed process. Be honest, self-critical, and disciplined in this examination and consider getting help from a consultant.

CORE INCOMPETENCE

The principal of DD Architects may indeed be prone to the risk-taking that is consistent with her entrepreneurial spirit. While this may serve her well at times, it also may blind her to other options and smarter choices.

This points out the importance of remembering the common self-help adage, "Your habits are your destiny." Every person and organization has core competency and capabilities, but people and organizations also have what could be called "core incompetence." Notice what is done over and over again and consider whether these behaviors are resulting in positive outcomes. Some firm owners deal with their failings by finding a partner who is good at what they consider to be their weakness, and that can be a good strategy. In the typical scenario, a "design partner," gifted at creativity, may be paired with a "managing partner," good at organizing and running projects. And this may work, although it does not improve the core incompetence of either partner and may result in an "organizational incompetence," like a misalignment of values: Is design or profit more important? This could easily result in confusion of purpose and mixed messages to the staff.

The weaknesses and "bad habits" of firm leaders have a significant impact on operational effectiveness of the firm. For instance, consider the case of RH, a small firm owner who is very poor at time management. He is rarely on time for any of his meetings, internal or external. Accordingly, his consultants and his clients have learned this behavior and do not show up on time either. His staff, in fact, sets ahead the clock in the office by a half-hour to try fooling the principal into being on time. Nevertheless his inability to think realistically about time continues to influence his relationships with his staff, which can never know when he will be available and as a result, are completely frustrated.

It is easy to see how improving this core incompetence is a point of leverage with huge upside potential. And it is not that difficult—there are lots of time management books and methods and calendars and new technology that can help. However, it is a habit and as such, hard to change. This is especially true when the habit belongs to the person in charge and everyone around "enables" him, to use a pop-psychology term. Colleagues and coworkers of RH accommodate him by also coming late, changing their schedule to meet with him, etc., and nobody helps him make a change. Can you imagine the effect if he said to his staff, "Well I know I have a problem with time management and I want you all to help me change." The whole firm might soon function significantly better.

In many small firms these types of problems are common. Rest assured that most of the challenges of small firm management are not unique to any particular firm. Some patterns are widespread, like the archetypes shown in Chapter 1. Other patterns reflect the culture of the design professions and the nature of work in professional service firms, and they underlie much of what is seen on the surface.

WHOLE FIRM SYSTEM DIAGRAM

Figure 2.5 illustrates the interrelationship between the factors that universally influence productivity, and hence profitability in small design firms.

"Productivity" is shown in the center of the diagram because that is always going to be a main concern of firm management. Increase productivity and profits will increase, assuming there is a good backlog of work with new work consistently

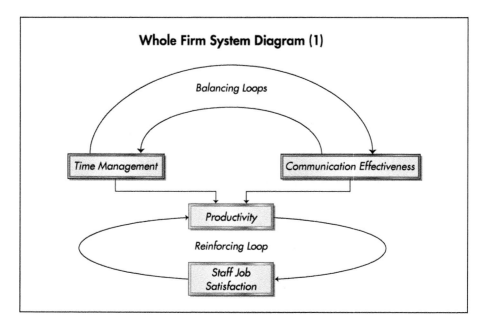

Figure 2.5 The factors that influence productivity are time management, communication effectiveness, and job satisfaction of staff and principals.

coming in. Productivity can be examined in any of the common work processes that firms engage in, whether it is a marketing process, such as preparing proposals, or an operational process, such as preparing contract documents.

The biggest influence on productivity in small firms is job satisfaction for both the staff and the principals. The principals must be included because their level of career contentment will have a profound influence on the other members of the firm. Job satisfaction and productivity have a very strong reinforcing relationship. When people are happy and enthusiastic they work better, when the work is going better, people are happier and more enthusiastic. It's a virtuous circle, which could change to a vicious circle overnight given the right circumstances. Generally in small design firms, much depends on the enthusiasm and willingness of all involved to work hard at executing projects with creativity, accuracy, and care. Job satisfaction is the engine of the firm that drives it toward achievement. This can carry a firm a long way, but there are limitations.

At the top of Figure 2.5 there are two important factors that impact productivity directly: time management and communication effectiveness. If time management is poor and communication not effective, then productivity will be negatively affected. Time management and communication effectiveness can also impact job satisfaction. If hard-working, enthusiastic people are constantly being frustrated by poor communication and time mismanagement, they will get burned out and not be able to function at their highest level. It is not uncommon for architects and designers to be willing to work all night because they are so interested in what they are doing. This can go on for a while, but eventually systems must be put in place so that people don't have to work all night, for example. If not, commitment, effort, productivity, and creativity will suffer. The limiting action of poor time management and communication systems will impact the principals' morale as well. Time management and communication effectiveness also have a direct operational relationship to one another. Good communication is essential for good time management which is vital to good communication.

Time Management

Time management for small firms means "coping with the unpredictable" because of the constant unpredictable demands on firm leaders' time. The sidebar *Time Management* summarizes some practical suggestions for improving time management in small design firms.

Time Management

Coping with the Unpredictable

- Minimize unexpected interruptions; consider establishing quiet time.
- Question unconditional availability to clients.
- Expect client-driven delays and deadlines.
- Examine the principals' tendency to micromanage.
- Set up specific times to manage/answer email.
- Use technology to help.

To minimize unexpected interruptions consider establishing "quiet time" of two to three hours each day. Use this time to focus on productivity—getting the work done. If a critical call is expected, make an exception, but exercise discipline. If instituted firm-wide, this can significantly improve productivity.

Since design professionals are generally not "emergency architects on call," question unconditional availability to clients. Be on equal footing with your client, doing business mostly during business hours, for instance.

Accept that there will be client-driven delays and deadlines. Workload fluctuations are common in small design firms so build in flexible staffing options. For instance, to prepare for a slowdown, see if there are staff members who are willing to work part time voluntarily, because it would serve their purposes as well. To prepare for work overload, interview some contract production workers or investigate onshore outsourcing. Taking these kinds of advance actions will build in the staffing flexibility that surely will be needed.

Some principals have a hard time letting other people do the work that needs to be done. They constantly look over the shoulder, always meddling. The most obvious symptom of this is a harried, overworked principal, who always stays late and works weekends. Principals need to be very strategic about what work they do themselves and what they delegate. Principals should do the work that only they can do. All other work should be delegated, including some of the fun and interesting work. If the principals feel they can do it better/faster themselves, then a more skilled staff needs to be hired, or more training and coaching must take place.

Email can take time from other work like no other distraction in the modern workplace. Set up specific times each day for management and answering emails—early morning and/or late afternoon, for example. Answer most emails soon after reading to avoid their loss under the next pile of new messages. Be disciplined about sticking to the set schedule.

Technology to help with time management is abundant: Time management software and calendars, BlackBerrys, PDAs, and many more devices are available. The more everybody knows about where everyone else is, the easier working together will be.

Communication Effectiveness

Communication Effectiveness

Timely and Accurate Information Exchange

- Know what information can be sent by memo, and what requires face-to-face contact.
- Routinize face-to-face contact between principal and project architect.
- Create filing and document storage systems that work and are used consistently by everyone.
- Have regular staff meetings.
- Use technology to help.

Make a distinction between the kind of information that is best sent by email and the kind that requires face-to-face contact, known as "rich information." Rich information exchange requires communication that includes body language, gestures, and eye contact. Now, technology can nearly replace in-person communication and these virtual meetings are likely to be used more in the future. Email is best for communication that needs documentation and that can be explained in list or bullet point form.

Principals and project managers/project architects need regular face-to-face contact with each other for rich information exchange. Make an effort to routinize this contact and be disciplined about its execution.

Research shows that significant time is spent at work by people trying to locate a document or some information when it is needed. Creating filing and document storage systems that work, and are used consistently by everyone, will improve productivity and reduce frustration.

Sometimes firm-wide staff meetings are time wasters, especially as the firm approaches 20. Some companies hold firm-wide meetings only once a month and have weekly meetings of project managers and principals, and/or weekly project team meetings.

Twenty-first-century technology is all about communication. Be sure to use it appropriately. Face-to-face contact is usually better than sending an email to a coworker who sits six feet away. With instant messaging and email, it is also easy to forget that phone calls are still an effective way to exchange information.

Job Satisfaction

Job Satisfaction

Level of Career Contentment

- Opportunities to design
- Control over one's own work
- Optimal variety and learning opportunities
- Challenge, recognition, and support
- Alignment of values and goals with that of the organization
- Feeling respected and well-liked by coworkers and principals

Job satisfaction is the element with the most direct influence on productivity—happy people work hard and try to do the best job possible. The dedication and excellence of a firm's staff is its most critical asset and the most important contributor to success in practice.

Based on studies of architects by sociologist Judith Blau,[3] several factors contribute to career contentment among architects. These are listed in the sidebar and include: opportunities to design, which should be available to everyone, including the principals; control over one's work, which is a significant determinant of satisfaction; optimal variety, meaning enough variety to keep work interesting, but not so much that it damages effectiveness; and learning opportunities which are critical to ongoing creativity and innovation.

Other important influences on worker satisfaction include an alignment of personal values and goals with the organization's, so people feel good about what they are doing; and a sense of being well-liked by coworkers and bosses, so that people feel respected, included, and empowered.

Time management, communication effectiveness, and job satisfaction are important influences on productivity and overall firm success. However, there is still something missing from this picture—the influence of work processes. Chapter 3, Routinize the Routine, offers a more complete look at the Whole Firm System.

ENDNOTES

1. Margaret Wheatley, *Leadership and the New Science*, Barrettt-Koehler Publishing Inc., San Francisco, CA, 1999, p.120.

2. Peter Senge, *The Fifth Discipline,* Doubleday, NY, 1990.

3. Judith Blau, *Architects and Firms: A Sociological Perspective on Architectural Practice,* MIT Press, Cambridge, MA, 1987.

CHAPTER 3

ROUTINIZE THE ROUTINE

Becoming intentional about the management of a small design firm almost always involves work process improvement. As discussed in Chapter 2, the positive influences on productivity may be limited or curtailed by operational missteps in areas such as time management and communication effectiveness (see Figure 2.5). Because design firms are project based, these missteps are most often manifest in the day-to-day execution of project delivery. When this occurs, profitability suffers along with productivity. This condition might be felt in a firm's apparent inability to advance financially, no matter how large its commissions become. Figure 3.1 is a chart of the income statements over time of a small firm in this kind of situation.

This chart shows that year after year, no matter the gross revenue, the expenses increased at the same rate as revenue leaving the owners of this firm with little or no profit. This shows that effective marketing, selling, and positioning the firm for larger projects will not necessarily yield firm growth and increased profitability. A chart such as this is a strong indicator of the need for operational improvements.

OPERATIONAL EFFECTIVENESS

Operational effectiveness comes first from recognizing the critical relationship between work processes design and productivity. Similar to the notion that buildings are the product of design; systems of effective production can also be designed. Figure 3.2 looks once again at the Whole Firm System Diagram (see also Figure 2.5), now showing the relationship of work processes to the other factors that influence productivity.

35

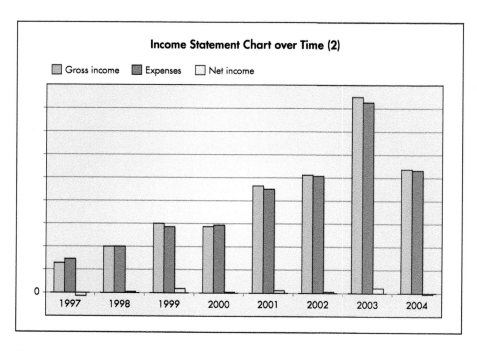

Figure 3.1 Some firms can't seem to advance financially, no matter how much their gross revenue increases.

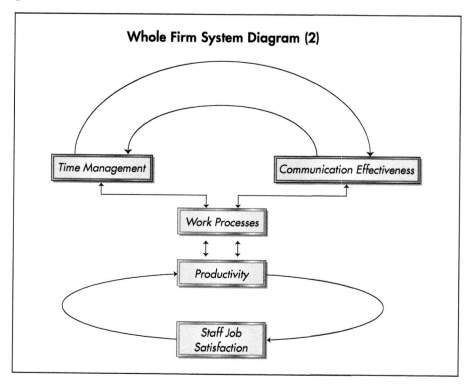

Figure 3.2 Productivity is mediated by the effectiveness of work processes.

Most small firm owners, including solo practitioners, would benefit from a careful review of their work processes. For example, PT Architects is an award-winning firm specializing in custom residential projects. The principal and the senior project architects are still doing most of their drawings by hand. Although this method seems inefficient and problematic, the architects are highly skilled and very traditional in their approach. The real operational problem is not the drafting method, but the fact that each of the project architects has their own way of putting together a set of construction documents. There are no standards for page layout and no checklists for what needs to be included in a complete set of documents. There are also no standard details in hardcopy or in electronic form. Each project includes considerable "reinvention of the wheel" which is handled with imagination by the very experienced architects involved. The owner of the firm is resistant to any kind of standardization because he is afraid that it will stifle the creativity of his project architects. Because this is an experience-based firm with complex and highly paid projects, the firm is still able to be profitable. However, it is worth considering what there is to be gained by identifying the routine aspects of the work and using standards and templates as appropriate. Rather than stifle creativity, this is likely to relieve frustration and free up time to devote to the truly creative work involved in custom home design. Higher profitability is also a likely result of these kinds of process improvement.

Work processes that may be ripe for improvement in any firm include production work related to project delivery; and also processes related to marketing and selling, such as preparing proposals. Other work processes in design firms involve gathering and documenting information, project startup, quality review, construction phase activities, and project close-out, to name a few. Identifying distinct work processes and mapping out the flow of work, noting bottlenecks and wasted efforts is one way to approach planning improvements. A more practical and expedient way is to start with processes that are presenting obvious problems. In most firms, identifying where to begin is usually not difficult.

THE TYPOLOGY OF WORK

To assess needs and to determine effective strategies for work process improvement, it is important to understand that there are different types of work. The analysis of work comes from the discipline of organizational design, specifically sociotechnical design, which considers how work process can be designed to provide the best match between social systems and technological systems. Much of the significant writing in this discipline happened in the 1980s, as companies began to integrate new office technologies (the computer) into their work processes. Because office technologies were first applied to the completion of repetitive work, work process designers needed to identify differences between routine and nonroutine tasks. As stated by Calvin Pava in his book *Managing the New Office Technology*, which was published at a time when office work was just beginning to be automated, "Routine office work primarily involves the management of structured problems. Such tasks are characterized by accuracy of detail, short time horizon, information with consistent formats, and narrow scope.... Non-routine office work, on the other hand, primarily involves the management of unstructured or semi-structured problems. The jobs are characterized by plausible but imprecise information inputs, varying degrees of detail, extended or unfixed time horizons, diverse information formats, and diffuse or general scope."[1] Pava goes on to explain that routine tasks are linear and sequential while nonroutine tasks are nonsequential and free-flowing.

Analyzability and Variety

Socio-technical designers have identified two qualities of work that help them recognize the difference between routine and nonroutine work. Four distinct types of work tasks and processes emerge. Figure 3.3 illustrates the two qualities of work and four types of tasks.

On the vertical scale is a quality of work known as "task analyzability." Analyzability means the ease by which a task can be described with simple directions—a memo or list of steps. Highly analyzable tasks are easy to describe, while low analyzability means that the task is not easily understood and is not linear. In general, nonroutine tasks, "above the line" have low analyzability, while routine tasks are highly analyzable. Similarly, the horizontal scale, task variety, is a measure of the level of sameness encountered each time a task is undertaken. Some tasks are very complex, but involve doing the same thing over and over again with increasing skill.

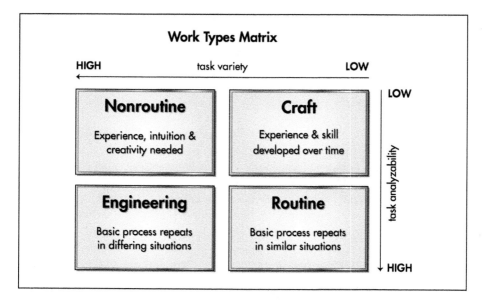

Figure 3.3   Tasks can be divided into four distinct types of work.

Routine tasks or processes, such as recording reimbursable expenses, are the same every time and are highly analyzable. **Engineering** tasks have high variety, such as the different loading or support conditions when sizing a beam, but are basically understandable through a step-by-step procedure. **Craft** is the opposite of engineering—low variety and low analyzability. Craft processes, such as rendering in watercolor, take practice to develop skill over time. The process, though complex, is virtually the same each time it is undertaken. Success depends on doing the same thing over and over again, with increasing ability. **Nonroutine,** such as complicated problem-solving, also demands experience and intuition, but there is high variety in the tasks presented. Success depends on ability to generalize and apply knowledge gained through diverse experience. All design solutions are a result of nonroutine processes as well as craft-based tasks, since the design process is basically the same each time. Although architects are sometimes unwilling to admit it, much of the work, and sometimes entire projects, could also be seen as routine.

By identifying and routinizing routine work, unnecessary "reinventing of the wheel" can be avoided. Creating systems, standards, and check lists that handle routine tasks in routine ways, will always create more time for the nonroutine work. For nonroutine work, "reinventing the wheel" might be fine as is often the case in complex and innovative design projects. The critical issue here is that firm leaders differentiate between these different types of work and apply the appropriate processes to each.

In addition to distinguishing between routine and nonroutine tasks, work processes may also be improved by looking for bottlenecks, wasted efforts, and blatant inefficiency. Take care to use technology effectively; thinking about what is appropriate for the size of the office and the work that is done.

Situational Leadership

From a management standpoint, understanding the different types of work gives rise to the notion that different work requires different management and leadership styles. Popularized by Ken Blanchard and Paul Hersey in books such as *The One Minute Manager*,[2] situational leadership explains that leadership and management style should depend more on who is being managed than on the disposition of the particular manager or leader. In the Blanchard/Hersey model, the balance between support and direction given by a manager should vary depending on the skill and motivation of the worker.

Examples of directive behaviors by a manager include clear instructions, fixed deadlines, and quality review of the work product. Supportive management behavior includes providing information, resources, and mentoring needed by those performing the work task. It may also involve an interpersonal and emotional component. For example, "coaching" involves high levels of both direction and support and is appropriate for the management of motivated learners. This style of management mimics the behavior of a football coach on the sidelines—calling the plays, but also encouraging the players, telling them, "You can do it!"

Inexperienced workers need direction more than support and managing them in a directive manner is fitting. They need to be given instruction about exactly what is expected and how to get there. For some leaders, being directive is more difficult than giving support, but according to Blanchard and Hersey, this is exactly what beginners need in order to succeed. In contrast, highly skilled and self-motivated workers no longer need direction and are best left alone to do the job their way. However, these peak performers still need support, often in the form of acknowledgment of their contributions. For emerging contributors who are ready for independent work, delegation may be the best management strategy. In architectural firms, much work is delegated to expert outside consultants who operate with little or no management direction or support.

Match Management Style, Staffing, and Work Types

Key to operational effectiveness is the correct match between task type, management style, and worker skill. There also needs to be a match between the firm's management style and the firm's business model, as discussed in Chapter 1. Entire projects and entire firms can be seen as routine or nonroutine and need to be staffed and managed with that in mind. Figure 3.4 summarizes the critical relationships between work type, management style, and staffing.

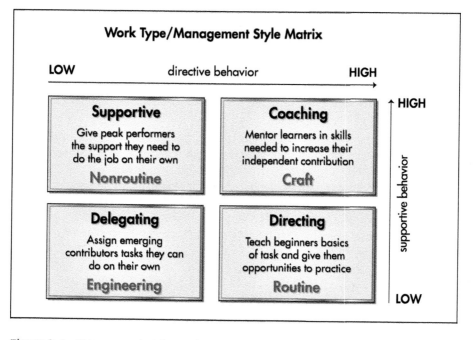

Figure 3.4   Management style needs to match the skill of staff and type of work being performed.

HOW TO ROUTINIZE

Figure 1.7 in Chapter 1 illustrates the Administrative Breakdown archetype, a system of problems common in many small design firms. The diagram shows the potential negative consequences of ineffective handling of administrative tasks—cash flow shortages, lost job opportunities, and unhappy clients. Administrative tasks and related inefficiencies in project management is an excellent place to begin routinizing the routine. Even if the administrative systems are not overloaded, there is almost always room for improvement, perhaps as preparation for firm growth. Figure 3.5 illustrates the influences on administrative process improvement efforts.

As demand grows, administrative overload can be improved through efforts toward office automation and systemization of some processes. Improvement efforts might include those discussed in this chapter—routinizing the routine; using performance management software; and creating a project startup process. Careful

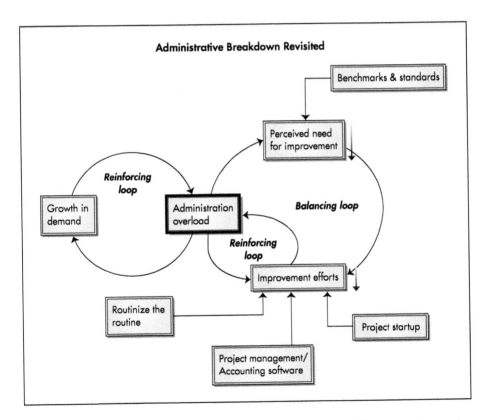

Figure 3.5 Administrative overload can be improved through office automation and systemization of processes.

thought should be given to whether additional administrative hours are needed to support the partners and professional staff. These hours could be provided by hiring additional administrative staff or by consciously shifting certain tasks to partners or professional staff. Hiring outside consultants or services, such as a marketing consultant or a payroll service, can also help accomplish some of the administrative tasks.

The perception of the need for improvement efforts is the balancing force at play in this system. As things improve the motivation to continue the efforts may decline, leading to a decline in efforts and the potential for backsliding. This danger exists in all process improvement efforts, so continuous improvement needs to be built into the culture of the organization. Care must be taken not to underinvest in critical systems. This tendency can be reduced by using standards and benchmarks to evaluate your progress toward tangible goals. In the case of administrative support, a significant benchmark might be the number of days between when work gets done and when the invoice for the work is paid. Industry average is a shocking 60 to 90 days.

Investment in administrative effectiveness also means investment in the continuing education of administrative staff. Organizations such as the Society for Design Administration (SDA), the Society for Marketing Professional Services (SMPS), and the Society for Human Resource Management (SHRM) can be excellent resources for education in administrative skills.

If firm growth and increasing firm value are strategic goals, then improving administrative processes is a critical strategy. This effort will move firms into a more professional posture, allowing consistently good service to clients and positive work experiences for staff.

Project Management/Accounting Software

One way to improve the administrative systems is to implement the use of project management/accounting software. These software products track ongoing performance of projects and the finances of the firm as a whole. Whether it is project profitability, staff utilization, or overall firm financial health, it is critical to monitor performance relative to expectations. When information about performance is available, firm leaders have the ability to anticipate what lies ahead and to make timely adjustments. Investing in performance management software that is project-based and created specifically for design firms is a huge step toward professionalizing firm management and reducing the time it takes to complete routine administrative tasks.

Performance management is defined as tracking execution in relation to what was expected or budgeted. In design firms performance management has two major components—accounting and project management. Accounting functions will give firm leaders big-picture information in regard to revenue, spending, and cash flow.

Performance Management: Accounting Functions

1. The firm as a whole—profit & loss reports, balance sheets
2. Payroll, payroll benefits, taxes
3. Customers and vendor accounts
4. Overhead and direct expense tracking
5. Cash flow and receivables tracking

Performance management for projects involves monitoring execution of projects in relation to budget and contractual obligations. Project management software collects data from electronic timesheets and can use that data to create invoices, project progress reports, and utilization reports.

Performance Management: Project Management

1. Project setup (fee basis, team makeup)
2. Project budget
3. Client contact information
4. Document filing
5. Team performance tracking (time sheets, utilization)
6. Overall project profitability
7. Reimbursable expense tracking
8. Invoicing

Accounting and project management overlap when it comes to tracking financial transactions. For example, a payment received from a client needs to be posted to both the general accounts and to the project. Likewise, if an expense is charged to a job it also needs to be noted in the general accounts. Project-based performance management software will do these tasks automatically, avoiding the need for double entry.

Project-based information, especially from time sheets, is vital to the development of accurate proposals for future work and for the creation of overall financial projections. This information needs to be readily accessible and visible in the general accounts. Without some integration between the two components of performance management, firm leaders cannot have a full picture of what is taking place in their firms.

Common Practices

Most often, in small firms, the accounting side of performance tracking is handled well with standard software for small businesses, such as QuickBooks®. However,

QuickBooks® and similar applications are not designed for project-based businesses. They have limited capacity when it comes to performance management of projects.

As a result, performance on projects is simply not tracked in many small firms. Firm leaders manage through experience and intuition, and firm performance is tracked as a whole—a conglomerate of performance on all projects. This is common practice for solo practitioners or two-person firms and often works well at that scale since the firm owner is intimately involved with every aspect of project delivery.

When project performance is tracked in small firms, it is often done by using "home-made" spreadsheets and employee time sheets. Many administrative hours are then spent entering time sheet data from one software application into another. Additional nonbillable hours are then required to enter the same data into other home-made spreadsheets designed to analyze performance of staff, projects, or the firm as a whole. This is further complicated by the use of different hardware platforms—it is not uncommon to see Mac and PC users sitting side by side in small firms.

This piecemeal approach makes it difficult for small firm owners without much administrative support to find the time to track and manage project and firm performance. Yet without this information, firm leaders do not have what they need to make basic business decisions such as what to charge on a given project; whether to hire another staff person; or which projects are in need of immediate corrective action.

Lack of project performance management can also cause problems and delay in the invoicing process. Since accurate and timely invoicing is directly related to cash flow, this can be a serious problem. Accounting software is not designed to collect project-based information and then transform this data into an invoice ready to be sent to a client. Without project management software, invoicing involves gathering data that may reside in many different places (billable hours, contract terms, reimbursable expenses, for example). This process is time consuming and can result in invoices being sent out late, sometimes with little verification of their accuracy.

Types of Performance Management Software

To reduce these administrative hours—often logged by the principals in small firms—there are many performance management software applications on the market. Some of these are designed for professional service firms, some specifically for architectural practice. Many are scalable and web-based and some are completely custom built to fit the needs of the firm.

The performance management software currently on the market for the A/E industry fall into two groups, based on how they handle the integration of accounting data and project management information. The two distinct approaches are:

1. Integrated: A fully integrated system that accomplishes accounting and project management with the same software. These systems often have modules designed for distinct groups of performance management tasks.

2. Project Management Only: This is software that tracks project-based information and provides a way to transfer data to and from accounting software. This allows an existing accounting system to remain in place eliminating the need to learn a new system or transfer accounting data from the old system to the new.

All these products provide electronic time sheets, automated invoicing, various financial and performance reports, and graphic tools for project tracking. All allow ready access to information on projects to project managers/architects, as well as to the principals. These systems also provide ways to make information private and available only to selected firm members. Which software application to choose depends on the firm size, its situation, and its strategic goals.

Integrated Systems

In general, the integrated performance management software is more complex, but also more customizable. As with all software, these systems can be time consuming and costly to implement and learn. Not only do current projects need to be entered into the system, but all accounting information as well. It requires significant administrative time to implement these systems and may take several months to complete. The software providers do provide assistance with this process, along with training and technical support.

If a firm has many employees, complex projects, or unusual business circumstances, the customization features of the integrated systems may be important. The integrated systems also can supply more sophisticated reports and graphics that combine information from accounting and projects. These can give firm leaders a snapshot of performance that is very rich and useful for decision making. The power and breadth of features in the integrated software can be impressive.

Vision by Deltek is the most well-known integrated performance management software. Deltek has been designing software for use by the A/E industry for over three decades—Vision is in use by many large firms—and is considered the industry leader. The product is sophisticated and has excellent graphic interface. This includes a unique graphic called Visualization, which shows the performance of all current projects simultaneously. Projects are grouped by building type and are shown as boxes sized in relation to their contract size. Troubled projects (those over budget) are shown in shades of red, progressing from light to dark as the problems grow more serious. High-performance projects are noted in blue, while breakeven jobs are left white.

The Deltek Vision web page **http://deltek.com/products/vision/default.asp** reveals the company's orientation to large firms with a sizable administrative staff and a managing principal. However, Deltek does offer a small business version of Vision and promises that it can be "ready to run right out of the box." Either version allows firm leaders to quickly understand performance of projects, staff, and the firm as a whole.

However, in most small firms the owners are architects, not business professionals. To fully use the capabilities offered by this software application, there would need to be strong interest in business development as an end in itself. As firms grow, this interest is no longer optional but in firms that intend to stay small (under 20), much of the capacity of the integrated software may go unused. When considering which software to purchase, firm strategic goals particularly in terms of growth become critical.

Another company that offers integrated performance management software for the A/E industry is Axium, **http://axiumae.com/products**. The Axium products include *Ajera,* the basic version, and *Portfolio,* a version that adds increased capabilities in firm-wide performance management. Axium has been developing industry-specific software for over 20 years and offers an alternative to Deltek for small firms.

For small firms, Ajera appears to offer excellent project performance management capabilities and a good graphics interface. In terms of accounting and financial performance management, it appears to be adequate, but not as powerful as standard accounting software such as QuickBooks. Full financial accounting capability is available in Axium's Portfolio.

Project Management—Only Systems

The alternative to an integrated system is a software application that offers only project performance management. These systems are not integrated, but they have the capacity to share information with existing accounting software. The advantage of these systems is that they are generally lower in initial costs and are easier to implement because the existing accounting system stays in place. Reducing administrative work in the implementation of a new system is a powerful benefit for small firms, especially very small firms under five members.

The obvious disadvantage may be potential glitches in the import/export functions between the accounting and the project management software. In addition, these systems seem to offer less customization than the integrated software systems and are not designed to track firm performance as a whole. To understand overall firm performance, it would be necessary for firm leaders to get standard reports from the accounting software and separate project performance reports from the project management software. Nevertheless, increased understanding of project performance will give most small firm owners a good sense of how the firm is doing as a whole.

ArchiOffice, **www.archioffice.com/**, is performance management software that was created specifically for small design firms. ArchiOffice can work on both Mac and PC platforms and, as stated on their web site, it was "created by architects for architects."

As reported by Michael Tardif, "Several years ago, Steve [Burns, FAIA] and his partner Gary Beyerl, AIA, set out to create a software tool for managing their firm, Burns + Beyerl Architects. Burns and Beyerl felt that the available tools for customer relationship management (CRM), accounting, and project management just didn't fit the needs of a typical small office. About one such application, says Burns: 'It looked daunting; I could never imagine myself using it. In our office it would have been like a jet engine in a Volkswagen bug.' The cost of many business management and productivity tools was also a barrier to making their technology available to smaller firms."[3]

How to Choose

Strategic goals may be the most important determinant of which performance management software to choose. If a firm is on a path of growth with business-oriented leadership, an integrated system with full accounting capabilities would make sense. New firms should also consider starting out with an integrated system in place. If firm goals involve staying small—fewer than 10—then a system may be preferred that minimizes administrative work at implementation and promises immediate reductions in ongoing administrative burden.

There are many resources for information on these systems, including referrals offered by the software vendors. Most of these systems have user forums where information is exchanged. Look for colleagues with experience in implementing and using the systems under consideration. The important point to remember is that these systems are designed to routinize the routine, as well as provide information for nonroutine decision making and this software can reduce administrative workload significantly.

Project Startup Process

The beginning of a project is critical to its successful execution. Effective project execution depends on creating a project work plan, budget, and staffing plan that reflects the project's goals, scope of work, and time frame. It also depends on careful documentation and the ability to retrieve critical information when needed. Although every project is different, the process of project startup is basically routine.

Routinizing project startup begins with the project acquisition process. It is important to set up simple systems to process and track job inquiries, and to institute a go/no-go procedure for deciding which project to pursue. A standard form will facilitate tracking of inquiries and a simple checklist of criteria can be helpful for the go/no-go decision. As an example of a tool that can be useful in making the go/no-go decision, see the accompanying sidebar. Although it comes from a large landscape and civil engineering firm, it is instructive for firms of all sizes.

Other examples of simple project evaluator tools can be found in publications such as the thirteenth edition of *Architects Handbook of Professional Practice*.[5]

Once a project is acquired, it is common for a binder to be created as a place to collect all hardcopy materials associated with the project. Typically the binder will have dividers with headings such as: contacts (client and team), contract, budget and schedule, program requirements, site information, regulations and codes, product research, and the like. Sometimes there will be sections for the phases of the project—predesign, schematic, design development, construction documents, negotiation and bidding, and the construction phase. These sections might be used to file hardcopy reductions of the drawings and any related documentation, reports, meeting notes, emails, or phone-conversation notes.

Potential Project Evaluator [4]

Project Name: Date:

Project No: Location:

Client:

PROJECT OVERVIEW

Briefly describe the client, their business, their needs and building type/program.

THE CLIENT	Yes	No	Unknown
Have we worked with the client before?			
Does this client have shared values and will they appreciate our leadership and qualifications?			
Is the client experienced, and do they have knowledgeable staff?			
Has the client identified a project manager or advocate for the project?			
Do we have personal knowledge of the client's financial stability and general reputation?			
Do their references indicate they would be good to work with?			

THE PROJECT			
Does this project fit our marketing and strategic plan goals?			
Did we know about the RFP before it was published?			
Do we offer unique value that stands out from the competition?			
Is the project of the type that we have worked on before both successfully and frequently?			
Do we know the full scope of work and fully understand the needs of the project?			
Is the project properly funded, particularly our portion of the work?			
Is the project practical considering the schedule, budget, program, profit?			
Are there reasons, other than profit, for pursuing the work? (Examples: developing new market niche; building client relationship; building consultant relationships)			
Is the project within easy traveling distance to our office or one of our offices?			
Do we anticipate additional work being generated for the firm from this project?			
Do we have a high probability of winning the project?			

THE TEAM	Yes	No	Unknown
Do we have a strong track record with this project type?			
Do we have staff with the right experience for the job?			
Are we able to handle the workload without strain on our staff/resources?			
Have we worked successfully with the proposed team before?			

CONTRACTOR			
Does the client have an outside contractor identified?			
Have they gone through a partnering process before?			
Do they have high-quality control standards?			

If the project is a GO, use space below to indicate ways in which any identified risks (Nos, Unknowns) will be mitigated:

Prepared by:_____

Signed by:_____

(Principal)

Source: BCNW Business Development Team: Ellen Southard, Karoline Vass, Rene Senos, Bob Walsh & Jane Dewell.

A parallel process in electronic form must also be initiated for each project. Firm-wide norms for file names and locations must be established. Without these conventions, information on a project can be very difficult to retrieve when needed. Research has shown that significant time is wasted in offices looking for missing documents and lost information. Being disciplined about project startup will establish a culture of attention to how information is documented and filed. Many of the project management software systems have project-based document and information filing systems that can facilitate this process. The software also requires that client information be recorded, project budgets be entered, and project team members be named.

Routinizing the project startup and documentation systems will contribute to excellence in project delivery by establishing a culture of attentiveness and accountability. Establishing and tracking the project budget, schedule, and quality will help all involved understand expectations and responsibilities. This will contribute to increased productivity, profitability, and overall operational effectiveness.

Capacity Utilization

In addition to performance management software and routinizing the project startup process, operational effectiveness can be augmented with attention to capacity utilization. Capacity utilization is the amount of the firm's total facilities and resources that is being used to execute the work of project acquisition and delivery. Typically a capacity utilization rate of over 90 percent will inhibit operational effectiveness. For example, if staff members are waiting to use the copy machine or a particular workstation with special software, this is a capacity utilization problem. Investment in a small amount of excess equipment and redundancy can reduce wasted time and production bottlenecks if targeted correctly. Proper balance between excess capacity and frugal use of resources must be found to maximize effectiveness of production processes.

Backup systems may prove invaluable in the event of failure or damage to critical infrastructure. Backups can prevent loss of the firm's intellectual property—whether in drawing, accounting, marketing, correspondence, personnel, or other files (digital or otherwise). Consider how the firm may be vulnerable or ill-equipped in a deadline-generated crisis (or any other crisis) and take action to remedy the situation. Investments in firm capacity and backup systems is not optional and should be part of any firm's annual budget.

In summary, firm leaders can take action to improve work processes by implementing some of the suggestions in the following sidebar, *Routinize the Routine*.

Routinize the Routine

- Treat routine work and nonroutine work differently.
- Pay attention to processes: Look for bottlenecks, wasted efforts, blatant inefficiencies.
- Project startup: Use standard forms and procedures.
- Consider performance management software for general accounting and project management tracking.
- Create standard forms for information that is gathered repeatedly, such as a form for recording project inquiries.
- Monitor capacity utilization carefully.
- Consider backup systems and security measures.

While the importance of operational effectiveness cannot be overstated, the real engine that runs design firms is its people and its leadership. How to motivate and maximize the efforts of intelligent and talented people is the topic of Chapter 4, Leadership Matters.

ENDNOTES

1. Calvin Pava, *Managing the New Office Technology*, The Free Press, NY, 1983, p.47.

2. Ken Blanchard and Paul Hersey, *The One Minute Manager,* William Morrow and Company, Inc., NY, 1982.

3. Michael Tardif, "Tools for Practice" *AIArchitect*, American Institute of Architects, Washington, D.C., November 16, 2007.

4. Belt Collins Northwest Business Development Team: Ellen Southard, Karoline Vass, Rene Senos, Bob Walsh and Jane Dewell, *Potential Project Evaluator,* Belt Collins Northwest LLC., Seattle, 2009.

5. American Institute of Architects, *Architects Handbook of Professional Practice,* 13th ed., Joseph Demkin, AIA, exec. ed., John Wiley & Sons, NY, 2001, p. 158.

CHAPTER 4

LEADERSHIP MATTERS

Although it may sound trite, people really are the most important assets of professional service firms. It is the technical knowledge, emotional intelligence, experience, drive, and creativity of all involved that determine the success of small design firms. The temperament of firm leaders, and their willingness to trust the people they have hired, creates both atmosphere and cultural norms at a firm. It is not uncommon to hear small firm leaders complain about the behavior of their staff, remarking on a lack of motivation or attention to task. They wonder how they can elicit voluntary commitment and encourage employees to strive for excellence and innovation.

The answers to these questions begin with understanding firm culture, cultivation of self-awareness among firm leaders, and appreciation of the unique challenges of managing organizations populated by creative professionals.

FIRM CULTURE

The definition of organizational culture is a subject of much dialogue among management consultants and human resource professionals who want to hire people who are a match to their companies' culture. It is often defined by referring to values, organizational structure, and the level of concern for employee well-being. Consultant Roger Harrison has defined organizational culture based on two factors—the amount of organizational focus on the individual versus on the group; and the tendency for an organization's management to be controlling rather than trusting of its workforce. This model is shown in Figure 4.1.[1]

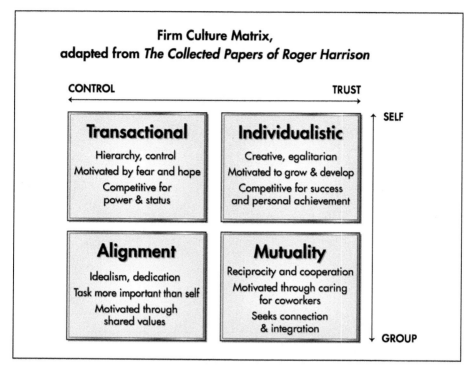

Figure 4.1 Organizational culture revolves around levels of control versus trust, and group versus individual concerns.

Transactional organizations, as the name implies, are based on transactions. People in this type of organization trade information and influence for power and status. These organizations are hierarchical with top-down control and are oriented toward benefit of self rather than the company. People in this kind of organization are motivated by a "carrot and stick" approach—fear of punishment and hoped-for rewards. Traditional corporate organizations and large corporate professional service firms often have this type of culture.

Individualistic organizations also encourage self-gain over the benefit of the company. However, in this type of culture there is a higher level of trust because people are motivated by personal achievement rather than acquisition of power. These are creative and egalitarian organizations where people compete on the basis of personal excellence and hard work. Broadly speaking, the culture of the architectural profession is highly individualistic.

Organizations with an alignment culture are ones in which the group takes precedence over the individual. Often these organizations are driven by an ideal, are focused on a mission that is more important than the individual. People in these organizations are motivated through a shared identity and belief system, and are often described as "true believers." Tight control from the top is replaced with zeal for the cause that gives people sufficient direction to do what needs to be done. Sometimes there is a tendency toward utilitarian ethics where the ends justify the means. Political or religious activists often form this kind of organization.

Finally, organizations that have a culture of mutuality place the emphasis on the well-being of the group through trusting the individual. These organizations motivate individuals by promoting caring, cooperation, and connection. Democratic management practices such as consensus are possible because of the underlying norms of compassion and fairness. Many family-run companies and many small closely held businesses have this kind of organizational culture.

Many small architectural firms have aspects of mutuality and individuality co-existing in their firm cultures. Both can be positive and which becomes dominant rests squarely on the disposition of firm leadership. There are also architectural firms that exhibit an alignment-type culture in which both staff and principals are dedicated to a certain ideal such as sustainable design or affordable housing. Of course, transactional architecture firms exist as well, mostly in the form of large corporate offices.

Field Theory

In the new science there is an idea known as "field theory." A *field* is defined as an invisible, nonmaterial influence, such as gravity or magnetism. Many scientists today believe that the universe is filled with such fields and this understanding explains many previously unexplainable phenomena.

The application of this idea to organizations is easy for most people to perceive. For example, it is not uncommon for people to walk into a store, a restaurant, or an office and comment on feeling "good energy" that has positive influence. And many have also had the experience of entering a place and immediately feeling that something was not right. These are fields at work, and in organizations fields manifest themselves as culture and atmosphere.[2]

Understanding firm culture allows firm leaders to become aware of the "field" they have created and to consider if it accurately reflects their personal values and vision for the firm. For example, a firm may be highly individualistic and competitive despite the firm leader's espoused desire to have a firm based on collaboration and mutuality. This disconnect between aspiration and actuality may indicate a lack of congruence between the firm leader's message and the firm leader's actions.

Self-Aware Leadership

No matter what leaders may say, employees will imitate their behaviors. What is important to firm leaders becomes important to everyone at the firm. How leaders behave will be how everyone behaves. When leaders "walk their talk," their values will permeate the entire organization. When they do not, their lack of integrity will also be imitated. Leaders of small firms determine their firms' culture and set the tone at their firms through modeling behavior that (hopefully) is consistent with their values, vision, and purpose.

While it seems evident that leaders influence the feelings and actions of their followers, research in neuroscience is discovering the brain chemistry behind this phenomenon. As reported by Daniel Goleman and Richard Boyatzis in their article, "Social Intelligence and the Biology of Leadership," scientists have identified cells known as *mirror neurons* which are found throughout the brain. As explained in the article, "This previously unknown class of brain cells operates as neural Wi-Fi, allowing us to navigate our social world. When we consciously or unconsciously detect someone else's emotions through their actions, our mirror neurons reproduce those emotions. Collectively, these neurons create an instant sense of shared experience."[3]

The importance of this discovery to small firm leaders is the recognition that they must be very aware of what they are doing and what subtle messages are being sent. If staff members continually behave in ways that displease firm leaders, either the staff doesn't understand what is expected and they need some training or coaching; or perhaps, the staff is mirroring unintended or unconscious direction from the firm leaders.

Research reported by Goleman and Boyatzis shows that the tone of delivery in giving feedback, for example, is actually more important than the content of the feedback—those leaders who are positive, in a good mood, and quick to smile are more likely to bring out the best in their employees. Goleman and Boyatzis write, "If leaders hope to get the best out of their people, they should continue to be demanding but in ways that foster a positive mood in their teams. The old carrot-and-stick approach alone doesn't make neural sense; traditional incentive systems are simply not enough to get the best performance from followers."[4]

Whether it is the result of brain chemistry or field theory, firm leaders can use their ability to model values, vision, and ethics as a management tool. Robert Haas, CEO of Levi Strauss & Co., calls these "conceptual controls . . . it is the *ideas* of a business that are controlling, not some manager with authority."[5]

Control versus Trust

Because most small architectural firms are fairly egalitarian in their management structure, the problem is sometimes not too much control, but not enough guidance. Take the case of CC Architects. The principal there is highly respected as a cutting-edge creative designer. Her practice has been built on her design talents and now she has a steady supply of clients who come to her because they like her unique style. Unlike many "star designers" she is easy-going and well liked and runs her firm of almost 20 without any heavy-handed autocratic structures. There is a clear sense of identity, fostered by the design reputation of the firm, and an observable feeling of freedom among the staff to do their work as they see fit, with one notable exception.

The project architects complain that although they try to make their work fit with the concept developed by the principal, they often "get it wrong and don't really know what she wants." Since design takes place throughout the entire design process, and the principal can't do all of it, a disconnect keeps occurring between what the principal wants and what actually gets drawn. The result is rework, redo, frustration for the staff and principal, and too many demands on the principal's time.

The solution to this problem lies in the realm of mentoring, training, and coaching. There is no problem with clear vision; the principal has plenty of that, both as a designer and firm leader. The problem is lack of knowledge and understanding of the vision throughout the firm. An action that might improve this situation is a series of in-house "design classes," where the principal discusses and illustrates her design methods and ideas. She needs to familiarize her staff with her tendencies, her personal preferences and approaches to design issues. Doing this along with bi-weekly "design crit" get-togethers will go a long way toward helping her staff design more effectively and more congruently with the "firm style." The whole office learns together and also learns to share their knowledge with each other.

While this approach may work for some firm leaders, it will not work for everyone because of their managerial disposition. The principal of CC Architects may never really be able to give up control of design decisions, no matter how skilled her staff becomes in understanding her approach. Or, she may be quite willing to guide and mentor her staff and to trust their decisions and approach.

Self-awareness as a leader must include understanding a personal comfort zone when it comes to empowering others. How much trust and how much control feels comfortable to a leader is a function of their personality and proclivities. And, as illustrated in the narrative about CC Architects, the comfort zone may vary for different types of decisions.

Leadership styles in business organizations range in a continuum from authoritarian to democratic, based on the extent to which staff is empowered to make decisions. In boss-centered leadership, managers make decisions and announce them, or perhaps allow some questions from the staff. In staff-centered leadership, the manager gives guidance, sets limits, such as deadline or budget, and authorizes staff to make decisions and get the job done.[6]

Firm leaders who have self-awareness about their place on this continuum are more likely to manage with integrity—to say what they mean and to mean what they say. Small firm leaders with integrity and self-awareness can successfully shape their firm in their own image. Based on the work type/management style matrix introduced in Chapter 3 (see Figures 3.3 and 3.4), if a more autocratic and directive style is preferred, then projects that involve more routine work and junior staff may be favored at the firm. If a leader leans toward a more collaborative approach, with a more supportive style, then focus on nonroutine projects or integrated processes may be more appropriate.

Of course this is not a rigid analysis and there are many ways that a leadership style preference may express itself in project choice and business model. Highly controlling persons may choose to be solo practitioners or leaders of very small firms where they can be completely in charge. Leaders who enjoy empowering others may find that they excel in project acquisition and can build their firms on the technical and design knowledge of their employees.

Regardless of the leaders' style, firm culture provides norms of behavior and basic guidelines to professional staff. Employees need these guidelines to refer to, so they understand what is expected of them. This is not only about design vision, it may be about how things are drawn, or technical aspects, or it may be in the realm of ethics, or how a client is treated. If staff has clear models from their leaders, then they can also have freedom to make decisions on their own. This will happen automatically in a firm as staff members mimic the behavior of the principals, similar to children who copy their parents. So like parents, firm leaders have to be very aware of what they are doing.

Career Contentment

As discussed in Chapter 2, job satisfaction, including the career contentment of firm owners, is a primary influence on productivity. This reinforcing relationship is true in all knowledge work, as stated with certainty by Goleman and Boyatzis, "And, everyone knows that when people feel better, they perform better."[7]

For architects, the primary contributors to satisfaction are opportunity to design and to have autonomy over one's work. Knowing this, it's easy to understand why there are so many sole proprietors and very small firms in the design industry. For small firms, retaining employees who hold technical and organizational knowledge and motivating them to provide enthusiastic commitment, is vital to firm success. For solo practitioners, success may depend on retaining passion for the work, and on creating new opportunities for challenge and learning.

Promote Career Contentment

- Provide opportunity to design or do other creative work.
- Provide stretch assignments to promising staff members.
- Provide acknowledgment and sincere appreciation.
- Communicate the purpose and values of the firm.
- Provide support for staff career goals.
- Provide support for continuing education and life-long learning.
- Provide opportunity for advancement within the firm.

Actions can be taken that promote career contentment for both staff and firm leaders. The first of these is to provide everyone in the firm with opportunities to design or engage in creative problem solving. This includes firm principals who often complain that managing their firms and acquiring projects leaves little time for design work. There are ways for principals to regain time for design, if desired, and these are discussed further in Chapter 5, Lifecycle of a Small Firm. Giving junior staff opportunities to design small projects or parts of projects will elicit enthusiasm and allow opportunity for new ideas and contributions.

Allowing for appropriate autonomy is the next important avenue to job satisfaction. By delegating responsibility and authority for a task to the lowest-paid person who could do the task, firms can increase profitability and offer stretch assignments that challenge its talented staff members. This may involve mentoring, coaching, and training to accomplish, but the pay-off can be significant in both staff enthusiasm and the bottom line.

Providing acknowledgment and sincere appreciation is a no-cost action with big dividends in terms of satisfaction. Angeles Arrien,[8] renowned consultant and cultural anthropologist, has identified four universal arenas for acknowledgment and appreciation:

1. Skills, talents, abilities—a person's core competence and exceptional capability.
2. Character—a person's integrity, courage, dedication.
3. Contribution—an individual's ability to inspire and contribute to the success of the group.
4. Appearance—within appropriate bounds, people enjoy compliments on their appearance.

Professional employees also need to have meaning in their work. Clearly communicating the values and purpose of the firm will help staff determine if their personal values are in alignment with the organization. If alignment is present, meaning derives from working toward common goals which, in turn, stimulates dedication and commitment.

Learning and professional challenge is another significant component of satisfaction among architects. Firms can create a culture of learning by supporting the individual professional development of its staff and leadership. Continuing education and broadening of professional knowledge is beneficial both to the individual and the firm when their goals are aligned. This takes thoughtful consideration of the knowledge needs of the firm and a connection between firm strategy and professional development planning. Learning efforts can be supported financially, but learning can also happen through internal education programs, mentoring, and creating an expectation of knowledge sharing. In Chapter 9, Strategic Thinking, the notion of a "learning organization," where all are encouraged to gain and share knowledge, will be discussed as an important strategy for success. For solo practitioners and very small firms, learning is vital to remaining professionally relevant and personally engaged.

One of the most challenging aspects of career contentment in small firms is the ability to provide clear avenues for employee advancement within the firm. It is common for skilled and experienced architects to leave the firm that trained them in order to advance their careers. Firms can minimize this occurrence by clearly defining roles, responsibilities, and the knowledge needed for advancement; by including the promotion of existing staff as part of their strategic growth plans; and by making the process transparent and fair. Creating an ownership transition plan and the identification of likely candidates is also important and is discussed fully in Chapter 6, Transition Times.

Employee Retention

It cannot be overstated that retaining experienced employees and motivating them to do their best has an impact on the bottom line of small design firms. Excellence and enthusiasm can be nurtured by creating a firm culture built on the well-being and advancement of staff and firm owners alike. Firms that achieve a culture of mutuality, where people work hard because they care about one another are the most resilient over time. Some owners fear that if they provide professional development support to staff, it will represent a great loss if that person leaves the firm. However, providing professional development support is more likely to generate loyalty and voluntary commitment, especially if a path to advancement in the firm is evident.

Small firms often operate as if they are one big team. Collaborative work is an important aspect of operational effectiveness and team-building is a primary function of small firm leadership. Liking one's coworkers and feeling liked by them is another key to job satisfaction and employee retention.

There are many ways that effective team work can be encouraged. Angeles Arrien, in her research as a cultural anthropologist, has identified a "Universal Group Protocol" that applies when people work in groups.

Universal Group Protocol

From the Work of Angeles Arrien[9]

1. Any group can only go as far as its weakest link.
2. High-performance teams have high levels of trust based on staying current with each other.
3. Team members practice deep listening and genuine acknowledgment.
4. Avoid rescue, fix, unsolicited advice.

These are practical suggestions for behavior that can help people perform at their best throughout a project. The weak link alluded to in the first rule is not the person with the least skill, it is the person who is least engaged. Leaders should:

- Notice when someone is not engaged, always silent, or negative when contributing. Ask that person what is going on for them and why they are not fully contributing. Much can be learned from someone who is willing to voice what others are likely also thinking.

The second rule involves developing trust by staying current, which means not withholding information about feelings and thoughts from other team members. Arrien advises frequent check-ins and activities that promote familiarity among coworkers. Leaders should encourage team members to:

- Practice the 24/3/7 rule which means that if there is tension or outright conflict between two team members, it needs to be dealt with within 24 hours; if not, then within three days; and if not, then within seven days at the most. If the discord goes on for more than a week it can seriously damage team performance and personal relationships. In addition, if a conflict goes unresolved for too long, it will be difficult for those involved to remember what was said and what the whole problem was about.

Staying current by direct communication also avoids "triangulation" which happens when a third party is brought into a dispute between two other people. This can lead to allegiance building, a toxic situation for most teams.

Engaging in deep listening and giving genuine acknowledgment are the behaviors that make the previous suggestion work. Arrien points out that people need to be acknowledged for both their thoughts and their feelings and will continue to repeat themselves until both have been heard and recognized.

- Listen for both thoughts and feelings in what others say. For example, after a client presentation, a coworker might say, "I think that presentation went well." If the response is, "Yes, it did," the coworker is likely to repeat the statement one or two more times because only facts were acknowledged. If the response is, "Yes it did, and you did really well," (assuming that is true), then both facts and feelings are acknowledged and the coworker will feel heard. Small gestures can make a big difference.

The fourth rule is to avoid giving unsolicited advice and resist the temptation to try to rescue teammates. Unsolicited advice, fixing things for someone else, or doing their work for them are behaviors that can be used as a subtle way of asserting power or superiority. However, responding when help is requested is more than appropriate. Leaders should:

- Demand excellence and accountability from each member of the team as well as encourage teammates to seek help from one another when needed.

WORKING WITH CREATIVE PEOPLE

When working with creative people it is important to distinguish between perfection and excellence. Perfection is an absolute and by definition is rarely, if ever, achieved. Excellence, on the other hand, is a relative term meaning that something is done in the best possible way compared to other similar efforts. Design firms sometimes suffer from "excessive perfection" and this striving for the best is common among creative people.

Another quality that creative people share is a desire to contribute to the success of their organization and be acknowledged for that contribution. Given the opportunity, most design firm staff members will be anxious to contribute to firm development and improvement efforts. These efforts may involve visioning, branding, marketing, improving production processes, and enhancing sustainable workplace practices, among others. Firm leaders can use this willingness to contribute by involving staff in helping them determine and accomplish firm development tasks. One way to do that is through holding a firm retreat.

Effective Firm Retreats

Firm retreats can leverage the creativity of staff and increase organizational self-knowledge. Outcomes of effective retreats include development of strategic initiatives, activation of process improvement, and enhancement of morale. Effective retreats engage participants and encourage shared leadership. Chances of retreat success will be increased by using an innovative method known as Open Space Technology.

Developed by consultant Harrison Owen[10] in 1985, Open Space Technology (OST) is a nonproprietary method in use by organizations of every type and size throughout the world. OST is known worldwide as an effective group process for identifying critical issues, sharing knowledge, voicing concerns, and working collaboratively to find solutions. While other methods might be used to achieve these ends, many of them are proprietary and require the services of a facilitator certified in the system. OST has a do-it-yourself simplicity and is freely available to all comers.

For architectural firms, staff input is critical to organizational assessment, vision alignment, strategic planning, and process improvement. A retreat using OST will give firm leaders access to the intelligence, experience, and enthusiasm of their staff. Because the method requires shared leadership and collaboration, an OST retreat builds strong connections between principals, administrators, and professional staff. The method is most effective when used by firms of 15 to 50 members, but can also work well for very large groups.

Open Space Technology Method

The first step in planning an OST meeting is to determine and articulate a theme for the meeting or retreat. Usually this is done by the firm leaders, sometimes with the help of a consultant. Often it is wise to craft an open-ended calling question such as, "What are the issues and opportunities involved in achieving excellence in design and project delivery?" or "How can we better satisfy our clients and make this the best possible place to work?" A targeted issue can also be used effectively as a meeting theme. An example of a pragmatic retreat topic might be, "How can we improve quality control and quality assurance in our project delivery?"

Although OST methods are nonproprietary and easily learned, it is often advisable to retain a skilled OST facilitator to run the meeting or retreat. This will free firm leaders to participate fully without having to pay attention to anything other than the conversations in which they are engaged. In addition, a skilled OST facilitator can determine an appropriate length for the retreat; can usually recommend suitable venues; can help organize the retreat schedule; and can teach the OST method to participants.

In architectural firms, retreats conducted using Open Space Technology require a special role for firm leadership. Firm leaders must empower their staff to be honest and straightforward in the agenda formation and the small group dialogues. They must reassure those in their employ that there will be no negative consequences for things said or opinions held, and they must mean it. Morale and enthusiasm can be seriously damaged if the trust so requested is betrayed. For an OST retreat to be successful, firm leaders must be open to the perceptions of others, care about their feelings, and be willing to empower them to act on the ideas they generate. OST retreats can do more harm than good without sincere openness on the part of firm leadership.

With a theme determined in advance, participants create an agenda for the meeting during the first hour of the get-together. Any participant is empowered to suggest a topic for the agenda and to convene a small group meeting on that topic. Through simple organizational tools, a schedule of these meetings, including topic, time, and location, will be generated and displayed. Although a theme may be very broad, this process guarantees that all aspects of the topic that are important to those present will be discussed.

Small group conversations on the agenda topics take place in 45- to 60-minute sessions that are held in designated places and during distinct time slots. Each participant's time is their own to schedule, meaning that each person decides what conversation to attend, when to take a break, or when to talk to another person in a spontaneous interaction. Participants are also free to move from conversation to conversation ("Law of Two Feet"), insuring that they will always be involved in dialogue that is meaningful and interesting to them. Those moving from group to group provide the cross-pollination of ideas critical to creative outcomes.

At the concluding circle, each participant is invited to make remarks about their experience of the retreat. Because everyone has had the opportunity to spend the time in dialogue about ideas that are important to them, themes will begin to emerge and related issues will start to converge. These concluding remarks are often insightful, creative, energetic, and sometimes articulate specific action plans.

Outcomes of Effective Retreats

Typically, results from an Open Space Technology retreat fall into two categories. The first kinds of outcome are action items that can be accomplished immediately. These actions arise from the many good and practical ideas that are always generated when people converse about topics they really care about. An example of this might be a small change to a work process that makes it more efficient or a decision to implement a carpooling program. Because the process of OST identifies those who have passion for these kinds of ideas, it is simple to find the right person to facilitate their implementation.

The second kind of results are ideas, insights, and creative imaginings that require more thought or research before action can be taken. These outcomes sometimes will cause a taskforce of interested persons to be formed. Firm leaders will certainly be involved in these work groups if ideas surface that suggest a reconsideration of basic procedures or existing structures.

Another common outcome of an OST retreat is a significant increase in familiarity, enthusiasm, and commitment among participants. In architectural firms, these outcomes translate into improved productivity and collaborative processes. Sometimes, issues that involve the deeply embedded culture of an organization will unexpectedly surface, causing widespread surprise and transformative insight among participants.

While it is common for organizational change to be met with apathy or active resistance, when change is initiated as the result of an OST meeting, this is less likely to happen. The method allows all stakeholders to understand the intent of the change initiative and to contribute to its formation.

Open Space Technology is a tool that allows firm leaders to do more with less when planning and executing a firm retreat. Facilitation and planning costs are low in both time and money because OST is based on the principles of self-organizing by the participants. Because it engages both the enthusiasm and initiative of the participants, using Open Space Technology yields reliably positive, often inspired results. See Chapter 9, Strategic Thinking, for a case study of a strategic planning initiative that includes a firm retreat.

Plan Nonbillable Hours

The results of a firm retreat may lead to the formation of work groups tasked with the job of researching and/or implementing plans and projects for firm development and improvement. For example, a retreat focused on improving project delivery may result in work groups that focus on researching conversion to 3-D software; improving the project startup process; or organizing the detail library, to name a few possibilities. When these tasks are tackled by dedicated work groups composed of both principals and staff, things get done. These kinds of activities are value-added, meaning that they improve productivity and are worth the expenditure of nonbillable hours.

In small firms, owners benefit greatly from enlisting the help of their staff in firm development. There will always be nonbillable hours as part of professional service work, why not plan use of those hours, similarly to how billable hours are planned? About 15 percent of the workweek is not billable for the average project architect or project manager in a small firm. The key is to organize nonbillable work into discreet projects and assign staff to help research and implement firm improvements. This could be anything from helping with the website to putting up shelves.

Small firm leaders have the opportunity to see their staff as allies in the development and strengthening of their firms. This can be done, as discussed in this chapter, by providing self-aware leadership and intentionality about firm culture; by supporting and promoting the career contentment of the staff; by engaging staff assistance through firm retreats; and by planning nonbillable hours to benefit firm development.

While many small firms are led by just one person, it is equally common for small firms to be lead by partnerships of two or three. Partnerships present special challenges to firm cohesion and morale since firm culture mirrors the relationship between partners as much as it reflects the partners as individuals.

PARTNERSHIPS

Having good partnerships in small firms relies on three aspects of compatibility: operational, interpersonal, and aspirational. Despite inherent challenges, there are numerous motivations for entrepreneurial architects to form partnerships. Sharing a common narrative of what it means to succeed and having the ability to collaborate effectively are critical qualities of flourishing partnerships.

Entrepreneurial architects frequently start their firms as sole proprietors—often running the practice completely alone for several years. Many enjoy sole ownership, even as their firms begin to grow and they hire employees. Others find it unsatisfying and are drawn to partnering with a peer—another skilled architect who will bring to the firm contacts or knowledge that is currently absent. Of course many small firms also originate as partnerships of two or three. Some business partnerships are magical, as are some marriages, but most take hard work to be successful.

Why Partner?

Many sole-proprietor firm owners will form partnerships in the hope of expanding the firm's offerings or growing the firm. They may be ambitious new firm owners, or seasoned owners of well-established firms looking to create value beyond their personal scope. The new partner is likely to be someone with knowledge and market sector connections that the founding partner lacks. The new partner might also have large firm experience which the founding partner hopes will benefit the organizational structure and work processes of the existing firm.

In this scenario, it is often challenging for the founding partner to accept the changes a new partner brings to the firm. Although the founder often has good intentions, as stated in the partnership agreement, it is not unusual for resentments to build as the old firm is "reinvented." It is also not unusual for the new partner to disregard the importance of legacy processes and existing firm culture. Staff will feel the struggle between old and new influences as well and may begin to form alliances behind each partner, creating a toxic competitive atmosphere. Fledgling partnerships that go down this road are likely to be short-lived.

Sole firm owners may also look for partners who have skills and interests that complement their own. If they are naturally personable and gifted at acquiring work, they may look for a partner who excels in project execution and delivery. Similarly, if a firm owner is talented in design, he/she may look for a partner who is skillful in management. An intellectual, artistic firm owner may seek a partner who is action-oriented with a technical bent. This strategy can work well although it, too, has its challenges. The danger here is the enabling of each partners' weaknesses. "Designers" are granted permission to ignore budgets and schedules, while "managers" may become exclusively focused on the short-term bottom line. Misaligned purpose, values, and messages to the staff can be the consequences of this kind of partnership.

What Makes Partnerships Work

Whatever the reasons a partnership is formed, certain qualities will foster its success. First and most importantly, partners must share basic values and have complementary professional goals. It almost goes without saying that each must be competent, reliable, and have effective work habits, even if work style differs between the partners. Other aspects of operational compatibility include clarity of roles and responsibilities; and the ability of each partner to tap into different social networking arenas.

However, operational compatibility will only go so far. Often, the very differences that make people consider each other as partners will make it challenging for them to actually work together. Social science research has shown that different career paths will attract people with differing talents and personality types. Therefore, when you bring two professionals together who have divergent experience and knowledge, it's not surprising that there may be conflict, or at least differing points of view. This is where interpersonal compatibility becomes essential.

Interpersonal compatibility, as defined here, is a similarity in how each partner deals with relationships. Successful partners often possess a high degree of emotional intelligence about themselves and others. They have the ability to be honest communicators—to say what they mean and mean what they say. They also communicate frequently, in both structured and unstructured forums. Partners who are interpersonally compatible demonstrate a willingness to stay current about their thoughts and feelings with one another, avoiding hidden resentments and the "building of a case" against the other. This kind of compatibility is essential to successful collaboration over the long haul.

It is easy to see how a married couple might have an advantage in this aspect of partnering. A married couple is likely to be ahead of the curve when it comes to interpersonal communication and understanding. Expressing mutual respect and appreciation, and seeing the success of a partner as a personal success may likewise come easier to married firm leaders. Yet all partners that work well together must have a measure of these qualities—a willingness to accept their partners' differences and operate with a spirit of generosity.

The flip side to this scenario is not hard to imagine. Partners who differ greatly in interpersonal style are in for a rocky ride. For example, if one partner tends to be withholding of their feelings while the other is easily expressive, understanding between the two may be extremely difficult to achieve. Without mutuality that comes from appreciation and respect, unsavory emotions such as jealousy, envy, and competitiveness may arise, or worse, lurk dangerously beneath the surface. In this case, the partners may need the help of a skilled organizational psychologist, assuming they want their partnership to survive.

Rules of the Road

Before forming a partnership with another design professional, consider completing the following exercise together. Take a moment individually to write down answers to the following questions:

1. Describe a partnering experience in which you felt excited and satisfied with your involvement and the partnership's performance.
2. Describe what you value most about your contribution to the partnership.
3. What were the core factors that made the partnership a success?

Compare the answers that each prospective partner has prepared. Notice whether there is compatibility in terms of the contributions made to the partnership experiences described. More importantly, note each partner's definition of success and the central factors involved in its achievement.

This exercise will give prospective partners insight into their aspirational compatibility. It will help them to understand what makes each of them feel successful and it may reveal whether their values are aligned. The professional and personal goals of each partner must be compatible as well. While these aspirations need not be identical, they should be able to support one another over time. Surfacing and sharing these long-term visions up front should be part of any partnership formation discussion.

On the practical level, it is important that partners draft a written agreement which serves as a guide during the twists and turns of professional life. This is especially important considering the high likelihood of changes to a partnership over time. A consultant can facilitate conversations to help partners form an agreement and an attorney for each partner should be involved to draft and review a legally binding partnership agreement. At a minimum, partnership agreements should include:

- The name of the partnership and the names of each of the partners.
- A general description of the type of business that will be conducted.
- The powers and duties of the partners, including any limitations or restrictions.
- The financial contribution (cash, labor, and/or equipment) that each partner will make.
- How profits and losses are to be divided.
- How partners can leave the business and how new partners can be added.
- Ownership of intellectual property.
- Exclusivity: Is a partner allowed to work on projects outside of the partnership, which will not contribute to the income of the partnership?
- Dispute resolution process.

A partnership, as a legal entity, may have certain tax advantages over becoming a corporation. Careful consideration should be given to the choice of legal business entity. For example, in a partnership, it is necessary to understand that partners are personally responsible for all the debts and financial obligations of the partnership. Seek professional advice to become familiar with the legal and financial implications of forming a partnership.

What Makes Partnerships Fail

Scenario 1: Partnerships that fail quickly are those in which one or more partners misunderstand, and thereby misrepresent their own leadership style. The partners may think they want to collaborate on decision making, and they may believe that differing approaches will strengthen their firm; but in the day-to-day world of real practice, they may quickly discover otherwise. Entrepreneurial architects who are used to calling the shots can become impatient with one another, growing tired of drawn-out discussions and joint decision making. Sometimes détente occurs, with each partner taking control of separate aspects, of different "studios," or departments, within the practice. This is a functional, but by no means optimal solution.

Lesson Learned: Make sure you know your leadership style. If you like being "king" you may not like being a partner. Don't make promises about power sharing that you may not be able to keep over the long term. Partnerships don't always have to be 50/50.

Scenario 2: Partnerships are also at risk as firm owners enter mid-life and their firms have matured and stabilized. Partners who have always gotten along may find that their priorities are shifting and differences that were once workable have become untenable. Differing goals and different value systems suddenly appear to emerge. Many partnerships dissolve and reconfigure at this stage of professional life.

Lesson Learned: Prepare for change in advance. Partnership agreements must have an "exit strategy," one that is agreed to long before it is needed. Also, as advised by Jack Welch, famed CEO of General Electric, it's a good idea to "change before you have to."[11] Stay aware of shifts in personal interests and priorities and make adjustments before a crisis forces change.

Scenario 3: It is often said that business partnerships are similar to marriages. Let's not forget that nearly 50 percent of marriages end in divorce. Partnerships that are based on an alliance of two people who have very divergent professional experiences can be very challenging. All the stereotype dualities about different types of architects have some basis in fact—the creative designer versus the efficient project manager; the people person versus the brainy introvert; the scattered visionary versus the rational organizer. It takes a great deal of work to bridge these kinds of gaps in personality and professional approach. If partners are able to achieve mutual understanding, however, they can leverage their differences positively and create a flourishing organization.

Lesson Learned: Prepare to need professional help. It's reasonable to partner with someone who has very different work history, professional strengths, and personality style. But if you do, be prepared to work hard at accepting and appreciating differences. Make sure your prospective partner is willing to do so as well.

Consider soliciting assistance from an organizational psychologist to help you learn to collaborate effectively and efficiently. Otherwise, prepare for divorce court.

"Unintentional Enmity" Revisited

When entrepreneurial architects form business partnerships, they must be sure that they are ready to share decision-making power. They also must be ready for differing perspectives and must find a way to welcome them. They must understand that their priorities and interests may change over time and prepare accordingly. The potential for increased revenues, more diverse project types, expanded services, and the creation of a firm that has value beyond its founders are strong motivators. Just be sure to carefully evaluate compatibility of operational skills, interpersonal style, and aspirational goals before "tying the knot."

In Chapter 1, Archetype Three illustrated a situation dubbed "Unintentional Enmity." Partners may inadvertently find themselves in this situation due to incompatibilities that are discovered in the course of working together. As illustrated in the scenarios, it may take significant effort to turn the vicious cycles illustrated in Figure 1.8 into virtuous cycles illustrated here in Figure 4.2.

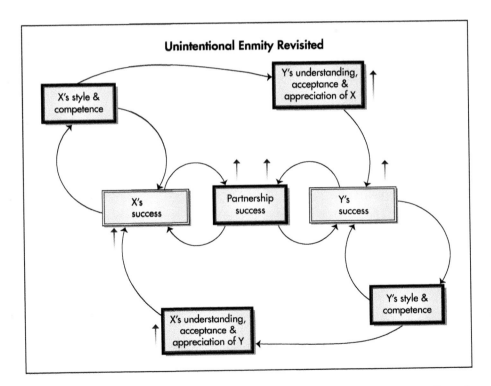

Figure 4.2 Appreciation of the other partner's style and contribution will benefit each partner and the partnership.

The "Unintentional Enmity" diagram has been transformed to show a situation in which each partner benefits fully from the style and competencies of the other partner, rather than feeling inhibited, blocked, or sabotaged. In this situation, each partner makes an effort toward improved communication and sincere appreciation of the other partner. This yields benefits to each partner in the form of personal growth and the increased likelihood of success for the partnership.

Transformation of the "Unintentional Enmity" archetype into this positive pattern can happen if there is awareness of destructive patterns and a willingness to change behaviors. Partners who realize how they sabotage the other, and therefore themselves, may begin to operate differently. Instead of resenting the other's success, for example, each might work harder to foster the other's accomplishments. In time, these positive behaviors will increase each partner's success and will be self-reinforcing. The virtuous cycles shown in Figure 4.2 require discipline, openness, and perhaps professional help to pursue the personal growth necessary to make partnerships work. See Chapter 10, Small Design Firm Practice Models, for a description of the qualities married couples often bring to running a design firm as business partners. The alignment of vision, mutuality of support, and effectiveness of communication that married firm partners often exhibit can be a model for all design firm partnerships.

Some partners take a different approach to making their partnerships work. As mentioned before, they do this by forging a relatively comfortable *détente*. Often, these partners will develop a way to manage separate areas of the practice in their own way, but without negatively impacting the other. Although probably less satisfying than learning to work collaboratively, partners who organize their practice in this way can create a successful firm as long as they continue to communicate well and feel positively about one another.

Success in Group Work

Whether it is the partners working together or a project team, success in group work among creative people is influenced by many factors. According to cultural anthropologist Angeles Arrien, success in group work is supported by the following conditions.[12]

- **Discipline:** not rigidity or perfection, but rather, rigor for achieving excellence. Remember perfection is not a relative term so it can never be achieved; excellence is relative, one outcome is excellent compared to another. Strive for excellence, not perfection.
- **Flexibility:** approach a task with curiosity and humor. Try not to take things too seriously; don't be too negative; see what there is to be discovered and learned; be open to new ideas and perspectives.
- **Follow what has heart and meaning:** focus on what is important. Try to divide work based on preferences of the team members, divide routine work fairly, and practice flexibility.

- **Place a high value on integrity and honesty:** this creates mutual respect; means that people tell the truth, and do what they say they will do.
- **Effective communication:** practice congruence—align words with emotional tone and body language. If there is a problem, deal with it immediately (24/3/7 rule).
- **Playfulness:** have fun and inspire each other.

Leaders of small firms can use this list as a guide for behaviors that motivate good work ethic and stimulate good relationships among coworkers. This, as much as any other influence, will help create small firm success.

ENDNOTES

1. Roger Harrison, "Organizational Culture and the Future of Planet Earth," *The Collected Papers of Roger Harrison*, Figure 14.1, Jossey-Bass, San Francisco, CA, 1995. © Copyright 1995, Roger Harrison, Harrison Associates, Freeland WA 98249.

2. Margaret Wheatley, *Leadership and the New Science*, Barrett-Koehler Publishing Inc., San Francisco, CA, 1999, p.120.

3. Daniel Goleman and Richard Boyatzis, "Social Intelligence and the Biology of Leadership," *Harvard Business Review*, Harvard Business School Publishing Corp., Cambridge, MA, 2008.

4. Ibid.

5. Margaret Wheatley, *Leadership and the New Science*, Barrettt-Koehler Publishing Inc., San Francisco, CA, 1999, p. 57.

6. Tannenbaum and Schmidt, "How to Choose a Leadership Pattern," *Harvard Business Review*, Harvard Business School Publishing Corp., Cambridge, MA, 1973.

7. Daniel Goleman and Richard Boyatzis, "Social Intelligence and the Biology of Leadership," *Harvard Business Review,* Harvard Business School Publishing Corp., Cambridge, MA, 2008.

8. Angeles Arrien, Ph.D., *The Four-Fold Way,* Harper San Francisco, San Francisco, CA, 1993.

9. Angeles Arrien, Ph.D., "Paths to Collective Wisdom" Workshop, Seattle, WA, 2003.

10. Harrison Owen, *Open Space Technology: A Users' Guide,* Barrett-Koehler Publishing, San Francisco, CA, 1997.

11. Jack Welch, *Fortune Magazine, 1989,* in *Becoming a Master Manager,* John Wiley & Sons, Inc., Hoboken, NJ, 1990, p. 29.

12. Angeles Arrien, Ph.D., "Paths to Collective Wisdom" Workshop, Seattle, WA, 2003.

PART **II**

BEST LAID PLANS

CHAPTER 5

LIFECYCLE OF
A SMALL FIRM

Founding owners of small design firms are entrepreneurs by nature, and have much in common with other small business owners regardless of type. According to Harvard researcher, Noam Wasserman, most entrepreneurs go into business seeking both wealth and control. Founders of architectural firms are more likely to say they want fair compensation and opportunity for design expression, but in essence this is the same. Most architect/entrepreneurs covet their control along with their earnings.

In his article, "The Founder's Dilemma," Wasserman reports on research involving 212 American startups from the late 1990s and early 2000s. His findings show that as a business grows, it inevitably outgrows the skills, energy, and resources of the founder. Basically, Wasserman has discovered that most entrepreneurs eventually must choose between "making a lot of money or running the show."[1] Architects who start their own firms are no different and are likely, at some point, to face this choice.

WEALTH OR CONTROL

According to Wasserman, founders come to a point where they must give up unilateral control in order to grow their business. Typically, in order to grow the business, they either need money from investors or, in the case of professional service firms, they need expertise from employees or new partners. Either way, they need to share control in order to acquire what is needed. Wasserman calls this the "rich versus king" trade-off and finds in his research that founders who share control with others build a more valuable company and are compensated better than those who don't.

While letting go of control may lead to greater return on investment, many founders find the "rich" choice to be extremely difficult. As explained by Wasserman, "The founder creates the organizational culture, which is an extension of his or her style, personality, and preferences. From the get-go, employees, customers, and business partners identify startups with their founders, who take great pride in their founder-cum-CEO status. New ventures are usually labors of love for entrepreneurs, and they become emotionally attached to them, referring to the business as "my baby" and using similar parenting language without even noticing."[2] As discussed in Chapter 4, leaders of design firms determine their firms' culture and identity and are no less attached than the CEOs in Wasserman's study.

Wasserman reports that most entrepreneurs tend to be overly optimistic about their potential for success. Many entrepreneurs believe that they are the only ones who are capable of running their company, even when there is evidence over time to the contrary. Architects and designers are particularly susceptible to this belief since they may have built their reputation on a unique talent, ability, or style. Research also shows that founders are willing to work with uncommon dedication at startup— 51 percent of founders earned less than at least one employee, even if they shared comparable backgrounds.

The Principals' Dilemma

Architect/entrepreneurs face similar situations. The first 10 to 15 years of an architectural firm's existence is usually spent working to establish a steady client base, a trustworthy staff, and reliable project delivery processes. In this period, the founders also establish professional reputations, build a network of strategic alliances, and gain a considerable amount of experience and knowledge. The startup firm is often organized in a pyramidal structure, with the principals at the top in control of all operations and decisions. The firm such as this will not be able to grow beyond the principals' capabilities and skill level, in terms of types and size of projects. Nonetheless, the firm can easily grow beyond the principals' capacity to manage, in terms of time and energy.

After around 12 to 15 years, firms often reach a plateau of stable maturity, with an established identity and foothold in the marketplace. When this happens, principals of architectural firms may face Wasserman's "rich versus king" dilemma.

If principals are uncomfortable delegating responsibility and authority it will be difficult to successfully grow the firm. Figure 5.1 illustrates the likely lifecycle of a firm where the founding partner is not interested in sharing control with a second generation of leadership.

Firm growth often depends on a redefinition of the partners' role and a redesign of the firm's organizational structure. A "reinvention" of the partners' vision for the

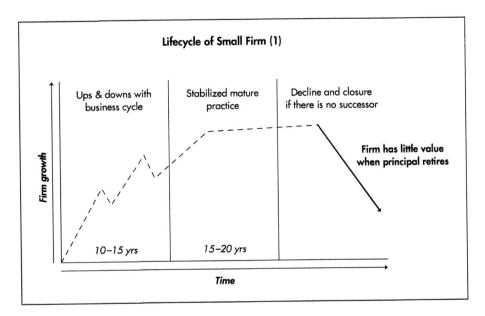

Figure 5.1   The founder retires and must close the firm if there is no transition to second-generation ownership.

firm is often necessary and is likely to be the most challenging aspect of this process. The payoff for principals in relinquishing unilateral control is the possibility of growing the market value of the firm and the potential for the firm to continue beyond the principals' active involvement.

Firm growth may also enable opportunity for larger, more diverse projects and for the inclusion of capabilities beyond the founders. These firms have the potential to create both financial and social equity beyond the reputation, core competency, and revenue stream established by the founding principals. Firms such as these allow the founders to retire with the promise of financial support provided by the ongoing firm, as illustrated in Figure 5.2.

Nonetheless, many principals are more comfortable being the "king" of their own domain, no matter how small. Practitioners who choose "king over rich" can have very successful practices and may accumulate enough personal savings and investments to retire comfortably without needing to build equity in their firm. Research suggests that these founders' personal sense of success may be dependent on always being in charge of their organization. On the other hand, if accumulating wealth is what makes a founder feel successful, relinquishing leadership toward that end should not be too difficult. The critical issue, according to Wasserman, is the founders' level of knowing the personal meaning of success. "Once they realize why they are turning entrepreneur, founders must, as the old Chinese proverb says, 'decide on three things at the start: the rules of the game, the stakes, and the quitting time.'"[3]

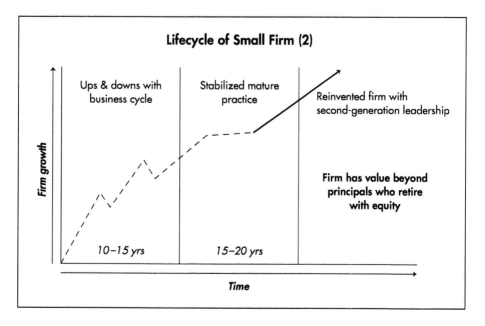

Figure 5.2 Transferring ownership to second-generation leaders has the potential to increase market value of the firm.

For founding principals of architectural firms, this choice may not involve "stepping down" or "quitting time" but it does mean a willingness to delegate authority in project management, client management, and even design to capable partners and nonpartner employees. It also means planning for retirement and for a smooth ownership transition to the next generation. Conversely, success may mean choosing to stay in unilateral control of the firm and to pursue financial security by fostering lucrative market segments or specialized, innovative expertise. Many independent small firm owners also pursue other sources of income, such as becoming developers, or investors in real estate, to increase their earning potential.

GETTING TO THE NEXT LEVEL

JJ is the principal of a small firm that has grown from four to 12 staff members in just two years. Despite the turmoil created by rapid growth, JJ dreams of heading a firm twice this size. He imagines taking on larger projects and creating a firm that has value beyond his personal reputation. He's seen other firms move up to the next level, but he wonders how.

Before the *how* question can be answered, the *what* question must be posed. What does the next level mean? As discussed earlier in this chapter, in order to increase market value, firms must continue to grow. But growth could come through expanded services, increased productivity, or cultivating expertise—not only through increase in firm size.

Be What You Want to Become

A firm keeps growing and moving to the next level by having the ability to change and reinvent itself. This is similar to the familiar self-growth adage—*be what you want to become*. Organizationally, a firm must act as if it already is what it wants to become.

Once vision is understood, there must be commitment. Getting to the next level takes discipline and actions such as strategic planning, commitment to continuing education, and sometimes, significant systemic change. Because architectural firms are project based, project delivery is often the first system that needs examination.

In many small architectural firms partners are the primary project managers. Partners do all the client contact and project tracking; all information flows through them; and they are the main decision makers. Not surprisingly, partners in these firms frequently work 60-hour weeks and complain about not having time to design. Although they may want to grow the firm, these firm leaders can't imagine how to manage more projects, employees, or even find the time to plan.

The Pyramid Problem

The project management model used by these firms is known as a pyramid structure. Partners, at the top of their pyramid, often become a bottleneck in the production process, causing delay and wasted effort. Because partners are frequently gone from the office, critical information can be missed and last-minute design changes may be common. If a partner were to disappear completely for some reason, much critical knowledge would also disappear, debilitating the projects and the firm.

In a pyramid model, illustrated in Figure 5.3, growth is only possible by adding more pyramids (partners), but growth through adding pyramids is limited. While the firm may get bigger, it is unlikely it will be more profitable, more productive, or more innovative. At worst, there may be a tendency toward competition for resources as each partner's pyramid becomes more separate from the others.

The Matrix Solution

To allow a firm to grow, partners need to focus on firm management, project acquisition, market development, and on building expertise or design innovation. In the matrix model, illustrated in Figure 5.4, professional staff members other than the partners become the primary project managers.

When a talented staff member assumes a project management role, they are given responsibility and challenge, inevitably resulting in increased commitment and enthusiasm. The partner in charge of a project can then support the project

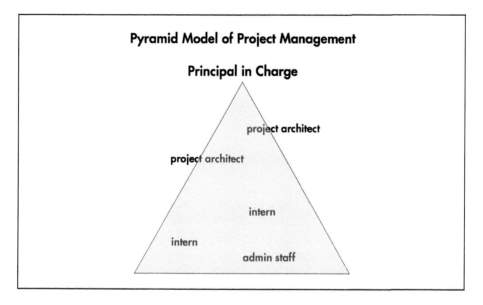

Figure 5.3 All project management and client contact is directed by and moves through the principal in charge of the project.

Matrix Model of Project Management

	Project 1	Project 2	Project 3	Etc...
	Project Manager	Project Manager	Project Manager	Project Manager
Predesign				
Schematic design				
Design development				
Construction documents				
Construction phase				
Project close-out				

Figure 5.4 Staff members other than principals are the project managers and follow a project from start to finish.

manager with mentoring and quality review. Sometimes partners will also serve on the project team as the lead designer, quality reviewer, or technical expert.

By letting go of project management, firm leaders are able to focus on work that enables a firm to grow, instead of dashing from deadline to deadline. Even in a firm of two people, one owner and one professional employee, a matrix model can be applied, freeing a sole proprietor to focus on design and market development.

Transforming Mental Models

Although the pyramid model often causes overwork and significant stress for firm leaders, many will tell you it is easier to manage projects themselves than to trust anyone else. They fail to understand the power of mentoring instead of managing, delegating instead of doing, and trusting instead of controlling. Transforming these mental models is as important to a firm's growth as changing the project management model, and the two shifts need to support one another.

Changing mental models of how things work is probably the most difficult aspect of this process. As discussed in Chapter 2, our habits can become our destiny. In small firms, the habits of the principals substantially influence every aspect of firm operations. These habits, good and bad, often become entrenched organizational patterns, copied and deepened by the staff.

Facing the weaknesses of an organization (and its leaders) and working toward improvement has huge potential for positioning a firm for growth and change. For a small firm to develop, firm leaders must grow to trust and support the intelligent people they have hired.

It's not hard for most designers to envision a preferred future, but actually taking the steps to get there may be another story. It is a process that takes discipline, personal commitment, alignment of purpose, and a willingness to be challenged. It must start at the top. To get to the next level, firm leaders may need to reinvent themselves along with their firms.

Everyone Is Dissatisfied Revisited

One theme emerges from the topics thus far discussed in this chapter—firm leaders' comfort with the notion of sharing authority and control will be the main determinant of a firm's lifecycle. This disposition is also manifest in day-to-day operations, particularly in how projects are managed and how information flows within a firm.

In Chapter 1, Archetype One, titled "Everyone Is Dissatisfied," was introduced (see Figure 1.6). It illustrated a situation where both the leaders and the staff of a small firm are overworked and dissatisfied. The archetype may, for instance, describe a firm that has grown beyond the principals' ability to be involved in all aspects of the work; but has not yet transferred project management responsibility away from the principals. When project management is conducted with a matrix model, as described earlier in this chapter, the vicious cycles shown in Figure 1.6 begin to unwind. In time, and with commitment to change mental models along with management structure, the system can transform, as illustrated in Figure 5.5.

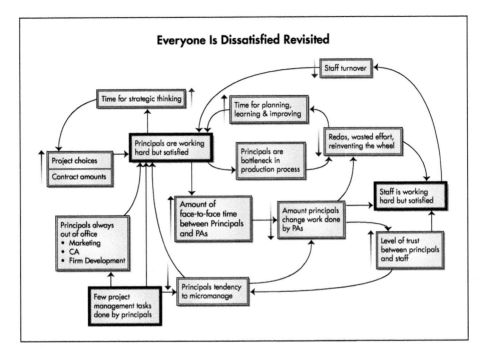

Figure 5.5 Vicious cycles unwind when project management responsibilities are transferred from principals to other professional staff.

Aspects of operational improvements such as those discussed in Chapter 3 will also positively influence this situation. Routinizing the routine will help reduce wasted efforts and "reinventing the wheel." Creating a routine practice of checking in with the project architects will also help. Freeing the partners of day-to-day project management will also give them more time for strategic thinking, firm development, and to make smart choices about projects and contract agreements. In addition, it is likely to result in less micromanaging, fewer last-minute changes, and more trust between staff and principals. This is likely to result in less turnover and more firm stability in general.

Small firm leaders depend on their next generation of leadership to help make the firm sustainable over time. Further exploration of firm lifecycle, the critical times of change for firm owners, and how ownership transition might be structured, is the subject of Chapter 6, Transition Times.

ENDNOTES

1. Noam Wasserman, "The Founder's Dilemma," *Harvard Business Review*, Harvard Business School Publishing Corp., Cambridge, MA, 2008.

2. Ibid.

3. Ibid.

CHAPTER 6

TRANSITION TIMES

C ertain times appear to be critical in the life of small design firms and their owners. After about 10 to 15 years in business there is often a reassessing, and perhaps a change of direction for one or more of the firm's founders. And again, when founders are within 10 to 15 years of retirement, there is a window for decision making that may ultimately determine a firm's long-term future.

THE 10-YEAR ITCH

Based on anecdotal evidence, as firms pass 10 years in business, they often experience a time of transition. This phenomenon is described by Cheryl Weber in an article titled "The Ten Year Itch" from *Residential Architect Magazine*.[1] "For most architectural firms, it seems that 10-year anniversaries come and go without much ado. . . . Even if architects don't think to celebrate this milestone, their firms do begin to undergo a transformation as they enter the double digits of their existence. This is the time when many architects sit back, look around, and ask themselves, 'Is this something I want to keep doing, or is it time to shift gears? Am I accomplishing what I had hoped, and if not, what's missing?' As owner, the issues you face now are different than they were ten, or even five, years ago. . . . Indeed, one of the hallmarks of maturing firms is the chance to be strategic rather than opportunistic. Do you grow for growth's sake, or do you think more about what you want to accomplish? Will too much growth diminish quality? Do you want to be all things to all people or stay focused on one thing in particular?"

Weber's article describes several firms that seem to have succeeded in their transitions to becoming more mature, stable, and strategic organizations. However, change is not always about creating a stronger practice; change can sometimes be about creating new possible futures for the founding owners.

When Partners Grow Apart: J/H Architects

RJ and BH have known each other for most of their careers, working together as young architects in the 1980s. In 1991, RJ started a firm in a western city and two years later, he invited BH to join him. BH left the East Coast where he had been working for a large, prestigious firm, and the two architects, with two employees, formed a new firm called J/H Architects in 1993.

J/H Architects created a niche for itself by being early adopters and advocates of sustainable design for institutional projects. RJ excelled in understanding building science, particularly daylighting and natural ventilation. BH added an intellectual and artistic approach to the projects, as well as an interest in the business side of the practice. Over time, their roles became more distinct: BH as the design and managing principal; and RJ as the sustainability expert and project lead.

With grounding in sustainable institutional work and master planning, J/H Architects grew from four to 11 staff members between 1993 and 2007. At times, each partner immersed himself in projects connected but somehow separate from the other partner and the firm. RJ designed and built his own house as a model and test case for advanced sustainable building systems. BH authored a book on sustainable institutional projects.

As the years passed, significant differences in aspirations and approach to firm operations began to emerge. RJ preferred to be more hands-on with projects, holding onto client contact and overall project management. BH, on the other hand, preferred to be the design lead and manager of the firm as a whole, allowing others to manage the day-to-day workings of the projects. This constituted a fundamental difference in approach to the role of firm leader and a divergence in comfort levels with sharing control.

In addition, BH began to have aspirations that went beyond how the firm was currently structured. He was interested in the notion of multidisciplinary collaboration and the idea of a building that would house many diverse creative professionals working side by side. He was inspired by the thought of a space where informal exchange and formal alliances could easily occur. BH even designed such a place before discovering a local developer was planning to build one. When, in 2006, the firm leaders learned that they would have to leave their current location, BH suggested they move their office to this innovative development. RJ showed only limited enthusiasm for this idea. RJ was more interested in the idea of purchasing a new office space to house the firm. Contemplating the long-term financial commitment that buying an office space would require caused both RJ and BH to reconsider the viability of their business partnership.

BH began to think seriously about leaving to start his own firm that could be located in the new "creative arts facility," as he called it. His partnership with RJ had left him feeling underappreciated and that his contributions to the firm were undervalued. In addition, BH was realizing that his other activities, specifically involvement with the local AIA component, provided him with more professional satisfaction than he was getting at the firm.

RJ, on the other hand, perceived BH as detached, not willing to fully engage in everyday billable work. He realized that he felt as if he worked alone, and that BH did not share his viewpoint that principals should directly manage project execution. RJ also believed that he contributed significantly to the design output of the firm. He didn't like the idea of being seen as the "sustainability/technical principal," thereby defining BH as the "design principal" by default. While both BH and RJ wanted to create a larger, more prominent firm, they had different concepts of their individual roles as principals and how those roles might evolve over time. They also had differing visions of where the firm's office should be located, influencing the firm's image and the context in which the firm practiced.

Facing this gap in aspirations, the partners soon realized that it was time to make a change. BH decided to leave the firm and establish H Architects, as a startup firm. RJ would retain the office and staff of the old firm, but would change its name to J Architects. They decided to work together to complete their jobs in progress, forming a Limited Liability Corporation (LLC) for that purpose. BH agreed not to take any of the existing institutional clients or staff with him to his new firm. Although this may seem an ill-advised decision, BH wanted a clean break from the old firm and reasoned that he could reenter the old firm's market sometime in the future, when he was ready.

The negotiations about the financial aspects of the separation—the price and terms for the buy-out of BH's 50 percent ownership—proved to be the most difficult aspect of the separation. The critical item in dispute was firm valuation. Believing that the firm value determined by their business development consultant was too high, RJ consulted another management consultant and had numerous meetings with the firm's accountant.

At issue was the value of the firm's reputation and goodwill, arguably created by both partners over the past 14 years. BH believed a premium over book value (net worth) should be included to represent the value of the reputation he helped build, but cannot take with him. RJ, on the other hand, felt strongly that the value of the firm should be its net worth, based on hard assets, such as furniture and computers, and accrued receivables. Positions soon became polarized and somewhat adversarial between the partners. Held resentments were voiced and old wounds reopened.

In the end, the separating partners agreed to a firm valuation equal to book value (see "Internal Sale" section, later in this chapter). Book value for J/H Architects included all hard assets and the value of work in progress and accounts receivables at the date of BH's departure from the firm. No value was attributed to firm reputation and goodwill, although much of the benefits of the old firm's reputation stayed with J Architects. A purchase agreement was struck that allowed J to pay H for his half of the firm over a period of three years, in monthly payments, without interest. Still compatible operationally, RJ and BH continue to collaborate on projects and have come away from their partnership with a cordial working relationship.

BH has succeeded in establishing H Architects as a viable enterprise operating in collaboration with a diverse group of design firms and other arts disciplines. He has created numerous strategic partnerships with others working in the "creative arts facility" in which his office is located. The economic downturn has presented challenges, particularly in reentering the institutional market of the old firm. BH advises others who are leaving a long-standing partnership to consider asking for more of its intangible assets, such as active clients and experienced staff.

Other lessons learned, according to BH, include the importance of crafting an ownership agreement that clearly outlines the basis for firm valuation and the process to be followed for the separation of a partner. Making this explicit in a partnership agreement while all are on good terms will be considerably easier than trying to work it out in a future adversarial atmosphere. This agreement should also include an articulate summary of partner roles and responsibility and the agreement should be revisited and updated periodically.

Like all startups, H Architects will take two to five years to stabilize, identify key collaborators, and find its place in the market. Although BH established his firm during good times, he could not have predicted the deep recession that began to be felt in late 2008. This only underscores that architects who leave established positions to start their own firm or pursue a mid-life career change need to be prepared for the risks involved. Manifesting one's vision is likely to require substantial investment. This investment might be in the form of sweat equity (not paying oneself), paying for critical advanced education (or financing it with debt), or simply supplying cash required to keep a new enterprise going. Nevertheless, outcomes are likely to be unpredictable, with both fortunate and unfortunate circumstances happening simultaneously.

A Cautionary Tale

Transitions usually involve courage and risk-taking, but they also can be motivated by seeking more security. However, even moves that seem safe sometimes don't work out as planned. Unforeseen conditions can derail even the most well-conceived strategy. The economic recession that began in 2008 was just such an event and it impacted many who were transitioning at that time.

WT is an architect in his mid-40s from an East Coast city whose path may be instructional to many small firm practitioners. Working in the public and nonprofit sector, his career began with a strong focus on large-scale urban design work. In the early 1990s, WT turned his attention to what he describes as "a focus on building and detail, to understand smaller components of the built environment." In 1991, he began a design-build firm in partnership with an experienced construction manager, DN. This was unusual at the time, but allowed the firm to operate in diverse urban markets. In 1999, in pursuit of higher compensation, DN left the firm for a career in the construction industry. WT continued with the design side of the business and within a year, took on a new partner, H. WT and H were able to build a successful practice during the boom times of 2000–2005. They became involved in large-scale international projects and enjoyed a highly profitable period.

Nevertheless, by 2006 things had begun to change in WT's life—he had more family responsibilities, was concerned that the boom time would not last and, "started to worry and look for a safe harbor." Even with the good years they had, WT knew that the cost of running his firm over its lifetime was more than the firm had ever earned. He recalls thinking, "Three or four good years could not make up for many bad years and for some disastrous construction jobs early on. I just wasn't sure the firm, or the good times, were sustainable."

WT began to investigate the possibility of joining a large firm. His experience in urban design and international projects enabled him to secure a position at a prestigious firm that operated in a global market. He went through a process of closing his firm by completing his own projects, communicating with his clients, and transferring joint work in progress over to his partner. H was happy to go his separate way and pursue his own interests which were somewhat divergent from WT's. H took over the lease on the office and leased WT's space to another architect. WT began his new employment at the large firm in February 2008. Unfortunately, due to the sudden and unexpected slowdown of late 2008, WT was laid off in November of that year.

WT is philosophical and upbeat about his situation, despite the short-term out-come. He had been teaching at a local school of architecture and feels fortunate that he did not give up that position when he got his new job. WT is slowly exploring new opportunities and acquiring new credentials, such as LEED accreditation. He is not even sure if he would accept the job offer if he was called back to the large firm. Although closing his firm did not work out as he had planned, he is not sure things would be that different had he stayed with running his firm. "I'm not even interested in taking on projects right now—I am open to opportunities, but I'm not into putting myself out there just yet. Sometimes you have to be in the unknown until the new path becomes clear."

Of course, the economic downturn certainly would have impacted WT had he not decided to close his firm. No one can know the result of other possible choices. The lesson here is not to avoid change, but to be aware that there are always risks involved. Be ready to be nimble, to be flexible, and be prepared with a "plan B." Success seems most likely when change is accompanied by strong passion, belief in oneself, commitment to excellence, integrity, and patience for the time it takes to build any new enterprise.

APPROACHING RETIREMENT

Ten to fifteen years into the life of a firm is likely to be the first major time of transition for its founders. The second time of transition is likely to be when the founders are within 10 to 15 years of retirement. Many small firm owners have a difficult time imagining retirement and tend to put off any consideration of the issue. This is an understandable tendency but it may result in a narrowing of options over time.

Anecdotally, it is known that many founders of small firms have satisfying prac-tices yet fail to earn enough for significant retirement savings. Small firms are

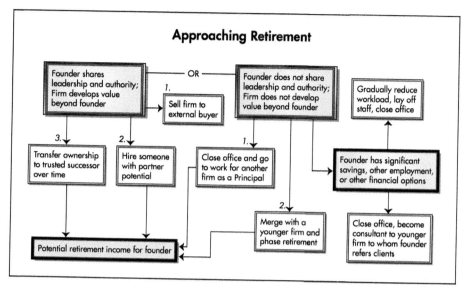

Figure 6.1 As retirement approaches, founders can evaluate their choices based on their comfort level with sharing leadership and control.

frequently successful in terms of excellent work product, but are often built solely on the talent, competency, and reputation of the founder. As a result, the firm has virtually no market value without the founder who sometimes faces retirement with little accrued equity and few financial resources.

10-Year Rule

To avoid this situation, founders of small firms must consider their options at least 10 years before retirement. Two important questions need to be considered in making choices about the future of their firms. First, has the founder accumulated significant retirement savings or investments, and second, is the founder ready to share leadership and power with successors? The answer to each of these questions opens up and closes off certain possibilities. There is no right or wrong answer to these questions—just self-aware choices that need to be made before the range of future possibilities become narrower. The key criteria and choices for founders of small firms are illustrated in Figure 6.1.

The two options involving the value of the firm at the founders' retirement are shown in the two uppermost boxes. Firms either develop value beyond their founder's involvement or they do not. Growing a firm's market value is only possible when people other than the founder are involved in job acquisition, client management, project delivery, and staff management. To grow firm value, founders must be comfortable with giving up absolute power and with delegation of decision making to others, especially potential successors.

Expanded Choices

If a founder is comfortable with sharing power then it is likely that greater market value and owner's equity can be built over time. Once the firm gains market value, three choices open to the small firm founder contemplating retirement, as shown in Figure 6.1:

1. Sell the firm to an outside buyer—this is unlikely unless the firm has an expert specialty or is in a market that can expand opportunities for another firm without the founder's continued involvement.

2. Hire someone with partnership potential and groom him/her over time—significant time may be required to insure the fit and capabilities of the potential partner.

3. Transfer ownership to trusted successor(s) over time—often the best option if available, successor(s) should be around 10 years younger than the founder, but care should also be taken not to disqualify anyone based solely on age.

Narrow Choices

If the founder's nature and personality is such that they prefer retaining control and leadership, the available choices are very different. It is unlikely that these firms will develop much market value beyond the talent and reputation of the founder. When the firm is closed, the founder takes its net worth with him or her and will be able to leverage the firm's value only in terms of personal and professional choices.

If founders do not have significant savings, or if they are just tired of the stress of small firm ownership, there are some options. Figure 6.1 shows two of these:

1. Close the office and seek employment at another firm at the Principal level. Many larger firms welcome mature, talented, and knowledgeable architects on their management teams.

2. Merge with another firm headed by younger leadership. A small firm's client base, built up over many years is an asset that can be transferred to the new firm over time and may allow for a phased retirement.

Both these options have the potential to provide some income when the founder finally retires.

If founders have significant savings, other employment possibilities, or other financial resources, they have some additional options. They can simply reduce activity and close their firm over time. Some of these founders may wish to continue working or wish to pass their client base onto a younger colleague. In that case, the option of acting as a design or technical consultant to another firm may be attractive. Neither of these choices is likely to provide additional retirement income.

Small firm owners in their 50s would be wise to consider their options for ownership transition and retirement. Self-awareness regarding one's comfort level with sharing leadership and power is a critical part of this planning process. Review of one's savings, employment, and financial options is another vital aspect in decision making about preferred futures. To be avoided is a lack of planning and a denial that retirement will eventually come. A comfortable retirement for small firm founders may hang in the balance.

CASE STUDY IN HAPPY ENDINGS: CAROLYN GEISE, FAIA

Carolyn Geise, FAIA of Geise Architects, has been a small firm practitioner in Seattle, Washington for almost 40 years. She started her career in 1969, during what she describes as "a depression—you know, the years when there was the sign outside Seattle saying 'The last one to leave Seattle, please turn off the lights.'" Carolyn describes how she learned to manage projects and the whole firm as a young architect working with the famed Jane Hastings, FAIA, the matriarch of the Seattle architectural community. "Jane was gone for extended periods over the four years of our partnership and left me in charge of the office and the projects. I learned that I could trust myself as a decision-maker and discovered that I could run a firm. I realized how much fun it would be to work for yourself and came to believe, at that time as a woman architect, that your name needs to be on the door to get respect from clients and colleagues." It wasn't long thereafter that Carolyn founded Geise Architecture. Carolyn's firm has been in business continuously since that time, growing to nine people in the 1980s when the firm was doing both public and residential work.

Over the years, Carolyn has thought about ownership transition, but found herself encouraging potential successors to go out on their own instead. Unlike many firm owners who complain about experienced employees who leave to start their own firm, Carolyn realized that employees make valuable contributions to the firm when they are learning and are challenged. When it became clear that a person had outgrown the firm, she supported an "up & out" approach. She generously shared resources and knowledge with long-term employees when they both agreed that it was time to leave the nest. "I made a serious effort [at partnership] with one person," she recalls, "but it worked out better for her to start her own firm after all. Also, the process of setting up a fair agreement between someone who is winding down and looking for more time off and another who is in mid-career and building a practice is difficult and time consuming. I was just never sure about the return on that effort." Carolyn recalls the excitement and exhilaration she felt at starting her own firm, and feels that she wouldn't want to take that experience away from anyone.

Like many sole proprietors, Carolyn is completely at home with the notion of owning her firm alone and controlling all its activities personally. She values team work in developing a project but "I like doing the projects, not bringing in projects and then managing others to do them," she explains, "and I especially like being able to shape the firm around my lifestyle choices. . . . I always have other projects going on [outside of the firm] —usually development projects on my own properties. Over the years, these activities have kept my staff busy when times get slow." Carolyn has had a life-long strategy of acquiring property and sees its appreciating value and the rent on her holdings as her primary source of retirement income. Among these is a "farm" on Whidbey Island, Washington, where she raises Alpacas for breeding stock and fiber and has created a vacation retreat rental that provides rewarding activity and rental income to offset expenses while the property continues to appreciate in value.

Carolyn is best known for her contribution to the revival of the Belltown neighborhood of downtown Seattle. Her building at Western and Vine, its adjacent streetscape, "Growing Vine Street," and the Belltown pea patch were a catalysts for the renewal of the neighborhood into a trendy, active, and densely populated residential area, unique for Seattle at that time. Carolyn has received considerable public recognition and acknowledgment for her contribution to urban community-building. This activity reflects her belief that "architects can be so effective when they become a vital part of their community by doing their own development. It can give them the freedom to go out on a limb a bit and it attracts others who are willing to do the same."

One of the outcomes for Carolyn from the Vine Street project was ownership of her office space and a second, smaller office in the 81 Vine Building. She believes that owning one's office is a great strategy for a small firm owner and comments that "[owning your office] removes the stress of committing to leases, and the fear of losing a lease, or being priced out of your space. Your rent payment is buying your own building instead of just an expense and your leasehold improvements are creating long-term value for you, not your landlord. It makes getting through the slow times much easier." Carolyn candidly advises all firm owners to try to purchase the space where they practice.

As Carolyn downsizes she has moved her practice into her smaller office condominium and is renting out her large former office space. She has part-time help from a young architect, in the process of starting up his own business, who supports her in many aspects of the work. She also has a bookkeeper/office assistant who works one day a week, and usually a part-time student intern. Carolyn is working on a number of projects that she describes as "engaging and fun" and says, "I still have a lot more I want to do before I close my office." This includes continued involvement with community-building (literally and figuratively) in the Belltown neighborhood and on Whidbey Island. She says her business has transformed to include "only the good stuff" and intends to keep working at it as long as that is the case. "After all," she concludes, "isn't retirement about getting to the point when you can do what you want to do?"

Carolyn Geise is representative of many architects who choose to keep their firm small and closely held. Her story validates the notion that activities external to the firm are likely to be crucial to a comfortable retirement for a sole proprietor.

OWNERSHIP TRANSITION OPTIONS

Taking on new partners has implications for firm culture as well as its finances. A new partner may influence a firm's atmosphere and operations more than expected. Firm leaders must be prepared to share power and decision making with the new partner(s). Processes for communication and designation of roles may need to become more structured and transparent than it was for the founder(s). Some founders may come to relate to the words of Carolyn Geise lamenting "all the need for talking about everything," but it will be necessary for the partners to have conversations about how they will work together. For internal sales, these conversations are critical to empowering new partners in their new roles as firm owners, rather than employees.

Internal Sale at Retirement

While many small firm owners look to existing staff to take over their firms as they approach retirement, the first hires of entrepreneurial founders may tend to be people who are more comfortable in a support role than an ownership role. This may mean that firm leaders will need to look to the next generation of employees—younger, perhaps more ambitious staff members. Identifying those who have an interest and natural inclination toward owning a business is likely to be as important as noticing those who are talented designers or technically gifted.

As potential successors are identified, they can be groomed and mentored for their future leadership role. Project and client management is an important part of this training and, as discussed in Chapter 5, can be keys to firm growth and longevity. When a firm or part ownership of a firm is sold to those already working for the firm, it is known as an internal sale.

According to Peter Piven and William Mandel, in their book, *Architects Essentials of Ownership Transition*,[2] internal sales are usually 1 to 1.5 of book value (net worth), while external sales are likely to be 1 to 3 times book value. External buyers are willing to pay a premium in order to accomplish certain goals, such as quick entry into a market, acquisition of a competitor, or the gaining of a needed skill or talent. For small firm founders reaching retirement, external sale of their firm is unlikely since few firms can offer what external buyers are seeking, especially with the founder soon to retire. However, internal sales can be extremely beneficial to all parties involved, since successors can usually take full advantage of the reputation and "goodwill" of the established firm, and the founder can continue to mentor and influence firm direction as part of a phased retirement.

The problem with internal sales, and the reason the price is often discounted, is that the potential successors may not have the financial resources to actually buy the firm. Even at a discount, firms are commonly purchased internally by replacing the purchasers' salary raises and bonuses with stock compensation. Over time, as the number of shares accrues, the new partners have increasingly more ownership in the firm. Of course, this new status means that decision-making processes and even firm vision will also need to be revisited.

Firm valuation is usually based on a number of factors that include accrued book value, weighted average net revenue (gross revenue minus direct project costs), and weighted average net income (net revenue minus all expenses) of the firm. Weighted net revenue and net income are determined by taking an average of five years past, and adding more weight toward the recent years. Book value equals the difference between the firm's assets and its liabilities. On a typical balance sheet, book value is listed as owners' equity. In a small design firm, the largest component of book value is likely to be accounts receivable and the value of work in progress, since the physical assets of design firms are usually relatively minimal. A multiplier is then applied to the book value, the weighted net revenue or the weighted net income, to determine firm valuation. Often, all three metrics and some others are considered in determining the value of a firm. Additional information about firm valuation can be found in the fourteenth edition of *Architects Handbook of Professional Practice*.[3] Before undertaking an ownership transition process, it is advisable to retain a CPA to complete a comprehensive and professional firm valuation.

INTERNAL SALE CASE STUDY: LS ARCHITECTS

Over his 30 years in practice, LS has built a successful architectural firm of eight employees with a diverse project base of institutional buildings and ultra-high-end residential estates. He is turning 60 soon and knows that in five to seven years he will want to retire from running his firm. LS is fortunate to have two very capable senior architects on his staff who have expressed some interest in forming a partnership to acquire the firm. In addition, a third, younger architect has accepted an invitation by the prospective buyers to join the partnership as a minority owner in the third year of the ownership transition process.

LS has developed a lucrative practice and wonders whether it would be more advantageous for him to sell the firm to these potential successors or simply reduce the size of the firm incrementally over time and close the firm when he is ready to retire. He is currently earning far more than the average small firm owner—over $200,000 per year—due mostly to his work for extraordinarily wealthy private clients. He reasoned that just continuing at this pace for five more years could set up his retirement nicely, along with the potential income from owning the building where his office is located. Nevertheless, LS is open to an internal sale as long as it does not result in significantly less than what he might earn by simply continuing for five years and then closing the door.

With the help of a consultant, LS developed a scenario for ownership transfer to consider in his deliberations on how to proceed. Based on a report prepared by a CPA, the firm value for internal sale is determined to be $400,000. The firm valuation is divided by 500 shares to determine a price per share of $800. These shares of stock are distributed to the new partners annually in lieu of raises and bonuses. As a result, LS, the seller, can retain almost all of the annual net income (profit) of the firm during the ownership transition period and the price of the firm is fixed, no matter what the economy does in the next several years.

Table 6-A illustrates a scenario that gives the new partners around 30 percent ownership after three years. At the end of four years, the new partners own almost 48 percent of the firm, and at the end of 5 years, over 63 percent. At that point, if all goes according to plan, LS would retire and the new partners would make a final lump-sum payment.

LS would like the agreement structured so there was an opportunity for reevaluation after three years. If it appears that the partnership is not gelling, if clients are balking at the changes, or if there is not enough backlog to reasonably expect the firm to succeed, LS wants to be able to terminate the agreement, finish the remaining projects, and close the firm. However, the consultant points out to LS that while he is still at the firm, it is unlikely to be a true test of the new partnership's ability to run the firm, despite the amount of firm ownership being accrued by the new partners.

Instead, the consultant encourages LS to set the three-year mark as a point of mutual evaluation with everyone involved. All four parties would need to consent to terminate the agreement and close the firm. At that point, a division of firm assets would be determined based on the percent of firm ownership. LS agrees, and realizes that he will have to support the new partnership with referrals, strong personal references, and access to his network if they are to succeed.

If the new partnership appears to be strong, and moves into its fourth and fifth year, the new partners confront a significant challenge. They will be faced with investing cash resources into the firm in order to meet the final

TABLE 6-A: Internal Ownership Transition Scenario

LS Architects Buy-In Scenario						
Internal sale price: $ 400,000			$800.00 per share			
	Salary	Stock Compensation	Bonus	Value of Shares	Share of Ownership	Total Percent of Ownership Transfer
Year 1						
Partner 1	$85,000	10	12	$ 17,600	4.40%	
Partner 2	$75,000	10	12	$ 17,600	4.40%	
						8.80%
Year 2						
Partner 1	$87,500	10	15	$ 20,000	9.40%	
Partner 2	$77,500	10	15	$ 20,000	9.40%	
						18.80%
Year 3						
Partner 1	$90,000	10	15	$ 20,000	14.40%	
Partner 2	$80,000	10	15	$ 20,000	14.40%	
Partner 3	$70,000	5	10	$ 12,000	3.00%	
Total After Three Years		65	94	$127,200		31.80%
Year 4						
Partner 1	$92,500	15	15	$ 24,000	20.40%	
Partner 2	$82,500	15	15	$ 24,000	20.40%	
Partner 3	$72,500	10	10	$ 16,000	7.00%	
						47.80%
Year 5						
Partner 1	$92,500	15	15	$ 24,000	26.40%	
Partner 2	$82,500	15	15	$ 24,000	26.40%	
Partner 3	$75,000	10	10	$ 16,000	11.00%	
Total stock compensation after five years				$255,200		63.80%
At end of year five, LS retires with lump-sum pay-off Pay-off equals balance remaining on firm sale price				$144,800		
Alternative pay-off structure: $4,022 per month for three years, no interest						

pay-off requirement. The new partners have decided that partners 1 and 2 will each own 40 percent of the firm while partner 3 has a 20 percent share to start. Table 6-B shows each partner's equity and capital investment required at pay-off.

TABLE 6-B: New Partner Investment after Five Years

	Share of Ownership	Share of Final Pay-Off to LS	Value of Stock Compensation	Total Investment
Partner 1	40%	$54,400	$105,600	$160,000
Partner 2	40%	$54,400	$105,600	$160,000
Partner 3	20%	$36,000	$ 44,000	$ 80,000

How each partner will raise this cash contribution will be an individual challenge, signaling a commitment to the business in a tangible way. This involves serious risk and significant courage and confidence is required for such a move. Potential new partners in this situation should take care that they possess operational, interpersonal, and aspirational compatibility with their new partners, as discussed in Chapter 4 and again in Chapter 10. The new partners will also need to understand that growth will be required to support a firm with three partners, instead of just one. Their partnership agreements should include a growth plan, with financial benchmarks, that will enable the firm to combine existing strengths with new directions and opportunities.

Alternative pay-off structures can be negotiated based on the needs of the seller and buyer. The retiring founder may decide he would benefit from having monthly payments, and might even be willing to agree to no interest, as in the case of the RJ/BH buy-out cited earlier in this chapter. This is especially true if doing otherwise would prevent the deal from going through because the new partners cannot foresee being able to raise the necessary cash. In a time of tight credit and strict loan standards, this may be the only option.

Realizing that he may be asked for financial concessions to make the ownership transition feasible, LS began to have conversations with his consultant about his motivation to sell the firm. Financially, assuming the net revenue and net income continue at their current weighted average, LS would earn around $200,000 per year for the next five years, whether or not he sells the firm. If he does sell the firm, he receives an additional $144,800 at his retirement. If LS does not sell, firm closure is likely to yield its owner 75 to 90 percent of book value, according to Piven and Mandel. Assuming that there are outstanding receivables and LS is able to sell all the hard assets of the firm, he may walk away with as much as an additional $300,000. It seems from this analysis that LS could do somewhat better financially by just closing the firm when he is ready to retire.

Nevertheless, LS would enjoy being able to refer his long-time clients to a known quantity. LS can also envision using the newly constituted firm for some development projects he is considering. Primarily he is driven by the personal satisfaction he would gain from seeing his firm continue after he retires. Most importantly, he realizes that he has great respect and fondness for his senior staff and believes that they can succeed. For this reason, LS decides to go forward with ownership transfer. The next steps involve making an offer to the new partners, negotiating the offer and having the final agreement prepared by the seller's attorney, and reviewed by attorneys representing each party. Of course, creating new understandings in regard to roles, responsibilities, and decision making will also need to be part of this process. These agreements about firm management issues should be reviewed annually to ensure that they reflect the changing ownership percentages (and personal dynamics) over time.

Clearly, if LS felt that his senior staff was not up to the challenge of running a firm or were not compatible in critical dimensions, he would not go through with this sale. The risk would be too high and the rewards minimal. In a small firm where people often work closely together for years, most firm leaders will have an innate understanding of the risk involved in this kind of transaction. Ultimately for internal sales of a small design firm, level of risk is related to level of trust between seller and buyers.

The uncertainty and risk involved in such an ownership transition can be eased by planning for these eventualities earlier in a firm's life cycle. This will enable founders to identify likely successors and to foster their ability to lead the firm. This may be done through taking on a minority partner at least 15 years before retirement and by identifying and mentoring the next generation of firm leaders.

Taking on a Minority Partner

Firm founders can provide transparent ownership succession and leadership development by taking on minority partners long before they are ready to retire. This is an internal sale, similar to the process described above. However, this ownership transition takes place when the current firm owners are far from retirement and are still active in the firm marketing and operations. It has the advantage of creating a known path to advancement for valued and entrepreneurial staff. Although founders may take Carolyn Geise's approach of "up & out" to the professional development of staff, another choice is to keep experienced staff within the firm and plan to grow the firm accordingly. As discussed in Chapter 5, firm growth is critical to developing firm value beyond the founder's reputation.

Table 6-C shows a buy-in plan that results in a minority partner having a 20 percent stake in the firm at the end of five years. The figures shown are based on a firm's internal sale price of $500,000, divided into 500 shares at $1,000 per share.

TABLE 6-C: Minority Partner Buy-In Plan

	Year 1	Year 2	Year 3	Year 4	Year 5
End of Year Ownership %	4	8	12	16	20
Salary (2% Increase per Year)	$77,000	$78,540	$80,110	$81,713	$83,347
Stock Compensation (Value of Shares)	$20,000	$20,000	$20,000	$20,000	$20,000

Each year the new partner receives $20,000 in stock compensation in lieu of salary increases and bonuses. After five years, $100,000 is accrued, equaling a 20 percent share of the firm's value. Financial benchmarks for the new partner's contribution to project acquisition might also be part of a buy-in agreement.

Having a minority partner is likely to mean that power and decision making will also need to be shared and that operations and changes to firm-wide organizational design may need to be reconsidered. This move may be seen as part of a larger reinvention of the firm in which the minority partner has an opportunity to influence the firm's direction. As described in Chapter 5, this can lead to firm long-term sustainability and financial gain for the founder at retirement. See Chapter 9, Strategic Thinking, and Table 9-B for a case study of how this kind of ownership transition fits into a five-year firm growth plan and firm strategic planning in general.

ENDNOTES

1. Cheryl Weber, "The Ten Year Itch," *Residential Architect Magazine*, Hanley Wood, Washington D.C., June 2006.
2. Peter Piven and William Mandel, *Architects Essentials of Ownership Transition*, John Wiley & Sons, Inc., Hoboken, NJ, 2002, p. 45.
3. Hugh Hochberg, "Ownership Transition," *Architects Handbook of Professional Practice*, 14th ed., Joseph A. Demkin, exec. editor, John Wiley & Sons, Inc., Hoboken, NJ, 2008.

CHAPTER 7

FINANCIAL MANAGEMENT: BEYOND INTUITION

As a financial management tool, intuition has its limitations. While most small firm owners have a good sense of what's happening at their firms, operational indicators such as cash flow shortages or mounting receivables don't tell the whole story. Strategic decisions including hiring or moving to a larger office require understanding of financial trends on both a macro and micro level.

Financial management involves tracking and understanding the implications of financial indicators pertinent to firm financial health and using the information to forecast future performance. This work does not need to be done by firm owners themselves, but it is essential to overall firm development. Without some reasonable expectations of future income, expenses, and profitability, it is difficult to plan and make sound business decisions. Understanding financial trends helps firm owners to see what is currently occurring and what might realistically be expected in the future. Financial management, along with clarity of purpose and a sound marketing plan, is critical to creating a successful practice.

This chapter is meant to give owners of small design firms a working knowledge of the concepts and applications of financial management tools. However, this information is not meant to replace the services of a Certified Public Accountant (CPA) or any other finance professionals.

MACROECONOMIC INFLUENCES

To a great extent, what is possible in any design firm, at any given moment, is influenced by the national and global economy as a whole. As part of the construction industry, the business of architecture is cyclical—subject to the ups and downs of the business cycle. In the United States, the economy is said to be in a recession when economic activity, as measured by the percent change in the Gross Domestic Product (GDP), is negative for two consecutive quarters (see Figure 7.1). Since design is early in the development process, many architectural firms see the effects of an economic slowdown long before a recession is officially declared. Starting with awareness of economic indicators, both internal and external, small firm owners can anticipate and prepare to survive an economic slowdown.

Economic Indicators

Gross Domestic Product is the sum total of all goods and services produced in the nation. Figure 7.1 is a chart of the GDP from 1948 to 2008.[1] The postwar economy has seen several significant recessions—three in the 1970s alone. These periods of recession are indicated by the gray bars on the graph. Those who began their careers as design professionals during the 1970s may remember being hired and laid-off, over and over, as the economy see-sawed. Since almost all building projects in the private sector depend on borrowed money, the cost and availability of credit is a significant indicator of future design and construction activity. In 1980, when interest rates were in double digits, there was little construction or design activity. In the fall of 2008, a crisis in liquidity at major banks caused credit to become unavailable. As a result, there was a drastic reduction in activity even though interest rates were low. Both recessionary periods brought high unemployment—up

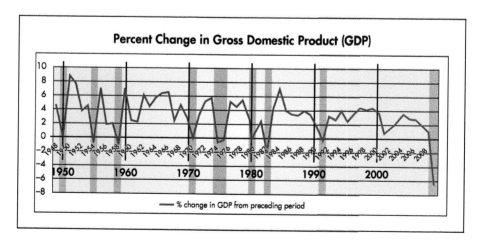

Figure 7.1   The change in GDP over time shows the ups and downs of the business cycle in the economy of the United States.

to 20 percent in design and construction. Loose credit can also portend a work slowdown if it leads to a frenzy of activity and eventually to overbuilding in a certain market or locality. In Figure 7.1, note the long period of economic expansion between 1994 and 2008. Some of the excesses that sparked the boom time at the start of the twenty-first century became the contributing factors to the deep recession that surfaced in 2008.

The Construction Business Cycle

Traditionally, the business cycle is seen as the interplay between supply and demand. When demand for goods and services outstrips supply, prices rise and interest rates follow, due to inflationary pressures. As prices and interest rates increase, demand for goods and services begins to weaken. Rising prices also encourage an increase in supply of goods and services and before long, supply begins to exceed demand, prices fall, and economic activity begins to contract. In time, as prices and interest rates fall, demand begins to increase and the cycle begins its upswing again. This basic business cycle is illustrated in Figure 7.2.

Although the basic business cycle may be impacted by globalization and extraordinarily loose credit, the important point here is every upturn will eventually lead to a downturn, which will in time, cycle into another upturn in activity. The more

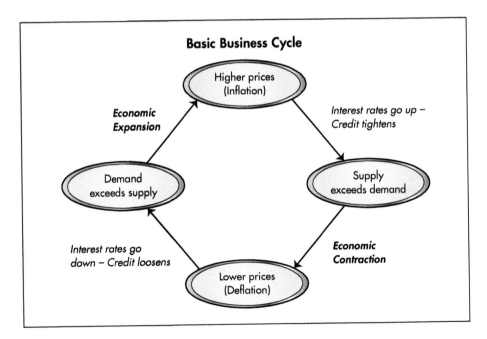

Figure 7.2 In the traditional business cycle, the interaction between demand and supply is critical and is heavily influenced by the availability of credit.

extreme and "overheated" an upside in the cycle becomes, the more likely it is that the downside will be severe.

When a recession occurs, or if the economy is expanding too quickly, the governments of the United States and other developed nations will often move to influence the business cycle. The U.S. government has two ways that it can impact the economy: (1) monetary policy, controlled by the Federal Reserve through setting interest rates; and (2) fiscal policy, controlled by Congress through taxation and government spending. Lower interest rates, lower tax rates, and government spending tend to stimulate economic activity while higher interest rates, higher taxes, and cuts in government spending will dampen an overheated economy.

For the construction industry, the business cycle includes a recognizable period of recovery between recessionary times and boom times. This recovery period is often sparked by lower interest rates and government spending on institutional building projects. When the recession has reduced commodities prices, interest rates are attractive, credit is available, and consumer confidence is on the rise, building and development once again become attractive. Another indication of the recovery is stabilizing rents on residential and commercial properties. This means that there are fewer vacant units on the market and demand is beginning to match supply. The construction industry business cycle is shown in Figure 7.3.

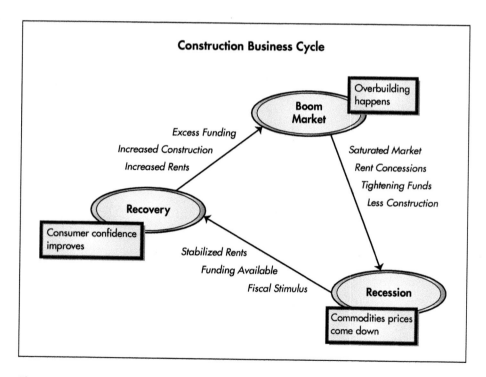

Figure 7.3   In the construction industry, a period of recovery follows a recessionary period and precedes a boom market.

The lessons here are clear: (1) beware of overbuilding and prepare for the coming recession during boom times; (2) recognize and prepare for the recovery when rents stabilize, credit loosens, and consumer confidence improves.

No matter what the economy is doing, all architectural firms experience ups and downs in work load as part of normal operations. Because firms operate in an environment of unpredictability, work load can be impacted by a variety of factors including client-driven delays, regulatory procedures, and gaps between project phases. Times of economic slowdown exacerbate this situation and challenge small firm owners to reexamine their business model, their vision, and the effectiveness of their operations.

How Small Firms Survive an Economic Slowdown

Many architecture firms grow and shrink along with the economic cycle, never breaking out of the up-and-down pattern dictated by macroeconomic conditions. Firm leaders who embrace a downturn as an opportunity to improve their firm's future can take positive actions to position their firm for financial success when the economy recovers.

To benefit from a downturn, firm leaders must have a vision of what they want their firm to be when the inevitable recovery occurs. Along with optimism, success in a slowdown requires imaginative strategic thinking. And, as the pace of work slows, time becomes available for reflective thought, work process improvement, and overdue professional development.

A firm can position itself for a strong recovery by having the ability to change and reinvent itself. Although a downturn is not a good time to enter new markets, it is a good time to expand professional skills and knowledge, and to research new possibilities and directions. Firms that succeed use "found time" to craft long-term strategies and implement long-needed changes.

During a recession, small design firms are particularly subject to economic stress. Many small firms operate with tight margins and little reserves. As revenues shrink due to reduced billings, smaller projects, and slower payments by clients, it may become more difficult for firm owners to pay salaries and other operating expenses.

Creating a plan for how to deal with diminishing revenues will help firm leaders prepare for a coming downturn. While unfortunate, the necessity of lay-offs provides small firm leaders with the opportunity to let their weakest performing staff members go. Because staff and principals work so closely together in most small firms, identifying the strongest performers, as well as those who are underperforming is usually easy to do. Care should be taken to not automatically equate number of hours in the office with strong performance. Otherwise, certain types of people may be unnecessarily targeted as underperforming, such as those who are parents of young children. Similarly, fewer years work experience does not necessarily result in weak performance. See Chapter 12, Big-Picture Trends, for further discussion of gender and generational issues in small firm management.

In most small firms, during a severe recession, firm leaders will choose a core group of critical employees to retain and then move to selective reductions in the work week or across the board pay reductions if conditions continue to deteriorate. Once the core group is established, the staff can become allies to the firm owners, participating in helping to control costs and support firm outreach. When staff reductions are accompanied by a review of organizational structure, firms can set themselves up for growth and a robust recovery.

External Economic Indicators

External economic indicators are important to watch in order to anticipate both the recession and the recovery. Particular indicators may track with certain market sectors. For example, a drop in the measures of consumer confidence may portend a drop in custom residential or retail projects. Similarly, a rise in interest rates or a lack of available credit may reduce the amount of commercial development undertaken.

Important economic indicators to watch include measures of the GDP, inflation, and construction activity in general. A drop in the GDP, such as was experienced late in 2008, will mean fewer goods and services are being purchased. This usually transfers into lower prices (deflation) and lower interest rates as the Federal Reserve attempts to stimulate economic activity. Observing economic trends over time will give firm leaders familiarity with general patterns that may impact the firm's business. This will improve ability to accurately forecast future revenue and staffing needs.

The American Institute of Architects provides industry-specific economic indicators such as the Architecture Billing Index that tracks the level of inquiries and billings by region. A drop in inquiries is a leading indicator of trouble on the horizon, while a drop in billings is an indication of a slowdown already in progress. Conversely, rises in either of these indicators may indicate a recovery is in the making. It is important to look at these reports by region since most small firms operate in a relatively small service area and the economic conditions will vary substantially from region to region in the United States.

External Economic Indicators

- Percent change in Gross Domestic Product: measure of economic growth
- Percent change in Consumer Price Index (CPI): measure of inflation
- Prime Rate: the cost of credit
- Consumer Confidence: especially critical for residential practices
- AIA Architects Billing Index: tracks monthly billing by region
- Housing starts; Number of permits; Unemployment rate
- Indicators specific to project type

Internal Economic Indicators

In slow times and to prepare for slow times, firm leaders must pay attention to metrics that are indicators of firm health. The first place that a slowdown is likely to be evident is the number of inquiries that flow into the firm. Setting up a system to track inquiries and the firm's "hit rate" (percentage of inquiries that become projects), will enable firm leaders to be alerted when things begin to soften.

As an economic slowdown deepens, projects that do come to the firm are likely to be smaller in scope and fee. Potential clients will be looking at fees more in their consideration of who to hire and it will be difficult to increase fees in this climate. Competition for projects will increase since larger firms may begin to "bottom feed," going after jobs they previously wouldn't have considered. Another indicator of an economic slowdown is that clients will be slow to pay invoices. Don't be shy about asking for payment and consider invoicing twice a month.

Internal Economic Indicators

- Fewer inquiries (leading indicator)
- Reduced size of potential projects
- More consideration of fee among potential clients
- Lack of ability to raise fees
- Longer time between proposal submittal and start of project
- Aging of accounts receivable (lagging indicator)

In good times, salaries and overhead will go up. So the silver lining of a downturn is that the opposite occurs, or at least, the pressure to constantly increase salaries is lessened. A slowdown may be a great time to renegotiate an office lease or look for a less expensive office space. And if a firm has work and is hiring, there may be an opportunity to hire talent let go by other firms.

Strategies to Prepare for an Economic Slowdown

The strategic keys to preparing for a downturn are:

- Stay aware of current macroeconomic trends.
- Leverage firm capacity to expand services to other project types.
- Build a cash reserve equal to three to six months of operating expenses (check with a tax advisor as to whether this reserve should be held in the firm's accounts or outside the firm in the owners' personal accounts).
- Establish a business line of credit (LOC) for short-term bridge loans (check with a financial advisor for guidance on how to determine size of LOC needed).
- Organize your staffing with the flexibility to handle the inevitable work load variations. Having prequalified contract workers on call or identifying staff

who are willing to go on temporary part-time are examples of flexible arrangements.

- Stay current with backlog and prospects—how much work is actually lined up? See the section on figuring backlog later in the chapter, but remember that backlog may need to be figured differently in slow times. According to Robert Smith, AIA, managing principal of CMMI Inc. in Atlanta, "One must be very objective—and probably very conservative—when making these judgments. In my experience, a higher percentage of backlog projects and prospects die during a recession than during normal times; and, during an expansion a higher percentage of backlog projects and prospects move forward than during normal times. It is wise to tailor our judgments around the actual circumstances taking place in the marketplace."
- Stay on top of cash flow and receivables.
- Expand marketing activities.
  - Undertake direct mailing (or blast email campaigns) to client base.
  - Expand networking and community involvement.
  - Establish professional alliances (contractors, other design professionals).
  - Submit projects for publication and awards.
  - Engage in teaching and writing to establish expertise.
  - Take existing clients to lunch.

Specific actions to prepare for a slowdown include:

- Be honest and objective with yourself about what's happening—resist overly optimistic assessments or straightforward denial of the situation.
- Communicate honestly and often with staff about firm workload situation.
- Research possibilities to "lend" employees to other firms.
- Identify the underperforming staff and be prepared to lay them off.
  - Rank all of your staff according to value and contribution—being very specific and explicit about the rationale used to make the ranking.
  - Prepare lay-off policies, such as severance pay and access to portfolio material.
  - Be fair, respectful, and communicate honestly.
  - Reconfirm commitment to valued staff.
- Check out employee preferences in case of a continued slowdown but be clear that the firm leadership will be making the final decisions on strategic actions:
  - reduced work week across the board
  - voluntary unpaid time off (with health benefits if possible)
  - voluntary temporary part time (with health benefits, if possible)

- Prepare to use employees to accomplish value-added tasks—tasks that will enable more effective marketing and work processes once the market recovers:
  - enhance marketing materials
  - update website
  - complete project close-out documentation
  - update detail library
  - improve systems for routine processes
  - organize files and hardcopy library
  - enter competitions
  - use slow time for learning new knowledge and adding competency—both for firm owners and for staff

Summary

During a work slowdown, resist the temptation to reduce fees. While an argument could be made that work at any price is better than no work, consider the opportunity costs of that decision. Since most architecture projects take some time to complete, a firm could be locked into discounted fee contracts long after the recovery has occurred. Small firms have a limit to their capacity for project execution, so the impact of discounted contracts can be long lasting.

Similarly, don't take just any job—working outside of the firm's comfort zone will not help the situation. And don't reduce the quality of the work or work for someone who seems untrustworthy. No matter what the circumstance, firm owners should always act as if they "don't need the money." Otherwise, they run the risk of making poor decisions. Awareness and strategic preparations can minimize this risk and enable small firms to weather an economic slowdown without compromise.

To fully grasp the impact of macroeconomics on a firm over time, it is important for firm leaders to track firm financial performance regularly. Understanding financial terminology as it applies to professional service firms is the first step.

FINANCIAL TERMINOLOGY

Financial terminology can be mysterious and sometimes different terms are used by different people in differing ways. In this book, specific financial terms and their intended meaning are as follows:

- **Gross Revenue:** Income from all sources.
- **Direct Project Costs:** Reimbursable, or pass-through, project-related expenses, such as consultants or printing.
- **Net Revenue**: Gross revenue minus direct project costs.
- **Direct Labor:** Cost of labor for work on projects.

- **Indirect Labor:** Cost of all labor other than direct labor.
- **Utilization Rate:** Direct labor divided by total labor, for an individual staff member—utilization rate can be calculated using either hours or payroll dollars.
- **Payroll Burden:** Costs associated with payroll, including payroll taxes, healthcare, and retirement plans.
- **Salary Expense:** Total of all salaries, both employees and owners.
- **General Office Expense:** Rent, utilities, maintenance, supplies, etc.
- **Overhead Expense:** General office expense plus indirect labor, plus payroll burden.
- **Net Income (*aka* Profit):** Net revenue minus salary expense, minus overhead expense before taxes and distributions.
- **Distributions:** Employee bonuses and owners' share of profit.

FINANCIAL PERFORMANCE INDICATORS AND BENCHMARKS

Some financial metrics are easy to observe and understand as part of day-to-day operations. These operational indicators include cash flow, accounts receivable (how much is owed to the firm and for how long), accounts payable (what the firm must pay to others, including outstanding taxes and payroll), and amounts billed to clients. Other indicators help firm owners understand firm performance in quantitative terms. These are usually expressed as ratios and can be compared to industry benchmarks. The following strategic financial indicators are important to track and are useful in projecting probable future performance.

- **Chargeable Ratio (*aka* Firmwide Utilization Rate):** Direct labor divided by total labor for the entire firm, expressed as a percentage. Past performance can be calculated using data from time sheet records of staff hours and how they were spent. If electronic time sheets are in use, this data is easily retrievable. For the purposes of forecasting and benchmarking, the chargeable ratio may need to be adjusted to reflect the reality that all direct hours are not actually billable. Industry benchmark is around 60 percent. On this point, Robert Smith, AIA, remarks, "utilization can be calculated using either 'hours' or 'dollars' and that the appropriate benchmark will differ, depending on which one you calculate—in my experience the calculation using hours will result in 2 to 4 percentage points higher than is the case when the calculation uses dollars. This is mostly important because industry surveys generally will report results using one particular calculation or the other. Those industry benchmarks need to be evaluated properly against the approach used by the firm so as not to produce meaningless, or confusing, interpretations."

- **Multiplier Achieved:** Net revenue divided by direct labor equals the earnings achieved for each dollar of direct labor. If the multiplier achieved equals 2.45, then the firm earned $2.45 for every $1.00 it spent on direct labor. A multiplier achieved of 3.0 has been a long-standing industry target.

- **Overhead Rate (before Distributions):** Total overhead (general office expense plus payroll burden plus indirect labor) divided by direct labor. Industry norm is about 1.5, but it can vary widely by region and circumstance. For instance, sole proprietors who work out of their home will probably have lower overhead rates, while architects with offices in major cities may exceed the average by a great deal.

- **Direct Labor Rate:** Direct labor divided by direct labor, always equals 1.0.

- **Break-Even Multiplier:** Overhead divided by direct labor plus direct labor rate (1.0). If the break-even multiplier is less than the multiplier achieved, the firm is being profitable; if the break-even multiplier is greater than the multiplier achieved, the firm is not operating profitably.

- **Profit Factor:** The complement of the profit goal divided into the break-even multiplier. For example, a billing multiplier that includes a profit factor of 15 percent will equal the break-even multiplier divided by .85.

- **Profitability Rate:** Net income (before taxes and distribution) divided by net revenue expressed as a percentage. A net income of $40,000 from net revenues of $400,000 equals a pretax, predistribution profitability of 10 percent. Industry benchmark for small firms is around 13 percent.

- **Net Revenue per Staff:** Annual net revenue divided by the average number of staff members at the firm during the year. This metric is useful for comparison to industry benchmark of $110,000 to $130,000 per person and as a predictor of realistic future performance.

Industry benchmarks are available through numerous organizations, including the American Institute of Architects. Other organizations that provide benchmarks information include PSMJ and Zweig-White Consulting.

FINANCIAL MANAGEMENT TASKS

For some leaders of small firms, financial management comes naturally. For others, it is a distracting burden from the "real" work of the firm. Regardless of attitude and aptitude, the information that comes from attention to financial metrics is vital to reaching strategic goals. To simplify and demystify the processes, this section provides a list of basic financial management tasks and instructions on how they are performed. Many of these metrics are easily generated by performance management software (see Chapter 3), available as reports and dashboard graphics. Nevertheless, understanding how the metrics are generated will enable understanding of their meaning and application.

Financial Management Tasks

- Track firm profitability.
- Track chargeable ratio and direct labor expense.
- Track general expenses and budget variance.
- Track break-even multiple and multiplier achieved.
- Track backlog and outstanding proposals.
- Develop income projections (see Chapter 8).
- Develop staffing needs projections (see Chapter 8).
- Complete annual financial checkup and financial performance review.

Track Firm Profitability

Firm profitability should be tracked monthly, if possible, and no less frequently than quarterly. It is easily generated by accounting software and is a big-picture look at what percentage of net revenue is left as net income after expenses are deducted, and before distributions and taxes. For example, net revenue: $361,000; net income: $27,000, equals 7.5 percent profitability.

Track Chargeable Ratio and Direct Labor Expense

Chargeable ratio is one indicator of firm-wide productivity. A higher chargeable percentage means that more hours are billable and more income will be earned. Chargeable ratio is usually calculated using salary expense rather than hours. To determine chargeable ratio, direct salary expense for all the staff including partners and administrators, is divided by the total salary expense.

It is not uncommon in design firms for individual staff members to report nearly 100 percent of their hours as billable in any given pay period. The only indirect hours reported will be for office meetings or distinct nonbillable tasks, such as work on marketing materials. However, even the most diligent worker cannot really be 100 percent billable. There is always down time of one kind or another in any work day, and the highest utilization rate possible is likely to be around 90 percent. Typically, utilization rates vary based on the job position of the worker. Partners and principals in small firms may only be 30 to 50 percent billable, while interns may realistically be close to 90 percent. Project managers and project architects will commonly have utilization rates that range from 70 to 85 percent.

To be a more accurate measure of firm-wide productivity, chargeable ratios may need to be adjusted to reflect the fact that not all direct hours will be billable. A method for adjusting chargeable ratio will be introduced later in this chapter.

To determine the chargeable ratio, compile a list of all firm members along with their total salary and target utilization rates, as shown in Table 7-A, for a fictional firm called MK Architects.

TABLE 7-A: Chargeable Ratio

Staff Member	Principal	Project Architect	Intern	Administrator (1/2 time)	Total
Salary Expense	$90,000	$60,000	$40,000	$20,000	$210,000
Target Utilization Rate	50%	75%	90%	0%	
Direct Labor Expense	$45,000	$45,000	$36,000	–	$126,000
Indirect Labor	$45,000	$15,000	$ 4,000	$20,000	$ 84,000

$$\text{Chargeable Ratio:} \quad \frac{\$126,000}{\$210,000} = 60\%$$

Estimate the direct labor for each person by multiplying the salary times the target utilization rate. Add them all together to determine the total direct labor expense. Divide the total direct labor expense by the total salary expense to determine the chargeable ratio. MK Architects has a chargeable ratio of 60 percent meaning almost two-thirds of the total hours are spent as direct labor on projects. This is in line with the industry benchmark for chargeable ratio of 60 to 65 percent.

For the purpose of this example, assume Table 7-A was created at the end of 2007 with the utilization rates drawn from data collected for the entire year. As such, this represents chargeable ratio achieved by MK Architects in 2007. Tracking chargeable ratio quarterly will give firm owners an ongoing sense of how the firm is doing in terms of productivity.

Track Break-Even Multiplier and Multiplier Achieved

Along with chargeable ratio, tracking the break-even multiplier and the multiplier achieved will give firm owners information about the outlook for profitability. Direct labor expense, overhead rate, and net revenue are used in these calculations. For the fictional firm MK Architects, assume 2007 net revenue is $361,000 and overhead expense is $208,000. The direct labor expense, as shown in Table 7-A, is $126,000.

2007 multiplier achieved equals net revenue divided by direct labor expense: $361,000 ÷ $126,000 = 2.87.

2007 overhead rate equals overhead expense divided by direct labor expense. Overhead expense includes indirect labor, payroll burden, and general expense: $208,000 ÷ $126,000 = 1.65.

2007 break-even multiplier equals overhead rate plus one: 1.65 + 1 = 2.65.

Because the break-even multiplier is less than the multiplier achieved, it is evident that the firm made a profit in 2007. Every dollar paid in direct labor returned $1.65 for overhead expenses and $0.22 in profit.

2007 net income equals $361,000 – $208,000 – $126,000 = $27,000.

2007 profitability, before distribution and taxes, equals net income divided by net revenue: $27,000 ÷ $361,000 (100) = 7.5 percent.

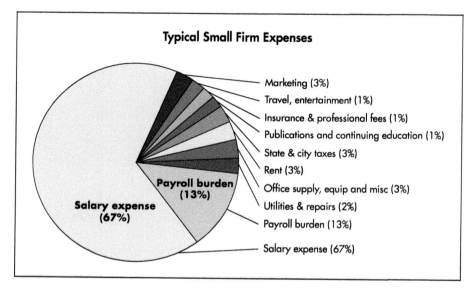

Typical Small Firm Expenses

Marketing (3%)
Travel, entertainment (1%)
Insurance & professional fees (1%)
Publications and continuing education (1%)
State & city taxes (3%)
Rent (3%)
Office supply, equip and misc (3%)
Utilities & repairs (2%)
Payroll burden (13%)
Salary expense (67%)

Payroll burden (13%)
Salary expense (67%)

Figure 7.4   Salary expense often accounts for two-thirds of the cost of running a small firm.

Track Overhead Expense and Budget Variance

Firm management must remain attuned to the basic costs of running the firm. This analysis could be done by an administrator, but firm owners should always be aware of trends and budget overruns in the firm's operations. Figure 7.4 shows the overhead and salary expense of a typical small firm. It's worth noting that labor and labor-related expenses normally comprise about two-thirds of a design firm's operating expenses.

Tracking overhead expenses will help firm owners understand how revenue is spent and enable them to create realistic budgets for the coming year or two. In general, budgets are useful even if they are not detailed—just general categories. Table 7-B shows the 2007 budget for a firm of 15 and an analysis of the first three months of 2007—January through March—to determine if actual expenditures vary from the budget expectations. The percentage of budget items in relation to net revenue is another way of examining the data on budget variances. This is especially helpful when, as in this case, the net revenue varies significantly from what was forecast.

This analysis reveals that total expenses were slightly more than expected. However, since indirect labor was significantly less than expected, total overhead expenses were also less than expected. And with indirect labor lower than expected, it follows that direct labor expense would be more than was expected, virtually evening things out for the first three months of 2007. The table also shows that in the first three months of 2007 the firm was more productive and more profitable

TABLE 7-B: Expense Budget Variance

Budget Projections and Variance: Jan – March 2007					
	January – March budget	% of Net Revenue	January – March actual	% of Net Revenue	Variance
Net Revenue January – March	$670,000		$800,000		$ 130,000
Marketing	$ 12,500	1.8%	$ 34,939	4.4%	($ 22,439)
Car/Truck	$ 3,750	0.6%	$ 6,287	0.8%	($ 2,537)
Insurance	$ 4,166	0.6%	$ 9,577	1.2%	($ 5,411)
Professional Fees	$ 16,666	2.5%	$ 16,565	2.1%	$ 101
Publications & Continuing Education	$ 6,250	0.9%	$ 3,960	0.5%	$ 2,290
State & City Taxes	$ 16,666	2.5%	$ 20,486	2.6%	($ 3,820)
Rent	$ 16,666	2.5%	$ 25,448	3.2%	($ 8,782)
Office Supply	$ 10,416	1.6%	$ 32,815	4.1%	($ 22,399)
Telephone/Internet	$ 7,083	1.1%	$ 7,376	0.9%	($ 293)
Office Equipment & Miscellaneous	$ 6,250	0.9%	$ 8,599	1.1%	($ 2,349)
Utilities	$ 2,083	0.3%	$ 2,142	0.3%	($ 59)
Repairs	$ 1,250	0.2%	$ 1,629	0.2%	($ 379)
Travel & Entertainment	$ 6,250	0.9%	$ 3,013	0.4%	$ 3,237
Total General Office Expense	$110,000	16.4%	$172,841	21.6%	($ 62,841)
Payroll Burden	$ 79,056	11.8%	$ 70,273	8.8%	$ 8,783
Indirect Labor	$160,671	24.0%	$ 38,844	4.9%	$ 121,827
Total Overhead	$349,727	52.2%	$281,959	35.2%	$ 67,768
Direct Labor Expense	$234,612	35.0%	$304,535	38.1%	($ 69,923)
Total Expenses January – March	$584,340		$586,495		($ 2,155)
Total Net Income January – March	$ 85,660		$213,505		
Profitability Rate	13%		27%		
Total average monthly "nut" equals: $195,498 ($586,495 ÷ 3 months)					

than expected. A result like this should be cause for firm leaders to investigate why the significant variances between the actual and forecast amounts for net revenue and direct labor occurred. Were the revenue forecasts too conservative? Were the target utilization rates too low? It is important to compare forecasts against actual results over time to evaluate the accuracy and effectiveness of forecasting methods.

Creating an annual budget and tracking it throughout the year will help prevent costs from slipping out of control and will give small firm owners an ongoing knowledge about the financial state of affairs at their firms. The "monthly nut" noted at the bottom of the table is the minimum amount needed each month to run the firm.

Track Backlog and Outstanding Proposals

Backlog is defined as the remaining unbilled (or unearned) value of signed contracts. For example, a firm may have a contract for $50,000 to design a custom home and has completed the predesign and schematic design phase worth 20 percent of the contract amount. The backlog for this project would be $40,000. Backlog is revenue the firm owners can rely on and use in forecasting income with relative confidence. However, since all work is uncertain until completed, only 90 percent of remaining contract amounts is counted in revenue forecasts.

Because it can be reasonably assumed that projects are continually being acquired by a firm, it is important to track outstanding proposals and include some proportion of them in forecasts of income. However, even if prospects (job possibilities that are more than 50 percent likely to come through) have high probability of success, it would not be reasonable to assume that all prospects will convert to signed contracts. Therefore, only 50 percent (or a number informed by the firm's data on actual "hit rate") of the estimated contract value of prospects should be counted in revenue forecasts. Similarly, suspects are the outstanding proposals that seem less likely to succeed. Because some of them will be won regardless of the odds, 10 percent of the estimated contract value of suspects is included in the forecast.

Gross revenue forecast from backlog and pending proposals equals: backlog times 90 percent, plus prospects times 50 percent, plus suspects times 10 percent. Table 7-C is an example of a spreadsheet used to track backlog and proposals pending. This kind of table should be in constant use by firm owners, continually updated to track the likely revenue stream for the firm. Compare the net revenue forecast to the "monthly nut" to see how many months this income will support the firm.

Year-End Financial Checkup

The beginning of the year is an excellent time to assess the financial health of a small firm. Firm owners can look back over the past year in order to form reasonable expectations of future income, expense, and profitability. An annual fiscal review can form the basis of an annual budget and help firm owners make business decisions such as when to hire or move to a larger office. An annual financial examination, along with reflection on firm purpose and a review of the marketing plan, is critical to creating a successful practice.

Annual Financial Checkup Components

- **Profitability Achieved:** Net income divided by net revenue, expressed as a percentage. Example: 60,000 net income ÷ 600,000 net revenue = 10 percent profitability.

- **Overhead Rate Achieved:** Overhead expense ÷ direct labor. Example: 340,000 overhead expense ÷ 200,000 direct labor = 1.7. This number is useful in projecting next year's operating budget.

TABLE 7-C: Backlog, Prospects, Suspects

Backlog, Prospects, Suspects		Date:		
	Phase	**Contract Amount (gross revenue)**	**Amount Billed**	**Contract Amount Remaining**
Backlog				
RK Residence	Schematic Design	$ 50,000	$ 7,500	$ 42,500
Doctors Clinic	Const. Documents	$120,000	$ 48,000	$ 72,000
Multiuse Commercial Building	Design Development	$400,000	$120,000	$ 280,000
ST Residence	Construction Phase	$ 55,000	$ 49,500	$ 5,500
Total Backlog				**$400,000**
Prospects (proposals pending)		Estimated Contract Amount (gross revenue)		
MH Residence		$ 80,000		
Tex-Mex Restaurant		$ 30,000		
Multiuse Commercial Building		$500,000		
Total Prospects		**$610,000**		
Suspects (less likely to win)				
Co-Housing Development		$600,000		
Train Station Renovation		$100,000		
Total Suspects		**$700,000**		
Gross income forecast equals (backlog x 90%) + (prospects x 50%) + (suspects x 10%) = $735,000 Net income forecast equals gross income forecast minus estimate of direct project expenses				

Note from Robert Smith, AIA, "Just because there is $735,000 of forecast gross income, there still may be timing issues with respect to start dates and hold periods and other delays that may cause an uneven flow of work—and uneven flow of revenue—over the period of time being considered. There also are issues related to how long it might take different clients to pay. All of these imponderables must be pondered in order for an income forecast to become highly informative with respect to the firm's future operations."

- **Break-Even Multiplier:** (Overhead expense + direct labor) ÷ direct labor. Example: (340,000 overhead expense + 200,000 direct labor) ÷ 200,000 direct labor = 2.7. This firm must charge $2.70 for every $1.00 it spends on direct labor to break even. This number is useful in profit planning.

- **Multiplier Achieved:** Net revenue ÷ direct labor. Example: 600,000 net revenue ÷ 200,000 direct labor = 3.0. Is the answer greater or lesser than the firm's break-even multiplier? If greater, the firm is operating profitably.

- **Net Revenue per Staff Member:** Net revenue ÷ number of staff members. Industry norm varies by region and firm size; likely to be $110,000 to $130,000 per person. This number will give an estimate of the net revenue needed to support or grow the firm.
- **Forecast Net Revenue for Coming Year:** Sum of backlog, prospects, and suspects minus estimated direct expenses:
  - Estimate the percent of gross revenue that goes to direct expenses such as consultants. Historical data on profit and loss statements will be a source for this information. This may be 10 to 20 percent depending on the type of practice.
  - Determine gross revenue estimate for coming year:
    i. Backlog: Take 90 percent of the remaining value of contracts already signed but not yet completed;
    ii. Prospects: Add 50 percent of value of proposals that have a high probability of success;
    iii. Suspects: Add 10 percent of value of proposals or possibilities that have lower than 50 percent probability of success.
  - Subtract the estimated direct project expenses from the gross revenue forecast to determine the net revenue forecast.
  - Compare gross revenue and net revenue estimates to previous years and consider macroeconomic conditions.

Compare net revenue forecast to the annual net revenue per staff member for a sense of how the firm stands relative to the income needed for the coming year. Compare net revenue forecast to the "monthly nut"—the amount of cash needed to operate each month—to get a sense of how long the expected work will support the firm. Twelve months' worth of backlog and prospects is comfortable for most firms.

Tracking Financial Health

Strategic Indicators
- Chargeable ratio (total direct labor/total labor)
- Net multiplier achieved (net income/total direct labor)
- Overhead rate (total overhead/total direct labor)
- Profitability (net income/net revenue)
- Backlog (unbilled value of projects under contract plus some prospects)

Operational Indicators
- Cash flow
- Aging receivables
- Proposals pending
- Monthly billings

Additional Financial Checks

In addition to the basic financial management tools already introduced in this chapter, there are other financial metrics that should be checked periodically. These metrics are particularly important for financial forecasts and for deeper understanding of productivity.

Realizable Income and Net Revenue

Realizable income is the total income that could theoretically be generated by the firm based on hours worked, utilization rates, and billing rates of all billable staff. The utilization rates are generated from the records of direct and indirect hours posted on time sheets. If realizable income for a future year is being forecasted, then the utilization rates are considered targets and should be based on past performance.

Differences between realizable income and actual net revenue are usually due to the fact that some direct hours are not billable. This may be because of contract limitations, or simply because work needs to be done on projects that can't be charged to the client. It may also be that more direct hours are reported than are actually worked, which is not uncommon and not necessarily intentional. For whatever reason, it is likely that most staff utilization rates are actually somewhat lower than documented.

The relationship between realizable income and actual net revenue is important for financial forecasts and for a realistic view of productivity. As shown in Table 7-D, at MK Architects, only 83% of the realizable income was actually billed to clients in 2007.

For the principal of MK Architects, Table 7-D could be a wake-up call indicating that productivity is not as good as it appears to be on time sheets. It is likely that all the staff members are recording more direct time than they are actually doing and it is also likely that much legitimate direct labor is not chargeable to the client for one reason or another. Judging individual staff members based only on utilization rate is not recommended due to the many factors that could influence the metric. If an individual employee is underperforming in a small firm, it is usually obvious without quantitative measures.

TABLE 7-D: Realizable Income and Net Revenue

	Principal	Project Architect	Intern	Total
Actual Net Hours Worked per Year	2,280	2,104	2,104	
Actual Utilization Rate	50%	75%	90%	
Billing Rate	$150	$90	$65	
2007 Realizable Income	$171,000	$142,020	$123,084	$436,104
Actual 2007 Net Revenue				$361,000

Percent of realizable income actually billed to clients: $\dfrac{\$361,000}{\$436,000} = 83\%$

TABLE 7-E: Cost Rate and Billing Multiple

	Principal	Project Architect	Intern
Gross Annual Salary	$ 90,000	$ 60,000	$ 40,000
Payroll Tax (15%)	$ 13,500	$ 9,000	$ 6,000
Health Insurance	$ 6,000	$ 3,000	$ 3,000
401K Match	$ 2,700	$ 1,800	$ 1,200
Net Cost per Year	$112,200	$ 73,800	$ 50,200
Net Cost per Week	$ 2,158	$ 1,420	$ 965
Gross Hours per Year	2,480	2,264	2,264
Vacation	120	80	80
Holiday/Personal Leave	80	80	80
Net Hours Worked per Year	2,280	2,104	2,104
Net Hours Worked per Week	43.85	40.46	40.46
Net Cost Rate per Hour Worked	$ 49.03	$ 35.09	$ 23.85
Billing Rate	$ 150.00	$ 90.00	$ 65.00
Billing Multiple	3.05	2.57	2.72

For MK Architects, Table 7-D lets them know that realizable income will need to be adjusted by 83 percent in financial projections, assuming that productivity and overhead expense remain substantially the same. The process of creating reliable and accurate financial projections will be discussed more completely in Chapter 8, Scenario Planning.

Cost Rate and Billing Multiple

To determine if the billing rate charged to clients is high enough to cover salary, overhead, and also yield some profit, it is necessary to know the actual hourly cost of each billable staff member. This metric is known as the cost rate. It is determined by dividing the net cost per year (salary plus payroll burden) by the net hours per year (hours worked minus holidays and other paid time off). Once the cost rate is determined, it can be compared to the billing rate for each staff member and the billing multiple can be calculated. Table 7-E illustrates this process for MK Architects.

Periodically, it is advisable to check if the billing multiples being charged are in line with profit goals. Table 7-E can be useful in profit planning and scenario planning.

Profit Planning

For MK Architects, the comparison between the break-even multiple (2.65) and the multiplier achieved (2.87) for 2007 revealed a profitable operation. For every dollar spent on direct labor, 22 cents net income was earned.

As calculated earlier in this chapter, net income for MK Architects in 2007 equals: $361,000 (net revenue) − $208,000 (overhead expense) − $126,000 (direct labor expense) = $27,000 (net income).

2007 profitability equals net income divided by net revenue: $27,000 ÷ $361,000 (100) = 7.5 percent.

However, 7.5 percent predistribution/pretax profitability rate is well below the industry standard of 13 to 15 percent for small firms. The principal of MK Architects would like to earn 10 percent profitability in the coming year. To determine the billing multiple that would be needed to achieve 10 percent profitability for MK Architects, assuming that the overhead rate remains unchanged, follow these steps:

1. Determine the complement of the profit goal: .90 is the complement of 10 percent.

2. Divide the break-even multiple by the complement of the profit goal: 2.65 ÷ .90 = 2.94.

MK Architects would need to achieve a billing multiple of 2.94 to earn 10 percent profitability, assuming that the overhead rate remains unchanged. In 2007, the firm achieved a billing multiple of 2.87, so this is likely to be an achievable goal. How this goal might be reached will be explored fully in Chapter 8, Scenario Planning.

ENDNOTE

1. U.S. Bureau of Economic Analysis, **www.bea.gov/national/nipaweb/Index.**

CHAPTER 8

SCENARIO PLANNING

In Chapter 7, the principal of MK Architects was faced with a gap between the firm's current profitability, and where the principal would like it to be. Gaps such as these are often the motivation behind strategic planning activities. These activities include assessment of the current situation and clarification of short- and long-term goals. Once the gaps between where a firm is now and where it wants to be in the future are identified, intentional actions can be planned and implemented.

To a great extent, strategic planning and building design are parallel processes. Architects would never consider designing a building without clear purpose, place, and financial criteria. This same thinking can be applied to the design of design firms. Figure 8.1 illustrates the similarities between business planning and building design.

Strategic planning allows firm leaders to be intentional about creating a preferred future for their firm. In an environment of unpredictability, the last phase shown in Figure 8.1, "evaluate and adjust" is the most critical. Small firm leaders cannot afford to develop a strategic plan that sits in the drawer and is never implemented because conditions change. What is important is the awareness the process brings, which in turn, enables strategic thinking. Strategic thinking allows firm leaders to evaluate opportunities and make management decisions that are aligned with identified goals. Goals approached in this way are more likely to be achieved.

To evaluate different courses of action, strategic planners use a technique known as scenario planning. Similar to schematic design, scenario planning is a process by which a number of "organizational plans" are developed as possible futures. For instance, if a firm wants to grow 20 percent over a period of five years, a number of scenarios can be developed to outline staffing, revenue, and marketing

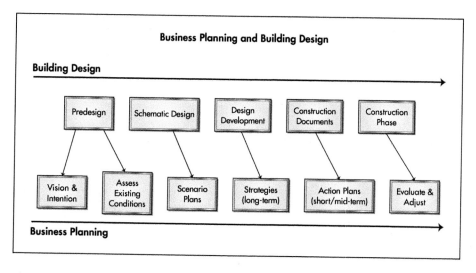

Figure 8.1 Business planning is a parallel process to building design.

requirements for each year, depending on the rate of growth and other factors. These can then be evaluated for feasibility, market positioning, and probability of success. Once a plan is chosen, it can be refined and steps for implementation developed.

Scenario planning is a tool that can be used to explore specific operational issues, such as strategies for increasing profitability, the goal of the principal of MK Architects. The quantitative aspects of this process will be discussed later in this chapter, but first, it is important to understand the factors that influence profitability.

INFLUENCES ON PROFITABILITY

Even in boom times, when there are plenty of projects and overall revenues increase, profitability may still be difficult to achieve. Figure 3.1, in Chapter 3, illustrates an income statement of a firm where the net revenue may go up in any particular year, but the overhead expense increases by nearly the same amount. The outcome of this situation is little or no increase in net income year after year. This situation is not uncommon in small firms and usually an indicator of low productivity, as discussed in Chapter 3. In a situation like this, no matter how much work is done or how big the fees are, satisfactory profit margins will never be achieved.

Productivity in economics is defined as the rate at which a company produces goods or services, in relation to the amount of materials and employee time needed. In architectural firms, one measure of productivity is the relationship between net revenue (what the company produces) and direct salary expense (what it took to produce it) of partners and staff (e.g., multiplier achieved). The cost of nonbillable

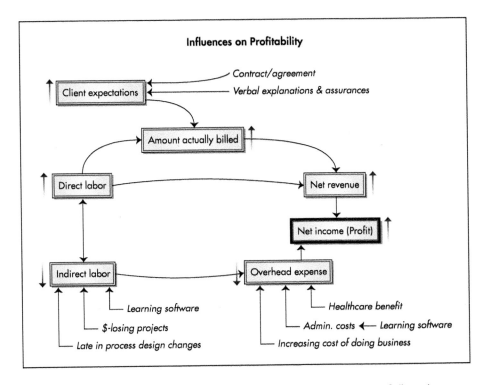

Figure 8.2 Net income is influenced by client expectations, number of direct hours, and amount of overhead expense.

hours (indirect labor expense), whether they are spent working on a project or on firm development, is a component of overhead. When productivity is low, overhead expense increases as the direct labor expense decreases. As a result, there are fewer hours to invoice to clients, and projects take longer (are more costly) to complete. If this goes on year after year, the inevitable outcome is stagnation in terms of profitability and potential for firm growth.

Figure 8.2 illustrates the major influences on profitability. In its simplest form, profit (net income) is the difference between net revenue and all expenses (direct labor expense plus overhead expense). When overhead increases profit will fall. Similarly if overhead expense remains steady, direct hours increase, and most are billable to a client, net revenues will increase and profits will follow.

Client Expectations

One way to improve the number of billable hours that can actually be charged to a client is to ensure that fee agreements are carefully structured to provide adequate revenue for the work that needs to be completed. Profitability is influenced by client expectations as much as by staff productivity. These expectations are conditioned by written agreements and verbal assurances. The fee agreement will determine the amount that can be charged (absent changes to the project scope), no matter how many hours are required to complete the work, unless a project is charged by the hour. Even with hourly contracts, it is not unusual for firms to discount the number of hours actually worked.

The impact of client expectations on profitability cannot be understated. When appropriate, clients can be charged for additional services, but only if included services are well articulated, the need for additional services communicated effectively and permission for additional services is granted. Be sure to use accurate historical data from similar projects as a basis for new proposals and contracts, as well as an understanding of the market value of the services offered. Many small firm owners have a tendency to undercharge, to lack clearly articulated agreements, and to not carefully consider whether a potential project is likely to be profitable.

As explained by Robert Smith, AIA, managing principal of CMMI Inc. in Atlanta, "It is important to make our expectations explicit—as a reflection of our understanding of the client's expectations. For example, we should define how many schematic design schemes we will provide; how many trips per month we will make to the site during CA (Construction Administration), etc. By making these assumptions explicit during scope and fee negotiations, the client is forced to focus on what his/her expectations might be with respect to service level desired. Without dragging these expectations out onto the table for mutual examination, the client probably is making assumptions that are not consistent with our own, but which will impose on us service levels we did not intend when we quoted the fee and which we cannot afford to provide, given the fee arrangements made."

Contractual arrangements that are not really adequate to do all that is required and expected is more likely to be the cause of losing money on jobs than any productivity failure on the part of the staff. Fixed fee contracts limit the amount that can be billed to the client, no matter how many hours are recorded as spent on the project and this will impact the amount of direct labor recorded on time sheets that is actually chargeable. In Chapter 7, it was shown that MK Architects charged only 83 percent of the direct hours that were recorded on time sheets. As diagrammed in Figure 8.2, this may have been due to the limits of contractual agreements and/or the lack of effective production processes.

Influences on Net Revenue

- Client expectations
  - Contractual agreements
  - Verbal agreements and assurances
- How much direct labor is actually billable?
  - Important to track
  - Substantial amount of direct labor may not be billable

Overhead Expense

As defined in Chapter 7, overhead expense is the sum of general office expenses, payroll burden, and indirect labor. Each of these components can have a significant effect on profitability. Although a significant contributor to overhead—remember that some indirect labor is necessary—not all indirect labor is bad. Principals need indirect labor for marketing, continuing education, and business development. Among staff, indirect labor is needed for professional development, process improvement, and to allow time for familiarity and team building. Learning and implementing new software for production and/or administrative processes can add significantly to indirect hours. In-house, sometimes frivolous changes to a project's design during the late stages of production are another way that indirect hours sometimes accumulate.

Overhead expense is further impacted by payroll burden, which includes the cost of providing health insurance for partners and staff. Other common elements of payroll burden include payroll taxes and retirement plans. These costs can easily be 20 to 25 percent of the total salary expense. General overhead is also constantly in danger of increasing and should be tracked carefully.

Influences on Overhead

- Amount of indirect labor
  - Utilization rates of staff (direct hours/total hours)
  - Overall firm chargeable ratio
  - Administrative staff expense
  - Learning and implementing new software
- Payroll burden
- Benefits
- Amount of general overhead expense

STRATEGIES FOR INCREASING PROFITABILITY

By understanding and using the strategic indicators that follow, a number of necessary management decisions become easier. If profitability is too low and the break-even multiplier too high, there are steps that can be taken for improvement.

For example, if chargeable ratio is below industry benchmark, analysis of work processes to identify bottlenecks and wasted efforts can yield good results. This can be especially effective if the professional and administrative staff is involved. A process improvement effort is an excellent opportunity to empower and engage the staff while taking advantage of their intelligence and know-how. In slow times, process improvement is a value-added activity.

Realizable Revenue

Improving revenue and profitability may also involve actions to assure that most direct hours are both meaningful and billable. These actions may include reviewing the entire proposal process; making sure that fees are adequate to allow for excellent job performance; establishing clear and frequent communication with clients; and instituting a go/no-go process for deciding which projects to pursue based at least in part on whether the project is likely to be profitable. If it is not, there needs to be another very compelling reason to take on a job.

To properly manage a small firm it is essential to engage in profit planning and use financial ratios to understand how to meet profit goals. MK Architects, for example, has a 2007 profitability of 7.5 percent, with a profit goal of 10 percent for 2008. To determine how that could be accomplished, begin with the realizable revenue for the staff as it is currently configured, shown previously in Table 7-D and again in Table 8-A.

Whether a firm is working for clients hourly, or on a fixed fee basis, there is likely to be a gap between the value of the hours worked (based on billing rate) and the amount that can be charged for the work accomplished. Client expectations impact the size of this gap to be sure, but another underlying cause may be the natural tendency for both staff and partners to record more time working on projects than actually occurs. Utilization rates and chargeable ratios are therefore unreliable markers, unless they are adjusted to reflect the reality of the situation more closely.

From Chapter 7, we know that MK Architects had a net revenue of $361,000 in 2007, direct labor expense of $126,000, and overhead expense of $208,000. Net income in 2007 was $27,000 and the profitability (profit ratio) was 7.5 percent. It was also determined, in Chapter 7, that a multiplier of 2.94 would be necessary to achieve a profitability of 10 percent. It can be reasonably assumed that if the staff size remains the same, salaries remain the same, and utilization rates remain the same, the amount of direct labor expense in 2008 also will remain the same. Therefore, by multiplying the direct labor expense by 2.94, the net revenue needed for 10 percent profitability can be determined.

The above model assumes that salaries will be the same in 2008, but actual salaries are likely to increase by an average of 3 to 5 percent per year, unless the

TABLE 8-A: Realizable Revenue

	Principal	Project Architect	Intern	Total
Net Hours Worked per Year	2,280	2,104	2,104	
Utilization Rate	50%	75%	90%	
Billing Rate	$ 150	$ 90	$ 65	
2007 Realizable Revenue	$171,000	$142,020	$123,084	$436,104
Actual 2007 Net Revenue				$361,000

Percent of realizable income actually billed to clients: $\dfrac{361,000}{436,104} = 83\%$

TABLE 8-B: Direct Labor Expense Calculation

	Principal	Project Architect	Intern	Total
2008 Salary Expense	$90,000	$62,400	$41,200	$193,600
Target Utilization Rate	50%	75%	90%	
Direct Labor Expense	$45,000	$46,800	$37,080	$128,880

economy is in a downturn. At MK Architects, the principal decides to hold his own salary steady, increase the project architect's salary by 4 percent and the intern's compensation by 3 percent. The impact on direct labor can be easily calculated using a spreadsheet such as the one shown in Table 8-B.

Net revenue required for 10 percent profitability in 2008 can be estimated by multiplying the direct labor expense by the multiplier determined in Chapter 7: $128,880 times 2.94 equals $378,907. This is an increase of $17,907, or 5 percent over the 2007 net revenue. This seems like an attainable goal especially when, as shown in Table 8-A, the potential realizable revenue for the staff could easily produce this amount of net revenue. However, it is evident from the results of 2007 that the actual net revenue was only 83 percent of the realizable revenue. Assuming this adjustment percentage will not change for the coming year, to get a realistic view of how to reach 10 percent profitability, the realizable revenue developed in every strategic scenario will need to be multiplied by 83 percent.

Increase Hours?

Many small firm leaders will attempt to increase profitability by simply working more hours, and asking the same of their staff. Table 8-C shows the impact of increasing hours to meet profit goals, assuming salaries, utilization rates, and billing rates remain stable.

This strategy appears to result in $24,000 more net income at the end of the year and easily reaches the desired increase in revenue. However, there are hidden costs to this approach. While asking salaried employees to work overtime is reasonable for a while, it is not sustainable. In addition, overtime is often rewarded with increased bonuses, so it can be assumed that some of the additional profit will be distributed

TABLE 8-C: Increase Hours for Each Staff Member

	Principal	Project Architect	Intern	Total
Gross Annual Salary	$ 90,000	$ 62,400	$ 41,200	
Hours Worked per Year	2,400	2,280	2,220	
Utilization Rate	50%	75%	90%	
Billing Rate	$ 150	$ 90	$ 65	
Annual Realizable Revenue	$180,000	$153,900	$129,870	$463,770
Net revenue forecast $= 463,770 \times 83\% = \$384,929$ Previous year actual net revenue: $361,000				

TABLE 8-D: Increase Billing Rates

	Principal	Project Architect	Intern	Total
Hours Worked per Year	2,280	2,104	2,104	
Utilization Rate	50%	75%	90%	
Billing Rate	$ 155	$ 95	$ 70	
Annual Realizable Revenue	$176,700	$149,910	$132,552	$459,162
Net revenue forecast = $459,162 × 83% = $381,104				

in this way. In addition, if an employee is not salaried, overtime can be very costly when paid at the legal rate. For example, if a technical employee is being paid hourly at $20 per hour and is working 120 hours per year overtime, this will cost $3,600 at the time-and-a-half overtime rate, plus additional payroll burden. Increasing hours may be a reasonable short-term solution but performance may suffer as burn-out mounts, causing ever diminishing returns.

Increase Billing Rates (Fees)?

If the market conditions allow, increasing fees is a sure-fire way to increase profitability. One method of determining fee proposals is by dividing the work into phases or tasks and projecting hours needed for each pay grade, for each phase or task. Increasing the billing rate will therefore increase proposed fees. Normally this figure would be compared to historical data (check direct hours as well as the contract amount) and to the market value of the work. Even if it appears that market conditions seem to make a fee increase impossible, it is not unusual for small firm practitioners to undervalue their services. Consider a small fee increase; perhaps try it on one or two proposals to see if it has any negative effect. Table 8-D shows that a $5 per hour increase in billing rates (that are reflected in fee proposals) across the board will nearly meet the profit goal sought for 2008, without any significant increase in operational expenses.

Increase Billable Hours?

For MK Architects, increasing the number of direct hours that are actually billed seems to be a strategy that has significant potential. Although utilization rates at MK Architects, as recorded on time sheets, are reasonable, only 83 percent of the realizable revenue was actually charged to the client in 2007. Because of this situation, it seems as if improvement to chargeable ratio should be possible. First, careful attention needs to be brought to contract agreements to ensure that fees are adequate for the scope of work. In addition, process improvement initiatives, such as those discussed in Chapters 2 and 3 are likely to help. As the amount of billable hours increase, the difference between realizable revenue and actual net revenue will decrease.

In 2008, MK Architects will have realizable revenue of about $436,000, if utilization rates, hours worked, and billing rates remain the same as 2007. If the percentage of direct hours that are actually billed increases from 83 to 88 percent, the actual revenue for 2008 will be around $383,600, and the goals for increasing profitability will be easily met. Of course, this assumes the additional work and fees actually are available. If the number of billable hours is declining because work is slow and indirect hours are mounting, this strategy will not be effective.

Increasing the number of billable hours with the same workforce, doing much the same thing is unlikely. Usually it takes serious and disciplined change initiatives involving work process improvement and client management. For forecasting purposes, it would be overly optimistic to assume these kinds of changes will actually take place. The success of change initiatives will be apparent over time. Even a small percentage change in the amount of direct hours that are actually billable will yield positive results.

Add Intern to Staff?

Assuming there is a work load to support the move, adding staff may be preferable to overtime. The question remains, will it increase profitability? Table 8-E shows how adding another intern to the staff does have the potential to increase realizable revenue and actual net revenue.

However, this strategy has associated costs that will reduce the profitability considerably. The direct labor expense is now $165,420. Adding a new employee will also cause overhead to increase. In Chapter 7, the overhead rate for MK Architects was determined to be 1.65. As a short-hand way of constructing a scenario, one could assume that the overhead rate remains stable. In reality, as Robert Smith, AIA, comments, "Rent usually doesn't go up simply by adding one person to the studio; the firm won't need another receptionist; it's unlikely the computer network would need to be increased, other than maybe adding another workstation. Overhead does not necessarily rise on a linear basis—it tends to go up in big chunks—i.e., new office suite; new computer network; new administrative person. Adding one intern generally won't require a 'big chunk' increase in overhead—the actual overhead increase is likely to be only that new person's employee benefits, plus whatever equipment and software may be required to support the new person. Most likely,

TABLE 8-E: Add Intern to Staff

	Principal	Project Architect	Intern	New Intern	Total
Gross Annual Salary	$ 90,000	$ 62,400	$ 41,800	$ 40,000	
Net Hours Worked per Year	2,280	2,104	2,104	2,104	
Utilization Rate	50%	75%	90%	90%	
Direct Labor Expense	$ 45,000	$ 46,800	$ 37,620	$ 36,000	$ 165,420
Billing Rate	$ 150	$ 90	$ 65	$ 65	
Annual Realizable Revenue	$171,000	$142,020	$123,084	$123,084	$559,188
Net revenue forecast: $559,188 × 83% = $464,126					

adding one design professional to a small firm probably would result in a slight reduction in the overhead rate for that firm because the basic fixed overhead is being spread across a larger number of direct hours."

For forecasting purposes, taking a linear approach to increasing overhead based on adding another employee accounts for a worst-case scenario which could include some unexpected "big chunk" increases. If it is assumed that overhead rate is the same, the overhead for the additional staff member at MK Architects could be calculated as the overhead rate times the new direct labor amount: 1.65 x $165, 420 = $272,943. This is an increase of around $65,000 from the 2007 overhead of $208,000, and represents a very conservative approach. Compare this to the likely overhead expenses incurred by a new employee—indirect labor ($4,000 minimum), payroll burden (+/− $8,000), additional workstation and software ($20,000 to $40,000). This adds up to about $50,000, which is equivalent to an overhead rate of 1.56, ($258,000 ÷ $165,420). The more that is known about likely overhead expenses, the more accuracy is possible in constructing this scenario. For MK Architects, $50,000 in additional overhead seems like a reasonable estimate.

Profitability can now be calculated as follows:

1. Net revenue minus overhead expense, minus direct labor expense equals net income: $464,000 − $258,000 − $165,420 = $40,580 net income.
2. Net income divided by net revenue equals profitability:
   $40,580 ÷ $464,000 = 8.7 percent profitability.

Although the net income increased, this strategy does not reach the profitability goal of 10 percent. If there is a backlog to support increasing the size of the firm, this can be a good strategy for increasing the net income and for increasing the compensation of the firm owner. However, it won't necessarily increase profitability significantly, especially since there are likely to be overhead costs that are not accounted for in this scenario. For example, the target utilization of the new intern is 90 percent, but the hours that are billable are likely to be about 83 percent of that, based on past performance of the firm. This means the real utilization is likely to be closer to 75 percent, so the indirect labor for the new employee could actually be about $10,000, not $4,000. In addition, there will be increased indirect labor for other staff members involved in training and orienting the new intern.

Add Skilled Staff?

As shown in Table 8-F, instead of adding an intern to the staff, a project architect is added. This may be appropriate when the new projects require additional skill or when a firm is beginning to transfer project management responsibilities away from the principal and to the project architects, as discussed in Chapter 4. In this scenario, it is assumed that a new project architect may come in at a starting salary of $55,000 and a utilization rate goal of 85 percent. The existing project architect also receives a raise to $65,000. Along with the salary increase, the billing rate for the existing project architect is also increased to $100/hr.

TABLE 8-F: Add Skilled Staff

	Principal	Project Architect	New Project Architect	Intern	Total
Gross Annual Salary	$ 90,000	$ 65,000	$ 55,000	$ 41,800	
Net Hours Worked per Year	2,280	2,104	2,104	2,104	
Utilization Rate	50%	75%	85%	90%	
Direct Labor Expense	$ 45,000	$ 48,750	$ 46,750	$ 37,620	$178,120
Billing Rate	$ 150	$ 100	$ 90	$ 65	
Annual Realizable Revenue	$171,000	$157,800	$160,956	$123,084	$612,840
Net revenue forecast: $612,840 × 83% = $508,657					

The net revenue for this scenario is forecast to be about $508,657. Assuming a relatively conservative overhead rate forecast of 1.6, overhead would be 1.6 x 178,000 (direct labor) = $284,800. Forecast net income will then be approximately: $508,657 − $178,000 − $284,800 = $45,857. This yields a profitability of 9 percent, a little better than the 2007 profit ratio. And, with $13,600 more in net income than in 2007, this represents an increase of a significant increase in potential distribution to the firm owner.

If these sorts of scenarios are laid out in spreadsheet software such as Excel, variations can be explored to see which ones yield more net income and more profitability. This exercise demonstrates clearly that for MK Architects the most effective strategies to more profitability are to increase billing rates/fees and to increase the number of actual billable hours. If there is an increase in gross revenue on the horizon, indicated by a backlog of signed contracts, then growing the firm is likely to yield the best results. Whether an intern or a project architect is hired will depend on whether it takes skilled staff to effectively complete the work at hand. While it is tempting to hire less expensive (and less experienced) employees, it will only translate into more net income and profitability if the new employee is a good match to the kind of work that needs to be done.

SCENARIO PLANNING STORY PROBLEM

To further understand how scenario planning can be used to help make business decisions, a scenario planning story problem follows. Table 8-G shows the staff of a small firm called AH Consultants (AHC). This firm specializes in highly technical acoustic design of performance venues. As such it is an expertise-based firm and is somewhat top-heavy in its staffing.

As shown in Table 8-G, actual net revenue for 2007 was $785,874. In 2007, AHC had an actual total overhead expense of $400,000.

The firm had a profit goal of 15 percent in 2007; and for 2008 the profit goal will remain the same. Based on backlog of signed contracts, AHC has forecasted a net

TABLE 8-G: Story Problem

	Principal	Senior Designer	Senior Project Manager	Project Architect	Intern	Office Manager	Total
Gross Annual Salary	$150,000	$100,000	$ 80,000	$ 60,000	$ 40,000	$45,000	$475,000
Net Hours Worked per Year	2,280	2,280	2,080	2,080	2,080	2,080	
Utilization Rate	30%	65%	75%	85%	90%	10%	
Direct Labor Expense	$ 45,000	$ 65,000	$ 60,000	$ 51,000	$ 36,000	$ 4,500	$261,500
Billing Rate	$ 180	$ 150	$ 120	$ 90	$ 65	$ 40	
Annual Realizable Revenue	$123,120	$222,300	$187,200	$159,120	$121,680	$ 8,320	$821,740

2007 actual net revenue = $785,874

Adjustment to forecast net revenue: $\frac{\$785,874}{\$821,740} = 95.6\%$

revenue of $950,000 for 2008. This represents an increase of about 20 percent from the previous year.

Story Problem Challenge

1. Figure the overhead rate, the break-even multiplier, and the multiplier achieved for the year just completed. What do you know based on the result?

2. Based on the actual net revenue for 2007, figure the gross profit and the year-end profitability. What should be done with the profit?

3. The principal of AHC has determined that two new project architects are needed to complete the contracted work for 2008. Based on the information provided, can AHC afford to hire two new project architects? Assume the same salary, hours worked, and utilization rates as the current project architect in determining the answer.

Consider working out the answers to verify understanding of the use of financial ratios in helping to make business decisions. Answers to the Story Problem Challenge follow.

Story Problem Answer:

1. Overhead rate equals overhead expense divided by direct labor expense: $400,000 ÷ $261,500 = 1.53; break-even multiplier equals overhead rate plus one: 1.53 + 1 = 2.53; multiplier achieved in 2007 equals net revenue divided by direct labor expense: $785,874 ÷ $261,500 = 3.01. Because the multiplier achieved is greater than the break-even multiplier, the firm made a profit in 2007.

2. The net income for 2007 equals actual net revenue minus overhead expense, minus direct labor expense: $785,874 − $400,000 − $261,500 = $124,374. This is also called profit before taxes and distributions. The 2007 profitability equals the net revenue divided by the net income: $124,874 ÷ $785,874 =16 percent. This profit may be distributed in a number of ways depending on the disposition of the firm owner. It may be advisable to save at least half the amount to capitalize future growth and/or build a "rainy day fund." That leaves enough for generous bonuses to valued staff as well as additional compensation for the owner.

3. Follow this process to determine the answer:

   ▪ Each new project architect produces $51,000 in new direct labor expense. Increase to direct labor expense for two new project architects is $102,000, bringing total direct labor expense to $363,500.

   ▪ Overhead is also impacted by having two new staff members. Use 2007 overhead rate (assuming general office expenses are steady) to forecast 2008 overhead expense: 1.53 × $363,500 = $555,155 (the overhead rate could be discounted—using 1.53 amounts to worst-case scenario).

   ▪ With net income forecast to be $950,000, overhead expense and direct labor expense can be subtracted to determine the net income forecast for 2008: $950,000 − $555,155 − $363,500 = $31,345.

   ▪ By dividing $31,345 by the net revenue of $950,000, the forecast profitability for 2008 can be determined: $31,345 ÷ $950,000 = 3.3 percent.

Based on this analysis, the answer is yes, two new project architects can be hired, but at the risk of the firm having low profitability in 2008. It may be best to hire only one new PA and plan the work schedule for staffing at this level; if hiring two PAs is unavoidable due the project schedule, the strategic benefits may make it worthwhile to have low profitability for one year.

The principal of AHC might use scenario planning to investigate other possibilities. For example, what would happen to profitability (and production) if one project architect and one intern were hired? What would happen if the firm engaged outside consultants to do some of the work—this would reduce net revenue but may prevent the necessity of hiring new employees.

Move to a Larger Office?

If adding employees means that AHC has to move to a bigger office and upgrade equipment or furnishings, scenario planning can help firm leaders consider the costs and benefits of such a decision. In the story problem example, adding two new project architects will increase the size of the firm by 33 percent and direct labor expense will increase by $102,000. Overhead expense will increase by $156,000, (1.53 × $102,000) and this increase includes all aspects of overhead expense: indirect labor (~$18,000), payroll burden (~$25,000), and general office expense

(~$113,000). So the total additional cost for each new project architect is $129,000 ($51,000 + $78,000). This total is in line with the industry benchmark of $110,000 to $130,000 average annual cost per employee. Using the overhead ratio makes it likely that any general office expense costs associated with a new employee, including increased rent, will be encapsulated in the overhead expense that is calculated for the larger workforce. This assumes that the firm actions will be consistent with past choices about spending.

Many of the one-time expenses involved with moving to a larger office will not be accounted for in general overhead expenses. New furniture and office equipment such as computers and printers are considered assets and are therefore show up on a firm's balance sheet. These expenses represent a capital investment in the firm and should come from the capital funds of the firm. If these funds are not enough, then a move will need to be funded by excess cash flow, by cash investments made by the owners, or by a bank loan. For a complete scenario plan, these costs and how they are funded would need to be outlined. In addition, gross revenue forecasts for the coming years should be developed with consideration of the macroeconomic climate. It is important to remember that strategic decisions should not be made based on one good year or one bad year.

PLANNING FIRM GROWTH

Scenario planning is a useful tool to plan firm growth and consider all the implications and consequences of a decision to grow the firm. As discussed in Chapters 4 and 6, firm growth requires power sharing and a spreading of responsibility and authority. Scenario plans can help firm leaders visualize a path to a preferred future for their firm.

Using AHC as an example, the scenario plans for growth over the coming four years can be outlined. For this example, assume Year One to be 2007 shown in Table 8-G, at the start of the story problem. Year Two is shown in Table 8-H and includes the addition of one new project architect. For simplicity, salaries are shown as rising at 3 percent per year, across the board.

Although the forecast revenue in this scenario falls slightly short of the projected work load, the principal of AHC believes that the scheduled work can be completed in a timely manner with this workforce. Because the number of inquiries is beginning to slow and the jobs on the horizon look smaller in general, the principal is cautious about Year Three of the plan and decides to make no changes. Therefore the scenario plan for Year Three would be the same as shown in Table 8-H for Year Two.

As the principal looks ahead into Year Four of the plan, he is optimistic that by then he can increase the market share that his firm handles, within its specialization. He feels that the conservative approach of Years Two and Three, and the marketing effort that he has planned will position the firm for significant growth in Year Four. Salaries have continued to rise over the last three years, and the principal knows that if he cannot increase fees/billing rates, net income and profitability will not keep

TABLE 8-H: Growth Plan Year Two: Seven Member Firm

	Principal	Senior Designer	Senior Project Manager	Project Architect	New Project Architect	Intern	Office Manager	Totals
Gross Annual Salary	$154,500	$103,000	$ 82,400	$ 61,800	$ 60,000	$ 41,200	$46,350	$549,250
Net Hours Worked per Year	2,280	2,280	2,080	2,080	2,080	2,080	2,080	
Utilization Rate	30%	65%	75%	85%	85%	90%	10%	
Direct Labor Expense	$ 46,350	$ 66,950	$ 61,800	$ 52,350	$ 51,000	$ 37,080	$ 4,635	$320,345
Billing Rate	$ 180	$ 150	$ 120	$ 90	$ 90	$ 65	$ 40	
Annual Realizable Revenue	$123,120	$222,300	$187,200	$159,120	$159,120	$121,680	$ 8,320	$980,860
Net revenue forecast: $980,860 × 95.6% = $937,702								

pace. Table 8-I shows the scenario for Year Four in which a new senior project manager and a new intern are hired and all billing rates are raised by $5 per hour.

This scenario tells the principal that if he wants to grow his firm to nine people, he needs to generate net revenue of around $1.3 million. Because, historically, direct project expenses have been about 10 percent of gross revenue, AHC can forecast that the gross revenue needed will be about $1.43 million. With this as an identified financial goal, the principal and senior staff can work out a marketing plan to achieve this goal, perhaps with the help of a marketing consultant.

Table 8-J shows a summary of the four-year growth plan.

Once scenarios are developed, reflecting on the long-term goals for the firm will be helpful in deciding if the scenario makes sense. Is growth desirable? Will market

TABLE 8-I: Growth Plan Year Four: Nine Member Firm

	Principal	Senior Designer	(2) Senior Project Managers	(2) Project Architects	(2) Interns	Office Manager	Totals
Gross Annual Salary	$163,909	$109,273	$174,836	$131,127	$ 87,418	$49,173	$715,736
Net Hours Worked per Year	2,280	2,280	4,160	4,160	4,160	2,080	
Utilization Rate	30%	65%	75%	85%	90%	10%	
Direct Labor Expense	$ 49,173	$ 71,027	$131,127	$111,458	$114,577	$ 4,917	$446,379
Billing Rate	$ 185	$ 155	$ 125	$ 95	$ 70	$45	
Annual Realizable Revenue	$126,540	$229,710	$390,000	$335,920	$262,080	$ 9,360	$1,353,610
Net revenue forecast: $1,353,610 × 95.6% = $1,294,051							

TABLE 8-J: Growth Plan Summary

Size Of Firm	6	7	7	9
Year	Year 1	Year 2	Year 3	Year 4
Net Revenue Forecast	$785,874	$937,702	$937,702	$1,294,051
Direct Labor Forecast*	$261,500	$320,345	$320,345	$ 446,379
Overhead Expense Forecast**	$400,095	$490,128	$490,128	$ 682,960
Net Income Forecast	$124,279	$148,157	$148,157	$ 167,265
Profit Ratio	15.8%	15.8%	15.8%	16.4%

*For simplicity, salaries rise 3 percent per year across the board each year.
**Assumes stable overhead rate of 1.53.

conditions be able to support a larger firm in years to come, or will new hires be soon laid off? How does ownership transition, as discussed in Chapter 6, enter into the scenarios? Scenario plans can provide the quantitative information for strategic planning and strategic thinking. Scenario plans can also become the basis for the financial aspects of an overall business plan.

While scenario planning is a useful tool, business planning for small firms is always challenging because of the unpredictable environment in which they operate. It seems that as soon as plans are made, conditions change. Because of this, firm leaders need to look at scenario plans and worksheets as "living documents." Use easy-to-update formats (i.e., Excel) so scenarios can be used, as necessary, to assess the implications of rapidly changing conditions. Some macroeconomic influences simply can't be foreseen by the ordinary person, such as the events of 9/11 or the subprime crisis that froze the flow of credit in late 2008.

Chapter 9, Strategic Thinking, further explores planning and strategy within an ever-changing business environment. The chapter includes a case study of one small firm's strategic initiative as well as a look at the strategic role of continuous learning.

PART III

LOOKING TOWARD THE FUTURE

CHAPTER 9

STRATEGIC THINKING

BUSINESS PLANNING FOR SMALL DESIGN FIRMS

Business planning is essential for actualizing goals and visions. One of the significant results of the business planning process is more awareness among firm leaders and staff of the overall purpose and aspirations of the firm. This awareness can lead to aligned action and can function as guidance for the many decisions that need to be made each day. Awareness also enables strategic thinking, which means making decisions based on how each choice might support or detract from strategic intentions.

For design firms, business planning can be divided into four primary aspects of business development: Purpose, Finance, Operations, and Marketing. Once purpose is understood, plans can be developed within each of the other three functional arenas. Please note that the business plans discussed in this section are not the kind needed for securing a bank loan. Those have a particular form that may need to be provided by the lending institution. Instead, these business plans are meant as documentation of intentions and the pro-active measures designed to accomplish goals. Business planning brings intentionality to the management of a small firm, which is a distinctly different approach than being moved primarily by external circumstances.

Elements of a Business Plan

A. PURPOSE/BUSINESS MODEL

- Philosophy/core values; be clear about vision
- Project types? Client types?
- Career contentment and disposition of owners
- Assess core competence and core weaknesses
- Assess market opportunities and threats to market position
- Firm size? To grow or not to grow?
- Firm future? Plan to transition ownership or not?

B. FINANCIAL PLAN

- Specify financial expectations of owners
- Revenue goals over time
- Operating budget expectations over time
- Profit plan over time
- Scenario plans for firm revenue and staffing over time

C. OPERATIONS PLAN

- Organization structure
- Technology upgrades and integration
- Project delivery model
- Knowledge acquisition and development
- Promotion, recruitment, and compensation

D. MARKETING PLAN

- External market conditions and competition
- Target market
- Key differentiators
- Image and brand
- Relationship marketing plan

Although the list in the sidebar makes the parts of the business plan seem separate and distinct, in reality they are interconnected. Each aspect is a part of a whole firm system and as such, they impact each other continuously. For example, marketing efforts must link closely with aspirations, which often determine operational choices; operational effectiveness will impact financial growth, and market position may determine what is possible financially. Figure 9.1 illustrates the

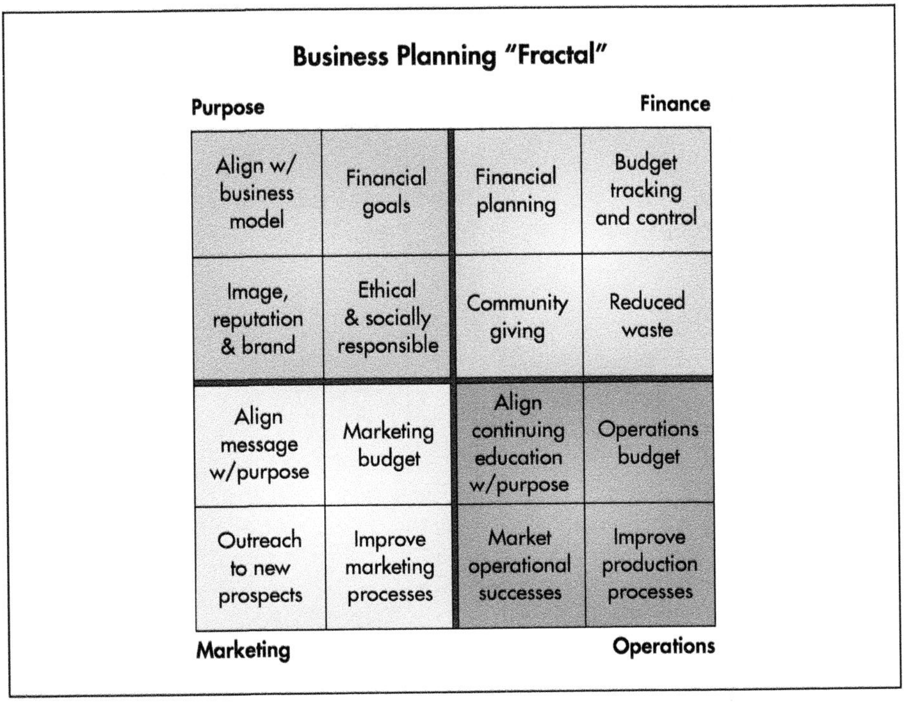

Business Planning "Fractal"

Purpose			Finance
Align w/ business model	Financial goals	Financial planning	Budget tracking and control
Image, reputation & brand	Ethical & socially responsible	Community giving	Reduced waste
Align message w/purpose	Marketing budget	Align continuing education w/purpose	Operations budget
Outreach to new prospects	Improve marketing processes	Market operational successes	Improve production processes
Marketing			Operations

Figure 9.1   Each box in this diagram represents a different yet interconnected aspect of business planning.

interwoven relationships between the parts of a business plan by using a fractal model. Each aspect of the business plan has the others within.

For example, consider the Marketing quadrant in the lower left-hand corner of the diagram. Each quarter of the Marketing quadrant is related to one of the major quadrants. The finance aspect of Marketing is a marketing budget (upper right corner); the purpose aspect of Marketing is alignment of the marketing message with vision (upper left corner); the operations aspect of Marketing has to do with improving job acquisition processes such as the proposal writing (lower right corner); and finally, the marketing aspect of the Marketing quadrant is outreach to new prospects and relationship marketing (lower left corner).

Similarly, each of the four sections in each quadrant can be assigned to their corresponding quadrant. So the operational aspects of Finance may be to reduce waste or conserve energy and the operational aspects of Purpose may be to deliver jobs ethically and to consider the firm's social responsibilities, and so on, with each lower right-hand quarter in each quadrant relating to operations. Each of the 16 items named in Figure 9.1 could be seen as a strategic project in itself. And this diagram can be customized by firm owners as they consider, for instance, what is the "marketing aspect of finance?" (shown here as community giving or pro-bono work). These strategic firm development projects will change as some are completed and some are altered by external circumstance. This fractal diagram can be used as a tool to plan and track firm development activities over time.

Marketing Plans

A marketing plan must be included in any business plan. However, the more important notion is to continually engage in marketing planning. In other words, the marketing plan made two years ago, may or may not be relevant today in the current market. So planning a marketing approach and adjusting it as circumstances change is likely to be more effective in the long run. Again, this is about a strategic process, not a static product. And, more than all other aspects of business planning, marketing activities must always be ongoing.

Smart Marketing

In order to market a firm effectively, firm leaders need to budget resources to the effort. Marketing professionals will tell you that the budget should be about 10 percent of your net revenue. This may sound like a huge number until it is understood that it includes the value of indirect labor dedicated to the effort by principals and staff. If consistent effort is dedicated to marketing, as it should be, indirect hours can add up pretty quickly.

With a budget number in mind, identify long-term goals, such as expanding the regional scope of the practice, and create a short-term marketing action plan to get there. "Short-term" means first steps and follow-up, well knowing that it may take time to bear fruit.

It is important to remember that marketing is distinct from selling. Interviews, for example, are "selling" activities. While selling lands the job, marketing creates job opportunities. The results of marketing efforts often don't show up for years after they are made, meaning marketing must be a consistent and ongoing effort, not just something firm leaders think about in a downturn. To facilitate ongoing marketing effort, it is best to create a dedicated team—usually the principals and skilled support. This support may be firm administrators, professional staff, and/or outside consultants.

In addition to creating the team, consistent time must be dedicated to the effort. Routinize the process as much as possible. For example, firm leaders may decide that every Friday, 9 AM to 2 PM, will be dedicated to marketing. No matter the size of the firm and no matter what economic conditions exist, firm leaders must dedicate this kind of time to marketing if they want their firm to thrive. By doing this consistently, firm leaders will find that opportunities seem to appear unexpectedly and from unexpected sources. However, this will not happen right away, which is why marketing needs to be done constantly, whether projects are currently plentiful or not.

These marketing efforts must be focused. It is important to identify target markets and the kind of jobs that will further firm goals. Many firm leaders will "take anything that walks through the door," and this is understandable, especially in slow times. However, unless circumstances are dire, consider whether a job opportunity is consistent with long-term goals, or is taking the firm off course. There is a danger of "opportunity costs" in doing projects that are outside a firm's identified target market. For example, another project might come along that the firm can't accept because it is too busy, or it may take staff away from other activities that advance the firm's goals. Even in slow times, it is worth considering the potential risks and possible benefits of accepting a certain job.

Market Constantly

Acquiring jobs is a primary task of firm owners and they should engage in marketing activities on a consistent basis. During the time that is set aside for marketing each week, firm leaders can:

- Maintain existing client relationships. Identify valued and repeat clients and take them to lunch.
- Develop new relationships. Do research on who the decision makers are for projects in the firm's targeted markets and take them to lunch.
- Identify and prepare proposals for projects that meet the firm's strategic goals and that the firm has a reasonably good chance of winning.
- Update and maintain firm website—the website is likely to be the first point of contact with clients and is an important communication and public outreach tool.
- If it is appropriate for the practice, enter award competitions and submit projects for publication.
- Engage in speaking and writing to establish expertise within the target market.
- Engage in volunteerism and civic-minded activities, and participate in social networking, both in person and online. This will bring contact with others of like mind and can be expansive and meaningful. And it might bring in some great project opportunities.

Purpose Matters

To engage in effective marketing, firm leaders must continually return full circle to the firm's purpose and vision. Why bother running a small firm if it can't be designed to be personally rewarding? Clarity of purpose guides choices on how marketing time is spent. Firm leaders can focus efforts on those tasks that further long-term goals. Insight into purpose can be gained by considering the following:

- What kinds of projects always interest and excite firm leaders and staff?
- What makes firm leaders and staff feel successful as professionals?
- What makes the work feel meaningful and satisfying?

If firm leaders know where they want to go, they will have more clarity on how to get there. Effective firm leadership then requires disciplined execution of strategic intentions.

Purpose and values may change over time as firm leaders grow older and move through their careers as professionals. It is important to revisit aspirations periodically and to have conversations about vision and values between partners and with staff. This is why business and marketing planning needs to be seen as a process, constantly requiring assessment, evaluation, and adjustment. In order to evaluate and adjust, the success of marketing efforts must be tracked. Set up simple spreadsheets to record the number of inquiries, as well as the other factors listed in the accompanying sidebar. If inquiries increase and begin to come from unexpected sources, it is likely that the marketing efforts are working.

Track Marketing Results

- Number of inquiries
  - Track over time
  - Benchmark to AIA Billings and Inquiries index
- Regularity of repeat clients (operational effectiveness counts here, too)
- Frequency of inquiries from unexpected sources
- Inquiries that are a clear result of a specific event, such as an award or publication
- Frequency of inquiries for project types that are preferred
- Percentage of proposals that become jobs (effectiveness of "selling" activities)

Value of Participatory Process

Marketing and strategic planning are primarily tasks for firm leaders, but professional and administrative staff can be and should be involved. There are clear benefits to doing so:

- Engage, empower, align staff with purpose
- Keep the action going—fight "plan in the drawer" syndrome
- Get help from the intelligent people you have hired—principals don't have to do it all
- Plan nonbillable hours—staff time on firm development is value-added
- Staff members can be champions of improvement efforts—they may have skills that leaders don't have

If strategic initiatives involve change, and most of them do, participatory processes can help smooth the way. If people feel empowered and involved, they will likely implement changes without complaint. However, if change is top down, it will be met with resistance—subtle sabotage, like gossip and allegiance building, and passive-aggressive acts, like just not going along.

Sample Business Plan Template

Traditional business plans include information about the firm's history and profile, as well as its purpose, marketing, financial, and operations plans. Although they vary, most formal written business plans include the following information:

Business Plan Outline

1. Executive Summary: One-page summary of business plan
2. Company Mission: Concise explanation of the business purpose
3. Company Analysis: Educates the reader regarding the company's history
4. Company Profile: Legal structure of the company
5. Industry Analysis: Description of the landscape in which a company is operating
   a. Trends
   b. Customers and competition
   c. Networking and promotional outlets
6. Competitive Analysis
   a. Identify the company's direct competitors
   b. Identify the company's key competitive advantages
   c. Learning from competitors—their competitive advantages
7. Management Team: Job description of key team members
8. Marketing Plan Outline: How the company will effectively reach its target market
   a. Describe products and/or services
   b. Customer Identification/definition/segments
   c. Customer demographics, needs assessment, and decision-making process
   d. Marketing action plan—newsletters, web optimization, networking, publications
   e. Customer retention plan
   f. Partnerships—Is there potential for partnerships, website links?
9. Financial Plan: Summary of the financial projections of the company
   a. Detailed revenue streams (from historical data)
   b. Pro-forma financial statements (future scenarios)
   c. Operating budget (annual)
   d. Marketing budget (annual)
   e. Validating assumptions and projections
10. Operations Plan: The action plan for executing the company mission
    a. Everyday processes—the processes that serve clients daily
    b. Business milestones—the overall milestones that measure company success

c. Professional development—the knowledge that needs to be acquired to continue to effectively deliver projects

11. Business Plan Appendix: Supporting documentation

Along with the templates and tools included in this chapter and Chapter 8, it is critical to remember that business planning as an ongoing process is one of the keys to success in managing a small design firm. Small firm owners have the power to create work lives that are personally satisfying and also provide satisfactory compensation for all involved. This is achieved by applying skill as designers to the process of business planning, by executing the plan with discipline and intention, and by having willingness to change with the unpredictable business environment.

PUTTING IT ALL TOGETHER: A CASE STUDY IN STRATEGIC ACTION PLANNING

SNB Architects is a successful firm of 15, operating in a small city on the West Coast. Started in 1986, with the original founder now retired, the success of this small firm rests on its established position within the local community. As one of two "larger" firms in the area, SNB produces a diverse portfolio of work, including public projects, mixed use/multifamily developments, and custom single-family homes. The partners, HN and GB, are active in the community and are committed to improving the local built environment through their work.

After more than 20 years in business, and over 10 years in partnership, HN and GB decided that it was time to be more intentional about the future of their firm. In some ways, the partners saw the firm as a victim of its own success. Its position in the local community, although stable, was beginning to feel limiting in terms of opportunity. The partners envisioned broader possibilities and wanted to expand their ability to attract more interesting and significant projects.

The staffing at SNB has also been stable over the years—many of the employees have been with the firm for more than a decade. The staff includes two full-time administrators—a receptionist/executive assistant and a bookkeeper, who have also been employed at the firm long term. While employee retention is generally perceived as a good thing, in this case it has had the unintentional consequence of creating a homogeneous staff where almost all staff members have grown to be similar in terms of their professional experience and skill. In 2009, the 10 professional employees included three registered architects and seven others who were in the process of taking their licensing exams. Because of a firm-supported initiative, almost all of the professional staff are, or are soon to be, LEED certified.

For a firm located in a small city, with two capable partners at the helm, it is understandable how this kind of staffing imbalance might happen. For one thing, employment opportunities for skilled design professionals in the local area are scarce, leaving employees with limited choices if they were to leave SNB. In addition, since the partners do most of the project management and design concept development, they have needed support from employees that are capable of carrying projects through the rest of the phases, mostly on their own. Given this operational pattern, it makes sense that the staff would eventually be populated by project architects with similar capabilities.

HN and GB could see that they were in danger of losing valuable staff if they could not provide opportunity for professional advancement, including elevation to principal or associate level. They have resisted creating organizational tiers in an attempt to be egalitarian, but there was, nevertheless, some evidence of declining motivation and enthusiasm among the staff. In particular, the partners worried about losing their most senior staff member, LN, an architect with significant experience and personal contacts that enabled him to bring "bread and butter" public work into the firm. LN had expressed a desire to become a partner in the firm and had implied that he would go out on his own if this opportunity did not become available soon.

All these factors brought HN and GB to the realization that they needed a strategic plan. They wanted to explore the path to successful firm growth with an eye toward solving existing organizational imbalances. They reasoned that a larger firm would be able to attract more significant projects and would give opportunity for advancement to some of their staff. They also understood that if they were to take on a new partner, an increase in revenue and net income would be needed to maintain their current level of compensation.

The firm leaders began their strategic efforts with an internal exploration of their mission and target markets. They developed a marketing plan that reflected their strategic goals of contributing to the community, expanding regional scope, and leveraging current strengths to attract new clients. These plans were implemented to some extent but were often held back by the demands of everyday practice on the partners' time. The partners continued to be concerned about the staffing imbalance, about the staff morale in general, and about LN's request to become a partner.

STRATEGIC ASSESSMENT

HN and GB engaged a consultant to assess the current situation at the firm and help chart a course for firm growth and continued success. The consultant conducted an assessment that included:

- Survey filled out by all staff and partners
- Individual and small group interviews with staff members and the partners
- Financial assessment

In general the consultant found the firm to be well managed and financially sound. However, some weaknesses in firm operations revealed obstacles to growth which implied that systemic change was needed. The initial findings were documented as a "Mind Map," shown in Figure 9.2.

The main findings of the assessment were:

1. Administrative processes of the firm need improvement and investment. While the financial accounting, tracking, and projections were excellent, other processes, particularly related to project tracking were less effective.
2. Partners' time for marketing is restricted by involvement in daily project and client management. This is likely to be the systemic limit to growth (see Figure 9.3).
3. Offer to potential new partner must be seen in context of overall growth plan with specific expectations for job acquisition by the new partner.
4. Both partners and professional staff are concerned about the current homogeneous staffing. Partners are concerned that they may lose valuable staff, while the staff is concerned that no professional advancement is possible within the firm.

In many ways, the situation at SNB is a classic "limits to growth" system,[1] as shown in Figure 9.3. The retention of experienced staff underpins the need to grow the firm and, at the same time, provides the capacity for growth (reinforcing loop). The amount of time the partners have for marketing and outreach is the limiting factor in this system (balancing loop). The partners' involvement in day-to-day project management places a constraint on the time for marketing. If the system does not change, any firm growth will create more demand on the partners' time for project management which will, in turn, decrease time for marketing and eventually stall growth. This implies that firm growth is dependent on relieving the partners of daily project management tasks and that the rate of firm growth will parallel implementation of this systemic change.

SNB Assessment Mind Map

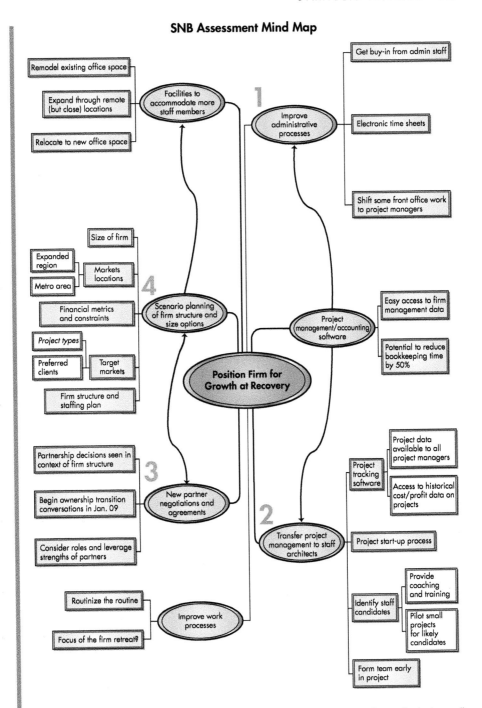

Figure 9.2 Findings of the assessment process can be expressed as a "mind map" showing the interrelationships between strategic issues at SNB Architects.

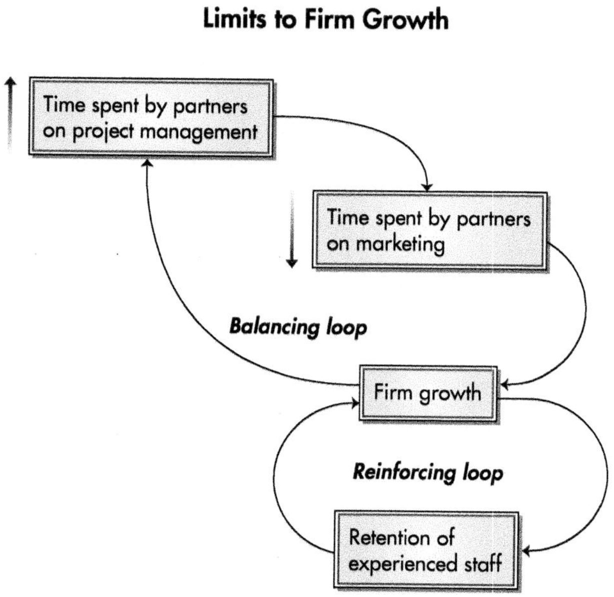

Limits to Firm Growth

Figure 9.3   Time spent on day-to-day project management limits the time that partners have to acquire projects and can stall plans for firm growth and retention of experienced staff.

GROWTH PLAN

To understand how the staff could be rebalanced as the firm grows, the focus of SNB's strategic process moved to the creation of a five-year growth plan (see Chapter 8). Because of the financial crisis in late 2008, the firm leaders decided to take a conservative approach toward short-term firm growth goals. It seemed likely that the firm would have to contract a bit, before it would be able to grow. Emphasis in strategic planning shifted to preparing for growth when the economy recovered.

Table 9-A shows a summary of the five-year growth plan developed for SNB Architects. It is based on annual scenario plans that specify the skill level of the new hires for each year (see Chapter 8), with emphasis on building project management capability. It reflects the financial realities of 2009 – 2010 when firm growth is not expected.

This growth plan includes a 3 percent salary increase per year across the board and reflects a stable overhead rate of 1.58 based on an average of past performance. The growth plan is meant to be viewed in tandem with the Minority Partner Buy-In Plan that is shown in Table 9-B. The buy-in plan

TABLE 9-A: Growth Plan for SNB Architects

Year	2008	2009	2010	2011	2012	2013	2014
Size of Firm	15	14	14	15	16	18	20
Gross Revenue	$2,418,200	$2,032,300	$2,041,700	$2,223,400	$2,395,600	$2,632,800	$2,956,800
Net Revenue	$1,820,000	$1,672,700	$1,680,400	$1,830,000	$1,971,700	$2,166,900	$2,433,500
All Expenses	$1,560,400	$1,443,200	$1,456,200	$1,601,700	$1,708,900	$1,868,700	$2,070,400
Net Income	$ 259,600	$ 229,500	$ 224,200	$ 228,300	$ 262,800	$ 298,200	$ 363,100
Profit Ratio	14.3%	13.7%	13.3%	12.5%	13.3%	13.8%	14.9%

TABLE 9-B: Minority Partner Buy-In Plan

New Partner's:	2010	2011	2012	2013	2014
Project Acquisition Goal (Gross Revenue)	$81,600	$177,800	$287,400	$421,200	$591,300
End of Year Ownership	4%	8%	12%	16%	20%
Salary (2% Increase per Year)	$77,000	$ 78,540	$ 80,110	$ 81,713	$ 83,347
Stock Compensation (Value of Shares)	$20,000	$ 20,000	$ 20,000	$ 20,000	$ 20,000

gives stock compensation to the new partner in lieu of bonuses and larger salary increases (see Chapter 6). This will transfer 20 percent of firm ownership to the new partner over a five-year period. Along with ownership, expected contributions to project acquisition by the new partner are also outlined in the plan. These project acquisition goals grow in tandem with ownership percentage.

With the growth plan, the minority partner buy-in plan, and the assessment as background for consideration, SNB held a firm retreat designed to explore staff ideas for strategic improvement.

FIRM RETREAT FOR STAFF INPUT

The firm retreat was held using Open Space Technology (see Chapter 4). A theme crafted by the partners and their consultant was left intentionally open-ended: "How can we position the firm for growth when the economy recovers and how can we attract interesting and stimulating projects?"

Because the retreat was designed to solicit the concerns of the staff, much of the conversation revolved around issues that impact their job satisfaction as architects (see Chapter 2). They discussed the need for creative expression, for autonomy over their work, and for opportunity to contribute to the local community. This gave rise to a notion of firm-sponsored outreach projects that are suggested, planned, and implemented by staff members. Seen as a way to boost morale and engagement, HN volunteered to take the lead in setting up criteria and reviewing requests for project funding by the firm.

At the retreat, all were in agreement about the need to improve internal knowledge sharing and information management. Seen as a way to improve project delivery, a task group headed by LN was empowered to work on this operational issue.

The most significant result of the retreat arose from staff concerns about their advancement and professional development. The undercurrent was visible—widespread anxiety about how the problem of homogeneous staffing will be resolved. While most staff members seemed to agree that growth will create opportunity for advancement, there was a high level of unease about how that would actually happen.

Central to this conversation was the need for a transparent path to career advancement at the firm. Here the fundamental dilemma facing the leaders of SNB was revealed: In order to grow the firm, project management responsibility must be transferred to the next generation of firm leadership. To do this, these individuals must be identified, fostered, mentored, and trained. The key question then becomes: "How can employee morale be maintained if some of the 'equal' are singled out for promotion to a new organizational tier?"

An answer to this question may reside in another idea suggested during the retreat: a personalized professional development initiative. This initiative would involve tailoring a professional development program to the individual interests of each staff member, while keeping in mind the strategic goals of the firm. The idea is to give each staff architect the opportunity to pursue knowledge, skill, and/or networking activities that interest them and also benefit the firm. Since learning is central to career contentment among architects, a professional development initiative is likely to help employees feel appreciated and supported, even if they do not receive a promotion. It is also likely to benefit the firm by expanding its knowledge acquisition capabilities.

The retreat outcomes validate the systemic changes identified in the initial assessment as fundamental to firm growth, and provide a blueprint for strategic action. This action plan includes a professional development initiative for all staff, while simultaneously identifying next-generation leaders to assume project management tasks from the partners. It includes integration of the minority partner and consideration of organizational tiers, as well as an initiative to improve internal knowledge sharing.

LESSONS LEARNED

Table 9-C summarizes the strategic action plan developed for SNB Architects. It documents the progress of the strategic planning process and outlines ideas to be considered as well as actions to be taken. It is a snapshot in time representing a cautious approach to change, taking shifts incrementally with attention given to bottom-line impacts. To complete this plan, specific time frames should be set for implementation and completion of each short-term action.

The challenge SNB now faces is implementation—how to make these changes happen and continue delivering projects. The truth is that it takes discipline to execute strategy and act differently than the well-worn patterns of behavior. Consultants can help by bringing a knowledgeable outsider's viewpoint into the mix and by helping to keep the momentum of change going. Assigning staff or a workgroup of staff to spearhead and take responsibility for implementing some of these action initiatives will empower and align staff with firm strategic goals.

It is clear from the story of SNB that if this firm is to grow, systemic change will be required. It may be necessary for the firm leaders to question their mental models about the "way things have to be." Espoused theory about egalitarian structures may come head-to-head with theory in practice that requires roles, responsibility, and authority to be assigned. Or long-held beliefs about client management may need to be challenged and updated by younger professionals, as societal norms change. This is difficult but can be accomplished if motivation is strong enough. This is why envisioning long-term goals is so essential to change.

The SNB case illustrates that intentionality in regard to staffing is as important as being intentional about clients and project choice. Firm leaders sometimes forget that their professional staff also has aspirations and need for meaning and satisfaction in their work. The traditional model of young architects switching firms to grow professionally is counter-productive for both firm and individual, and is often unavailable to those who practice in small communities. Firms that want to grow must foster their next-generation leaders with stretch assignments; share responsibility and authority, and act with sincere generosity so that all staff feels valued for their contributions.

The experience of SNB also points to the strategic importance of learning in professional service firms. In SNB and all other small firms, learning is both a professional necessity and a significant component of job satisfaction among architects.

TABLE 9-C: Strategic Action Plan

Goal	Strategy	Mid-Term Objective	Short-Term Action
Outreach to Target Markets & Development of Expanded Regional Scope	Greater % of partners' time is spent on networking, firm development, and marketing tasks	Transfer everyday project management from partners to selected staff	1. Identify staff for intensive PM training
			2. Devote resources to internal and external PM training & mentoring
		Improve administrative processes	3. Research, purchase, and install performance management software
Retention of Valued Senior Employee	Offer opportunity for minority partnership	Consider ownership transfer options for 20% ownership over five years	Make offer and negotiate agreement
Retention of Next-Generation Firm Leaders	Align professional development with firm goals and organizational design	Consider introducing tiers with associated roles/responsibility/ authority	1. Explore professional development interests of staff
			2. Create professional development plan for each staff member
			3. Determine professional development budget
Improve Effectiveness of Project Delivery	Improve processes for internal knowledge sharing	Empower task groups to spend time on improving internal knowledge sharing	1. Project close-out process
			2. Project startup process
			3. Internal lunch and learn sessions
			4. Design focused pin-ups

LEARNING IS JOB ONE

Considering how much project delivery has changed in the past 30 years, no one can doubt the significance of learning in an architect's career. Architects in their 50s and 60s in 2009 have spent much of their career hand-drafting, yet now find themselves in the world of digital modeling. New information technologies and communication methods become available regularly with the promise of improved productivity and expanded reach. In addition, these work process changes are fundamental to shifts in building design and construction due to climate change and growing scarcity of nonrenewable resources.

In the twenty-first century, leaders of small firms are challenged to be intentional about what they change and how they change. Investment in technology and training is becoming an ongoing necessity, as is the need to stay current with trends in building science and design. Learning is no longer optional and needs to be a continuous focus of professional service firms. As stated by David Garvin in his article "Building a Learning Organization": "In the absence of learning, companies—and individuals—simply repeat old practices. Change remains cosmetic, and improvements are either fortuitous or short-lived."[2] Garvin goes on to say that new knowledge and insights are most meaningful when they lead to new behaviors and new ways of doing the work.

For example, new knowledge about sustainable building practices might lead naturally to new ways of working with consultants. Instead of bringing consultants in after schematic design is complete, sustainable design practices encourage earlier collaboration. This may lead to an interest in Building Information Modeling (BIM) and a motivation to transform project delivery practices. According to Garvin, the most successful knowledge-based organizations are those that can transfer new knowledge into new ways of working. "These companies actively manage the learning process to ensure that it occurs by design rather than by chance. Distinctive policies and practices are responsible for their success; they form the building blocks of learning organizations."[3]

Learning by Design

Garvin would approve of the professional development initiative being contemplated by SNB Architects. His research shows that most organizations suffer for a lack of systems and processes that support learning and the integration of the new knowledge into daily operations.

Internal Knowledge Sharing

For small firms, improving and routinizing internal knowledge sharing is a low-cost, high-impact strategy. As the staff of SNB discussed at their retreat, much inefficiency and wasted effort comes as a result of one worker trying to find information that another worker may already know. Documenting and transferring project-based knowledge and lessons learned is challenging, even among people who work closely together. This is especially true if project management is dominated by the partners and project delivery is pyramidal (see Chapter 5). This is because the partners hold much of the organizational knowledge in their heads and the project architects may not even know what others in the firm are doing.

Specific activities that promote knowledge sharing are:

- Project close-out: document new learning and file project material at its conclusion so that lessons learned and field-tested solutions are available easily to everyone. Standards methods should be established for this purpose. Consider having a team member write a narrative case study of each project with "reviews" of the various project participants and project delivery methods.

- Staff meetings: hold staff meetings to exchange information about the status of the projects through a brief and informal check from each project manager/architect. This can be a rapid, informal opportunity to exchange timely information, not a lengthy detailed report.

- Lunch and learn: these sessions can be anything from manufacturers' representatives presenting their products to a "design class" given by one of the partners. This format is an excellent opportunity for in-house classes of any type—a chance for partners and senior staff to share how they do what they do, particularly in the area of client management. To make sure these sessions happen, one of the professional staff should be given the task of planning them, preferably someone who would be excited by the assignment.

- Design pin-ups: sharing work in progress among the staff is an opportunity for exchange of ideas about design. Dialogue about design concepts as well as code constraints and client management will flow freely in sessions such as these. This kind of informal knowledge exchange is critical in building the shared knowledge base of the firm and for giving everyone the chance to contribute to design outcomes.

Knowledge sharing can be accomplished through routine documentation, as in the project close-out process, but it really depends on opportunities for face-to-face exchange. Successful small firms dedicate time to these activities and consider them a vital part of firm culture. For instance, a staff meeting twice a month, a lunch and learn session once a month, and a design pin-up once a month add up to four to six hours of nonbillable time per month per person. This small investment has the potential to save countless hours of wasted effort and may even spark unexpected innovation. While small firms may not be able to set up internal "universities," they can create mechanisms that foster learning from one another.

External Knowledge Acquisition

The American Institute of Architects and many state licensing boards require continuing professional education for licensed architects. These requirements institutionalize the understanding that lifelong learning is a critical part of a design professional's career. For small firms, these requirements are an opportunity to align their strategic goals with the continuing education interests of the staff. Learning that is not grounded in big-picture strategic thinking will not easily be integrated into the way work is done.

For instance, at SNB Architects, the firm supported all its project architects to become LEED certified. Most of the staff have gained the credential but as yet, very little of the firm's work is LEED certified. SNB's developer clients have not yet shown interest in building green. Without client demand as motivation, work processes that would produce more sustainable buildings are not yet in place and are a low priority. While laudable in its intention, LEED certification for all may not have been the best use of professional development resources.

A budget for professional development should be determined along with budgets for marketing and operations. This can be distributed as a benefit that varies with individual compensation packages. Or it may be designated for certain uses, such as the licensing exam or software training. Creating a professional development budget also forces intentionality about how this money can be used to further individual and firm goals simultaneously.

Resources for continuing education are plentiful. They include offerings from publishers such as John Wiley & Sons, Inc., publications such as *Architectural Record*, and numerous offerings by AIA national, regional, and local components. *Architects Essentials of Professional Development* by Jean Valence is an important resource for firm leaders considering a formal internal professional development program.[4]

Learning as Competitive Advantage

According to David Garvin, "Learning organizations are skilled at five main activities:

- Systematic problem solving,
- Experimentation with new approaches,
- Learning from their own experience and past history,
- Learning from the experiences and best practices of others, and
- Transferring knowledge quickly and efficiently throughout the organization."[5]

To be successful, architectural firms must excel at all the activities on Garvin's list. "Systemic problem solving" and "experimentation with new approaches" are core competencies of design professionals. However, true competitive advantage comes to those firms that have mastered "learning from their own experience" and "learning from best practices of others." And, if knowledge can be "quickly and effectively transferred throughout the organization," the firm has the potential to build expertise, innovation, and a valuable firm-wide knowledge base.

Creating a culture of learning is necessary but not always sufficient to ensure a successful design practice. Strategies for small firm success embody a wide variety of organizational structures and leadership styles. Chapter 10 presents case studies representing some of the most widespread models of small design firm practice and the not-so-common models as well.

ENDNOTES

1. Peter Senge, *The Fifth Discipline,* Doubleday, NY, 1990.

2. David Garvin, "Building a Learning Organization," *Harvard Business Review*, Harvard Business School Publishing Corp., Cambridge, MA, 1993.

3. Ibid.

4. Jean Valence, *Architects Essentials of Professional Development*, John Wiley & Sons, Inc., Hoboken, NJ, 2003.

5. David Garvin, "Building a Learning Organization," *Harvard Business Review*, Harvard Business School Publishing Corp., Cambridge, MA, 1993.

CHAPTER 10

SMALL DESIGN FIRM PRACTICE MODELS

According to the Bureau of Labor Statistics (BLS),[1] most architects are employed in firms with fewer than five people. The organizational designs of these very small firms are not standardized, are very diverse, and are sometimes home-grown in near isolation from the professional community. These firms are the products of entrepreneurial vision born of passion for doing architecture, serving clients, and improving the built environment. Most small firm practitioners work in relative obscurity yet many have a profound impact on their clients and their local communities.

The most common type of very small firm is the sole proprietor—design professionals who own their firm alone. According to the BLS,[2] about 21 percent of architects are self-employed—more than 3 times the proportion for all occupations. Not all sole proprietors work alone, many have employees, but solo practice is very common. Architects who choose to "go-it-alone" face special challenges but they also have unparalleled opportunity to shape the quality of their work-life.

SOLO PRACTICE

Many solo practitioners wonder periodically about growing their firm. Would it be more profitable? Would it be more interesting? Would it somehow lead to new professional challenges? These musings may lead to other thoughts such as, "is it really okay for me to be doing this—am I being all I can be?"

If one looks to the AIA or the architectural press, it is easy to answer "no" to that last question. There is little or no attention given to solo practitioners and the work they do. Nevertheless, it is also easy to understand why solo practice is appealing to many architects. Opportunity to design and autonomy over one's work are critical to an architect's career contentment and both are amply available to a solo practitioner. In addition to these benefits, many solo practitioners find that they simply make more money by working alone. This is due, in part, to the ability to have very low overhead, to inherent efficiencies in work processes, and to the fact that many solo practitioners develop expertise practices over time. All these other factors aside, the primary motivations for licensed architects to continue to practice alone is freedom and autonomous control.

Solo practitioners are free from having to be responsible to business partners or employees which allows for a significant level of self-determination. More than any other group of design professionals, solo practitioners have the ability to design their firm in their own image. While they might make less money than their colleagues who are principals in larger firms, they are free to arrange their own work schedule and even take months away from work each year, if they please. They are also free to pursue other interests and organize their practice to suit.

Financially, compensation for solo practitioners spans the entire spectrum— from "just getting by" to doing extremely well. Their incomes tend to parallel all other architects whose median salary is $70,320 per year, as reported by the Bureau of Labor Statistics in May 2008. According to the BLS, only 10 percent of architects earn more than $120,000 per year and only 10 percent earn less than $40,000 per year. So the range of compensation that can reasonably be expected for a self-employed licensed architect is $50,000 to $100,000 per year.[3]

Economies of Small Scale

Consider the case of RMK, a "typical" solo practitioner. RMK practices alone, specializing in residential remodeling and doing business as RMK Architect. She has been in business for 15 years and has amassed a substantial portfolio and a sizable base of satisfied clients. Contributing to her success, RMK has excellent relationships with the local building department and strategic alliances with several experienced general contractors. Given her strong reputation and design skills, RMK is able to charge clients $125 per hour, which is about at the top rate possible for the middle-class market in which she operates.

Because of her experience and the fact that she does all the work herself, RMK is able to give clients accurate estimates of her fees and rarely exceeds budgeted hours for the design phases. She has learned not to overcommit, preferring breaks between projects to nonstop work. But breaks are rare since she discovered that clients are willing to wait for her. She now signs contracts for work months in advance and has a healthy backlog. This way of working ensures that her clients always receive a high level of service.

Without any employees to accommodate, RMK has been able to convert a backyard accessory building at her home into a small office. This keeps her general office expenses low, often under $15,000 per year. By tracking her hours, RMK knows that about 45 percent of her time is billable and the other 55 percent is spent in job acquisition, marketing, professional activities, and indirect labor on projects.

With this information, it's possible to calculate how much RMK would have to earn in net revenue to meet a particular annual compensation goal. For this example, imagine that RMK would like to take home a $75,000 annual draw. For solo practitioners, the equation is simple: $75,000 (owner's draw) + $15,000 (general expenses) + $20,000 (payroll burden, mostly self-employment tax and health insurance) = $105,000 estimated net revenue needed to break even. Anything over that means bonus compensation; anything less means not reaching the target earnings of $75,000.

To meet her goals, RMK has to earn $105,000 in net revenue, which at $125 per hour, equals 840 hours billed to clients (or the equivalent of 840 hours on fixed fee contracts). At a 45 percent utilization rate, to be able to bill 840 hours, RMK has to work 1,867 hours (840 ÷ .45). This translates into about 46, 40-hour weeks or about 38, 50-hour weeks. This leaves the equivalent of 6 to 14 weeks per year as time to pursue other interests.

As good as this looks for RMK, small changes will result in a significantly different outcome. This is why many sole proprietors will be conservative about paying themselves throughout the year. If RMK charged only $100 per hour, it would take 2,233 hours, or 46, 50-hour weeks to earn the net revenue required. Or if her hourly rate remained at $125, but her utilization rate dropped to 35 percent, (which is not uncommon among solo practitioners), she would then need to work around 2,400 hours per year to earn a net draw of $75,000. That would be 48, 50-hour weeks per year.

This vignette tells the story of the typical solo practitioner experience. Many self-employed architects do work 50 hours a week to earn the profession's median salary and also have the equivalent of four weeks off from work per year. However, many other solo practitioners settle for much less compensation in order to have more balanced lives, allowing time for children, family, and other interests. These other interests often assist the design practice through networking activities and are sometimes a source of significant additional income. For example, it's not unusual for solo practitioners to own and improve the building where they practice, gaining rental income and equity if the property increases in value. Some teach at a local university as a way to supplement their income, and some become building officials, small-scale developers, antique dealers, or all of the above.

CASE STUDY IN SOLO PRACTICE: NELSON BREECH NAVE, AIA

"All of the above" neatly describes Nelson Breech Nave, AIA, a solo practitioner from Kalamazoo, Michigan. In many ways Nelson is typical of the independent, energetic, creative, and entrepreneurial solo practitioner. Now 61 years old, Nelson started his practice in 1988 after going through what he describes as a mid-life crisis. He left a large firm in Indianapolis, where he was working on schools and hospitals, for a mid-size firm in Kalamazoo, and then went out on his own with a couple of small jobs referred to him by his former employer. He describes his current project type as "anything but schools and hospitals" and his current passion as historic restoration and adaptive reuse.

Like many solo practitioners, Nelson pursues a number of interests, some more related to his practice than others. He sells antiques out of the same building in which he practices and leases out space to others to supplement his income. Nelson volunteers his time on various local design commissions and is involved in city politics, applying his skills and knowledge as an architect to improve his community. In addition to these activities, Nelson is also a certified building official. In that capacity he consults with other designers as a code expert and plan reviewer. According to Nelson, this makes his relationship with local building officials cordial and cooperative, which is a great asset in his architectural practice.

Unlike some solo practitioners, Nelson believes in the importance of participation in professional associations and calls the AIA "a friend forever." He says that those who think the AIA doesn't serve them just need to get involved. Nelson describes his involvement in the national AIA Urban Design Committee and the AIA Design Committee as a source of much learning and intellectual stimulation.

As he approaches retirement, Nelson says he is beginning to tire of the constant demands of project delivery and looks forward to ramping down his firm by focusing on doing more consulting. Although he wonders out loud, "I don't understand why young architects aren't beating a path to my door," he expresses little serious interest in finding or grooming a successor. Nelson says that he is content to wind things down and eventually close the door on his design practice. He looks forward to more volunteer work and expects that he will simply refer design jobs on to others.

CHALLENGES AND OPPORTUNITIES FOR SOLO PRACTITIONERS

Nelson Breech Nave, AIA, is typical of the many self-employed architects around the country who are quietly crafting a satisfying professional life while making a difference in their community. He also represents the many that follow their passions, even if it leads away from profit and widespread recognition. While architecture may appear glamorous in the media, for all but a few "starchitects" the realities of everyday practice can be tedious. Being able to pursue other intellectual interests, other outlets for creativity, and other sources for income is one of the primary benefits of self-employment for architects.

Another benefit of solo practice is that work processes are often streamlined and highly effective. With one person doing everything, design and production processes often become merged giving project delivery the potential to be very efficient. This efficiency still relies on routinizing the routine, but as a solo practitioner gains experience, this usually becomes a naturally occurring process. These "routine processes" may sometimes be very customized, even eccentric, but as long as they work they will be repeated.

However, there are challenges inherent in developing a personal way of doing things and sticking to it. Blind spots to weaknesses are inevitable without input from others and professional norms to emulate. As suggested by Nelson Breech Nave, AIA, professional organizations can be the sole proprietor's "friend" by being a source for information on best practices and emerging professional knowledge. Professional organization can also help solo practitioners feel less isolated and stay in touch with trends in technology, building science, and design.

Another challenge faced by solo practitioners is the reality that their firm will never have economic value independent from its owner. Unless a successor is found and groomed, there is little likelihood that the firm will provide any income after retirement. Many, like Nelson, will simply move from project delivery to consulting and eventually close their firm. As discussed in Chapter 6, these architects must depend on income earned, saved, and invested while practicing or on savings or income gathered from other pursuits. So for self-employed architects, financial security at retirement may actually depend on the other pursuits that the very nature of solo practice can enable.

Not everyone is cut out to practice alone. It takes an ability to both acquire and deliver projects—tasks that are often distributed to different types of people in larger firms. Self-employed architects are often personable, confident, and able to easily win the trust of others. To be successful most are well organized and ambitious workers who are able to keep many projects (some not architectural) going simultaneously.

Some design professionals find alternatives to working alone that still affords a high level of self-determination. Some become part of loose cooperatives of solo practitioners that share office space and equipment. These arrangements vary, but often involve "leasing desks," and some level of mutual support. Design firms owned by married couples who share a common vision and complementary skills can also be as personalized as solo practice, but with the emphasis on "we" rather than "me." Although there are few statistics, anecdotal evidence shows that small firms owned by married couples are nearly as numerous as solo practitioners.

FIRMS OWNED BY MARRIED COUPLES

"Some people wonder how I can work with my spouse. I wonder how I could work without him," says Mary Johnston, AIA, of Johnston Architects in Seattle. This sentiment is typical of married design professionals who own a firm together. Like many of the other couples interviewed for this text, Ray and Mary Johnston share a passion for architecture that enriches their work and their lives. As explained by Ray Johnston, AIA, "We go on vacations to see architecture and we talk about our projects at home all the time. We never get tired of it because architecture is like a hobby as well as an occupation and our common interests seem to enhance our relationship."

As would be expected, common aspirations and values are powerful assets for most married firm owners. As expressed by Los Angeles architects Toni Lewis, AIA, and Marc Schoeplein, AIA, of Lewis/Schoeplein Architects, "We see each other as equals and we value each other's opinions. Although we sometimes have different perspectives, we hold a common vision and that helps us work things through." Toni and Marc met in graduate school, were married, and worked for other architectural firms for 10 years before Toni became pregnant and left the large firm where she was working. While at home she recalls, "projects just kept rolling in," and she never returned to her old job. Instead she started her own firm, working from home.

With the birth of their second child, Marc joined the firm. After practicing in their garage for 18 months, they moved to a nearby storefront and then to a larger office as their firm grew and took on employees.

Complementary Skills

Toni and Marc were able to bring diverse project types to their practice. Marc brought in single-family residences and Toni continued her institutional focus, designing educational and religious facilities. They were able to pursue their own interests, and provide support for each other, particularly in the beginning stages of design and in project acquisition. They make all go/no-go decisions together and have a strict rule, based on a bad experience, that both of them must go to every interview and community meeting. Since some of these engagements are at night, Toni and Marc are fortunate to have parents close by to stay with their kids.

Toni and Marc are also able to benefit from their complementary personalities. Toni is described as being more "high-strung" and Marc as more "patient" and "strongly interested in material and detail." Toni describes herself as, "a big-picture person," who is also the more "business-oriented" of the two. Working together and dividing work based on individual strengths seem to come easily to this couple.

Mary and Ray Johnston also benefit from their complementary strengths. While they differ in their management style—Mary tends to be more supportive while Ray is more directive—this amounts to a form of "situational leadership," as described in Chapter 4, where leadership tasks are divided based on what quality is required. Mary is the consummate "outside person," serving on the City of Seattle Design Commission and teaching at the University of Washington. She describes herself as having design vision and big ideas, but also as being a bit scattered and unorganized. Mary says, modestly, "Ray does all the heavy lifting." Ray, by his own description, deals with the "nuts and bolts" of the practice, manages the day-to-day affairs of the office, and often leads the larger projects undertaken by the firm.

Despite these differing roles, Mary and Ray describe their main strength as their common passion for constantly learning about design. As Ray put it, "We are interested in knowing why projects work to improve peoples' lives, we like variety in how design responds to client and context, and we always want to keep moving forward in our design thinking, not just repeating past successes."

Ease of Communication

All the couples interviewed describe their ability to understand their partner through unspoken communication and say they also check-in with each other constantly. Mary and Ray believe that it is important for married couples to resist using "short-hand ways of communicating that exclude other people at work." They say they are committed to combating that tendency although it is a natural result of their interpersonal relationship. Mary and Ray seek to be a model for their staff by showing how to work well together and respect one another. Making a similar point, Toni Lewis recounts a story of working for a married couple as a young architect. This couple did not get along well and were abusive to each other and to everyone around them. It's easy to imagine how this created what Toni describes as a "very bad work environment." Toni goes on to say that working together is not for everyone. "You may be a great couple and still not be cut out to work together."

Ruth Gless, AIA, of Lincoln Street Studio in Columbus, Ohio left a large firm to join her husband's small firm one year after they were married. Together they reinvented the firm to reflect their complementary skills and interests. On working with a spouse as a business partner Ruth says, "If you can't work together, how can you live together?" Ruth and Frank converted an old meat packing warehouse into both a home and office for their firm, and Ruth explains that the physical space is a reflection of the integration that exists between their home and work life. With a bit of a sigh she says, "Some people think we are odd."

However, among married small firm owners, this seems to be the norm. All the couples interviewed say that they talk about their projects and practice at home, although one couple commented "our children insisted we stop at dinner time, but we're empty nesters now so we talk about work whenever we want." Toni and Marc say they try to leave their work at the office but enjoy mulling over the "tasty bits"—the design concepts and ideas—at home where it feels more relaxed. Often they do their initial design sketches for a project in this atmosphere which Toni describes as "more creative because of its separation from the deadline-driven office environment."

Lessons Learned

In Chapter 4 in the section on partnerships, three qualities of partner compatibility were outlined: operational, aspirational, and interpersonal. Successful business partnerships seem to require complementary skills (operational), aligned passions and values (aspirational), and the ability to stay current with feelings and communicate effectively (interpersonal). Since there is little doubt that these qualities also contribute to a successful marriage, it's understandable that a married couple could work well as firm owners.

Like solo proprietors, couples who own a firm together can be challenged by "blind-spots." Differing perspectives may merge into one world view over time and can lead to overlooked warning signs and missed opportunity. Most importantly, couples who run small firms need to understand that their relationship will likely dominate the firm and influence all office dynamics. Being conscious of modeling respectful relationships is critical for all firm leaders, in all firms, but for married couples, ironically, it may be more challenging. Effort needs to be made to prevent personal relationship dynamics from coloring behavior in the office.

Married couples can experience "Unintentional Enmity" (see Chapters 1 and 4) but it is probably less likely since they see their individual achievements as a win for their partnership. Married couples often express a high appreciation for what their partner brings to the business and work hard at supporting each other's success. They can be a model of alignment and mutual support for nonmarried business partners.

Married firm owners can also model positive decision making and power sharing, as well as role differentiation for partners. The level of trust and compatibility that couples have may be hard to achieve among ordinary business partners, yet something similar is probably required for the smooth operation of small firms run by two or three partners. All this depends on effective and open communication among partners, also perhaps easier for married couples. Entrepreneurial architects should consider whether they are ready to "marry" a prospective business partner, meaning that there is a strong enough personal connection to ensure respectful communication, aligned goals, and mutual support.

SMALL FIRMS IN INTERNATIONAL PRACTICE

Although it might be assumed that small firms could not engage in international projects, in twenty-first-century practice this is neither uncommon nor impractical. BKBC Architects of Walnut Creek, California is a prime example. The firm is headed by Sanjiv Bhandari, AIA, an architect who has leveraged his experience designing shopping centers into participation in the master planning of large-scale retail and multifamily developments around the world.

Sanjiv regularly works 50 to 80 hours a week and spends every other week out of the country. He has been involved in projects located in China, India, Japan, and most recently, the new city of Songdo in South Korea. Songdo, notable in its intention to be a LEED-certified city, is a master planned city spanning over 1,500 acres of reclaimed land. BKBC is designing the Songdo City Retail Center, described on the firm's website as, "This two-level mall has over one million square feet of retail space with three levels of basement parking. Designed in contemporary architectural style, it is anchored by Lotte department store, Homeplus

Hypermart, Megabox Cinemas and Ice Rink." According to Sanjiv, the retail component has grown to be central to these types of new developments and retail malls are now known as "lifestyle centers." Sanjiv explains, "These are very complex mixed-use projects. Often, my role is to help mediate and balance all the conflicting interests."

Sanjiv's firm also does local projects, mostly urban infill residences and small commercial developments. He describes them as "useful to cover gaps in the international work and give the staff hands-on experience." Sanjiv also finds time to be active in the local community and local AIA components. He serves on public boards and policy-making bodies, including those that advocate for green building programs in the local municipality. Sanjiv believes that it is "important for architects to be leaders in their community, to understand how public policy is made, and use our knowledge to contribute to its formation."

When asked to reflect on his international practice, Sanjiv remarks that "the size of the project does not always reflect the size of the firms involved. Productivity of a small firm can be impressive and our agility is important to our success. Speed is often critical and there is a certain excitement in being able to participate." He goes on to say, "It is sometimes a problem in firms when people get dulled by doing the same thing year after year. It's important to step into a bigger, different arena to keep growing personally and professionally."

Much of Sanjiv's experience as a small firm practitioner in international practice is echoed by a leader of a large firm that regularly participates in the global marketplace.

Firm Size Is No Barrier

According to Friedrich Bohm, former Chairman of NBBJ, success in global practice depends on "agility, commitment and organization," and is not necessarily related to firm size. In an article, "New Opportunity Equals New Competition," he outlines best practices for firms wishing to take advantage of opportunities overseas.[4]

By agility, Bohm means the ability to compete in a marketplace where speed of project delivery is the dominant concern of clients. Local firms in emerging markets adapt quickly and offer clients an attractive alternative to U.S.-based firms.

Bohm goes on to explain that international clients are looking for long-term, committed relationships with design firms. As a result, clients look for firms that are compatible in terms of values and organizational culture.

Organization, according to Bohm, is the third key to success in overseas practice. Firms must research and understand the regulatory environment of each location; and they must clearly articulate roles and responsibilities of each party involved in the design process. Bohm goes on to outline key guidelines and best practices for overseas projects:

- Reflect on firm culture and evaluate possible international clients based on compatibility of beliefs and values.

- Look for potential growth markets to enter early in the development cycle. Bohm comments that in October 2008, Russia, the Gulf, and North Africa were areas of intense investment.
- Use known contacts to find entry into a market; this may be an existing client, a trusted consultant, or a local firm. Prestige and reputation may also enable firms to find clients in new international locations.
- Focus on a few places and put all effort into succeeding there.
- Research and analyze the situation before committing and be prepared to say no.
- Be adaptable, flexible, and respectful of the knowledge of local professionals.
- Have integrity, operate lawfully, and resist corruption; be clear about your operating principles.
- Support those who experience hardship of international travel and 24-hour business days.
- Have clear payment conditions and management control of those conditions.
- Establish a local reputation.
- Any size firm can do international work—what matters is talent and excellence.
- Explore the possibilities of applying sustainable design practices to international projects.

Bohm concludes the article by explaining that the international practice is becoming more competitive. U.S. firms of all sizes and firms from many different countries are entering the international marketplace. He suggests that U.S. firms consider focusing on specific market niches, and that they may be forced to do this by strategic necessity.

Another Calling

Rather than a strategic necessity, specializing in a market niche can be the result of personal passion and commitment to an idea. A small firm practitioner who exemplifies this approach is Kelly Lerner, principal of One World Design Architecture in Spokane, Washington. An early adopter and advocate of straw-bale construction, Kelly specializes in environmentally responsible design of single-family residences and remodels. Her book, *Natural Remodeling for the Not-So-Green House,*[5] authored with Carol Venolia, and her warm style as an educator, has made her a sought-after speaker on residential green building. In Spokane, her local practice is focused exclusively on the design of green residential projects.

It is Kelly's expertise in straw-bale building that opened the opportunity for her involvement in international projects, specifically in China. Working with the pioneers in straw-bale building in the mid-1990s brought Kelly in contact with development agencies in Mongolia and China that wanted to develop straw-bale prototypes for the regions. Starting in 1998, Kelly worked with the Adventist Development and Relief Agency (ADRA) to introduce straw-bale methods to China for the construction of schools and housing. To do this, Kelly has spent one to four months, sometimes more, in China each year since 1998. In 2005, Kelly received the United Nations World Habitat Award given by the Building Social Housing Foundation in recognition of her work on the Straw-Bale Energy Efficiency Housing Project which provides sustainable, seismically resistant housing to rural areas of cold northeastern China.

According to Kelly's website, "[In 2005] The project has built over 600 straw-bale houses and three straw-bale schools in five northeastern provinces in a project funded primarily by the Kadoorie Foundation of Hong Kong. Walls built from straw bales offer tremendous insulation value. The new houses require 68% less heating coal than the standard brick houses, thereby improving living conditions through reduced fuel costs, carbon dioxide emissions and air pollution. Engineering for the project was provided by David Mar of Tipping Mar + Associates of Berkeley, CA."

Kelly continues her work in China for ADRA, conducting feasibility studies for the application of straw-bale construction in other areas of China, particularly those prone to earthquakes. Her work demonstrates the role that architects can play in improving the lives of people in developing nations while introducing sustainable and environmentally responsible methods. Kelly models a different version of international practice, one that resides outside commercial, profit-driven enterprise.

Architects interested in participating in international sustainable development projects are encouraged to look into organizations such as Architects Without Borders (United States) and Architecture and Development (France). These organizations connect architects to nongovernmental, nonprofit organizations that are promoting sustainable development worldwide.

AIA members will find resources and support for international practice of all kinds through the AIA International Committee.

THE VIRTUAL OFFICE OPTION

Owners of small design firms are naturally entrepreneurial and prone toward looking for solutions to problems. This includes the problems of running a small design firm. This tendency sometimes gives rise to creative and forward-thinking business ideas. Though yet to be proven reliably profitable, one such innovative business model is being practiced by an architect in a rural area of northeastern Texas—Mike Leinback, AIA, of JML Architects.

Mike was motivated to find a new way to practice by difficulties that are not uncommon in small firms, especially those located away from major urban centers. Over its lifetime, his firm experienced wide swings in demand and resulting workload. In good times, it was difficult to attract qualified staff in his rural location. His client base wanted projects delivered quickly, and if JML Architects wasn't available, the work would go elsewhere. Because of this staffing pressure and unpredictable workload, Mike made the choice to incur debt in slow times, rather than let valued staff go. This up-and-down cycle caused his firm to be less than profitable year after year.

Twenty-First Century Opportunity

Technologies, not available until recently, allowed Mike to pursue a new way of delivering projects to his clients. The first of these technologies is Revit®, 3-D modeling software by Autodesk® which, according to Mike, makes electronic collaboration possible. "It used to be that you had to be face to face to do architecture together. Now Revit® and building information modeling (BIM) make it possible to have 'staff' spread out over a broad geographical area," Mike says, as he explains how his virtual office works. "My collaborators are located all around the USA. I wasn't really interested in offshore outsourcing. My connections are person to person and I spend a lot of time deciding who I will work with."

Mike came to this notion of a virtual office when a slow time forced him to lay off almost all his staff. When the jobs started to come in again he began looking for collaborators online, rather than employees. To do this Mike used social networking sites, the second new technology critical to creating a virtual office. These websites, such as LinkedIn, Facebook, and BIM user forums, enabled Mike to find design professionals who were willing and able to do the projects he acquired locally. Over time he has developed several reliable favorites and a host of others who can be called in when demand increases.

These "collaborators," as Mike calls them, work as consultants to JML Architects, in the same way that a structural engineer might. The collaborators do both design and production work with project information and quality review provided by Mike and his lone employee. Since many of Mike's projects are relatively routine, it is possible to apply standards, templates, checklists, and routine processes to the work, making it highly efficient and uniform among collaborators. Need for additional capacity is accommodated by adding more collaborators; when work slacks off, there are no employees to support.

The benefits of this virtual office model are obvious—it has the flexibility to expand or contract according to demand; and is perfect for an office located far from potential employees. Overhead costs can also be kept low since the physical office never needs to expand and payroll burden is kept to a minimum. In addition, the virtual office matches an architect who has work, (called a jobber in some industries) with architects who need work, wherever they are located. This capability could be positive for all involved, especially in a recession and for architects who want to work part-time from their home. Mike comments that he would someday like to start an "E-Harmony for Architects—a place where overworked practitioners are matched to those who need work."

In the big picture, this way of delivering projects could be seen by some as challenging to the architectural profession's image of itself and what it does. The success of JML Architects' "collaboration" relies to some extent on the widespread uniformity of office buildings, shopping centers, and speculative housing. Although the architectural profession likes to look elsewhere, this is the reality of the built environment in much of the United States. Moreover, this method of delivering design projects depends on the ability of any architect to design a "standard building" to go anywhere. It begins to treat architectural services more like a commodity than a customized professional service. Good or bad, the virtual office model does offer a way for small firm owners to handle work load fluctuation and keep overhead under control, as well as offering a new way for architects who need projects to acquire them.

Consider the Possibilities

Virtual 3-D modeling, BIM, electronic document sharing, and social networking sites are tools that enable a new way of working. Virtual tools are being used to create collaborative teams for huge international projects such as those on which Sanjiv works, and also for the design of the strip mall down the street. Virtual tools extend the reach of small firms and have the potential to change the nature of how all firms are organized. Some futurists predict that the number of self-employed people will increase as all work is done in far-flung teams that are formed around projects rather than within companies.[6] For architects, physical proximity to one another or to the construction site seems to be less and less necessary. These tools are likely to have both positive effects and unintended consequences on the design professions. See Chapter 11, Technology and Integrated Practice in Small Firms, for more discussion of the impact of virtual office tools on the practice of small firms.

ENDNOTES

1. Bureau of Labor Statistics, *Occupational Outlook Handbook*, 2008–2009 edition, U.S. Government, **www.bls.gov/oco/ocos038.htm**.
2. Ibid.
3. Ibid.
4. Friedrich Bohm, "New Opportunity Equals New Competition," *DesignIntelligence*, Greenway Communications, Norcross, GA, 2008.
5. Kelly Lerner and Carol Venolia, *Natural Remodeling for the Not-So-Green House*, Lark Books, NY, 2006.
6. William Bridges, "The End of the Job," *Fortune Magazine*, 1994.

CHAPTER **11**

TECHNOLOGY AND INTEGRATED PRACTICE IN SMALL FIRMS

M any small firm owners are early adopters of new ways of working. Like Mike Leinback of JML Architects (see Chapter 10), these entrepreneurial professionals are continually seeking ways to improve their project delivery capabilities and their bottom line. This chapter will highlight practitioners who have stepped out on a limb to try something new or different. They model a path that could be risky, to be sure, but has the potential for great rewards in both satisfaction and financial compensation.

ADOPTING BUILDING INFORMATION MODELING

By all accounts, three-dimensional (3-D) virtual modeling, enabled by software such as Revit® by Autodesk® and ArchiCAD® by Graphisoft® is creating a revolution in the design and construction industry. More and more firms of all sizes are changing their project delivery methods to take advantage of this new technology. As part of a bigger technological movement known as Building Information Modeling (BIM), 3-D modeling has the potential to greatly expand the production and design capabilities of the design professionals who use it. The use of BIM also fosters collaboration between architects and consultants early in the design process, which enables the kind of systems integration critical to sustainable and carbon-neutral design.

There are obvious advantages of BIM over two-dimensional CADD systems (and hand drafting). As explained in "Roadmap to Integration," the fourth of eleven essays that make up the *AIA Report on Integrated Practice*, "In CADD, as in hand drafting, one is simply adding lines to a sheet, lines that have no inherent intelligence. There are no relationships built between one line and another.... With BIM, representation gives way to simulation. The building is "modeled" as it would be built. Lines are not drawn to represent walls, but walls as assemblies of studs and gypsum board are placed virtually within the model as they would in the field. These assemblies are model objects with an inherent intelligence and interconnectedness to other objects within the model."[1] This means, for example, that any changes to a wall in the three-dimensional model, such as adding a window, would be instantly reflected in the floor plan, which is merely a horizontal section through the model.

Many see these tools as the path to transformation of the design and construction industry—a way out of outdated processes that create adversarial relationships and a significant waste of time, energy, resources, and money. As described in the *AIA Report*, "One of the most wasteful processes in the world today may just be the design process as it has evolved over recent decades—an all-too-inefficient progression of transforming the three-dimensional vision (the design) through a two-dimensional torture chamber (the drawing set) into a resultant three-dimensional reality (the building).... What BIM allows is the creation of a three-dimensional, fully-integrated model by the architect that is fully-transferable to the builder and/or manufacturer for direct construction or fabrication, sans torture chamber."[2]

While it is generally agreed that BIM has not fully achieved the promise of the previous sentence at the time of this writing, it already provides tools for automating functions such as interference checking which alerts designers to potential conflicts among building systems and components. In addition, data such as materials quantity and heat loss values of building components can be available as intelligent information that changes as the model is changed.

Small firm leaders who are considering adopting BIM and the use of virtual modeling software need to consider a number of factors. First among these, as always with strategic decisions, are the long-term goals and aspirations of the firm. Practitioners who have no interest in growing their firm and are content with the processes they are currently using may have no motivation to change. However, small firm leaders who are interested in growing their firms, increasing productivity, practicing integrative sustainable design, or those whose work is being built by construction companies using BIM, should seriously consider this new technology. Other considerations in converting to BIM include cost of the software, possible upgrades required to hardware, and the training time/process for learning to use the new system effectively.

According to Lance Kirby, an implementation consultant for Autodesk®, transferring to BIM software is easy. "With just a small amount of preparation and planning, introducing BIM into a small firm can be swift, painless, and highly effective."[3] He suggests a firm-wide roll-out, preceded by practice on an actual project as a pilot. He encourages training by professional instructors and suggests preparing for differences in how principals, staff, and consultants will work together to deliver projects.

While this advice is surely based on broad experience with firms that have converted to BIM software, anecdotal evidence suggests another process. In Chapter 1, Stan Schachne, AIA, described how he hired someone who was an expert user of the software and learned from his employee. Other small firms echo this notion of training an "office expert" who can then help all the other staff members with their on-the-job learning. So rather than "rolling out" the conversion so that all staff members are trained together and start using the new software on all projects, an incremental approach may be more effective.

This is the approach taken by Peter Stoner, AIA, of Peter Stoner Architects, a firm of eight located in Seattle, Washington. An early adopter of ArchiCAD®, he converted his office directly from hand drafting to virtual modeling in the late 1990s.

CASE STUDY IN BIM CONVERSION: PETER STONER, AIA

In the early 1990s, when many firms were making a transition from hand drafting to computer aided design and drafting (CADD), Peter Stoner, AIA, remained unimpressed. It wasn't that he feared new technology, even though he started his firm in 1978, well before computers were in widespread use. On the contrary, Peter is excited by new technology and had been using computers to help run his office since 1986. He could see that CADD had the potential to increase drawing productivity, particularly when standards are established and elements are repeatable. However, he remained skeptical of the usefulness of CADD to his practice which specialized in highly customized homes with little standard detailing.

Peter tried 2-D CADD by producing some projects himself using MiniCad, now called VectorWorks®. He concluded that it was, "functional, but nothing special, like drafting with a mouse." Even when using a 2-D program, it was apparent to Peter that CAD was essential for his practice. He continued his search for a computer drafting software that could deliver the potential he believed was possible, intending to start with software based on 3-D modeling.

By 1997, CADD software with three-dimensional capabilities was coming onto the market and these systems attracted Peter's attention. He was especially interested in the ability of 3-D modeling to facilitate changes to drawings—change one element on the 3-D model and it is automatically incorporated into every view. After educating himself about the software choices through seminars and user forums, Peter decided to "take a gamble on ArchiCAD®." Because of the software's small user base it was yet unclear whether it would survive and would continue to be supported by Graphisoft. He recalls that there were a few local ArchiCAD® users who had formed a support group, and that the assistance from Graphisoft® was excellent. "I bought one copy and turned out a couple of projects myself. I found it to be very straightforward and relatively easy to use."

From that point on, Peter orchestrated his firm's conversion from hand drafting to BIM software with an incremental and pragmatic approach. Beginning with the project architects that were competent with 2-D CADD, Peter purchased the new software one seat at a time, converting projects to ArchiCAD, one project architect at a time. Within two or three years, all the project architects had converted to the new software, even the most "old style" and initially resistant. In 2009, with over 10 years experience using the BIM software behind them, all the professional staff is reportedly pleased with the results. Rather than having one staff member in charge of process maintenance and improvement, all the architects work together during office meetings to share tips, exchange knowledge, and discuss application of standards. Through doing the projects, the architects add to the firm's library of 3-D objects and layers, and improve their 3-D component templates.

THE BENEFITS (AND CHALLENGES) OF BIM

The benefits of using 3-D modeling software are many according to Peter Stoner, AIA. Already mentioned is the operational ease of making changes to drawings. In addition, Peter says that it is easy to test initial schematic ideas with rough virtual models and he comments that with the 3-D software there is, "no kidding yourself, when things don't work it is all too apparent."

Ease of communication with consultants is another operational strength of BIM software. Sharing digital files instead of paper sheets eliminates a number of operational steps, such as making copies and physically transporting them to their destination. Information from surveyors can be easily imported into the model as its own layer, and consulting engineers can add their work directly to the model as well. Although Peter readily admits that he doesn't use all the BIM capabilities of the software, he does use features that allow "live updates" to schedules such as those for windows and doors.

Based on Peter's experience, it takes some trial and error to discover the effective use of 3-D modeling for client communication. While architects are enamored with "fly-through animations" and demonstrations of the action of daylight on interior space and exterior massing, many clients simply do not understand what they are seeing. As explained by Peter, "We would show these amazing "wow" effects with simple 3-D models, and the clients would respond by saying, 'Where are the trees?' or 'We really don't want a grey roof.' Some of them just didn't get it. I remember a time when the clients looked so confused by what they were seeing on the screen that I just made a quick little sketch of what the house would look like sitting by the water. Then they said, 'Oh, now we get it!' But some clients do seem to love the 3-D models and will gladly spend hours with the software looking at possible changes to the design. So we have learned to try to determine which kind of media will work best for each client and try not to make assumptions based on what we like."

LESSONS LEARNED

Peter Stoner Architects is representative of many small firms that have gone through an incremental conversion to BIM software, although the firm stands out as an early adopter and as an example of conversion directly from hand drafting to BIM, without the intermediate step of 2-D CADD. For late adopters, and there are many small firm practitioners who still use hand drafting, the experience of Peter Stoner Architects demonstrates that converting from hand drafting to BIM is feasible and perhaps worth the time, money, and effort.

For users of 2-D CADD programs, like AutoCAD®, conversion to Autodesk's BIM software, Revit® appears to be as easy as promised by industry spokespersons. The initial problem of poor interoperability in CADD software, 2-D or 3-D, between Mac and PC users, seems to have been mostly solved, making conversion simpler in most offices. Peter describes Graphisoft® as the "Apple of BIM software," with fewer users than Revit® by Autodesk®, which appears to be on its way to dominating the industry.

For Peter Stoner, the driving quest was to find out whether 3-D software could really deliver the power that computers have to offer. "Using the computer for managing my office was incredibly effective since it allowed a lot of administrative work to be done by the project architects themselves. I wanted something that would revolutionize project delivery in a similar way. My insistence on 3-D modeling has really paid off."

INTEGRATED PRACTICE AND INTEGRATED PROJECT DELIVERY

The advent of BIM technologies and the need for interdisciplinary coordination in sustainable design has given rise to an industry initiative known as Integrated Project Delivery (IPD). IPD is generally described as early stage collaboration between designers and builders to deliver a project as a joint venture under a single contract with the owner. Integrated practice refers to a way of working that institutionalizes and normalizes IPD. Integrated project delivery is the operational expression of integrated practice. While similar to design-build in some ways, integrated practice implies a multidisciplinary and highly collaborative approach.

For architectural firms and construction companies doing large projects for institutional and corporate clients, it is revolutionary to contemplate a transformation from adversarial relationships to collaborative partnerships. Because BIM technologies enable effective early stage collaboration, because IPD supports sustainable design practices, and because clients are demanding more effective project delivery, the AIA has taken an active role in promoting integrated practice. The AIA has published numerous white papers and best practice guides on the IP and IPD[4] and has published a series of contract documents designed to clarify risk and responsibilities among participants in Integrated Project Delivery.[5]

Of course, the partnering of designers and builders to deliver projects is not a new concept. As reported by Gary Tulacz, in an *Engineering News Report* article on IPD, "For many in the industry, the approach is old hat. 'In 1993, we had a poster that read: the world is turning to integrated design and construction,' says Walker Lee Evey, CEO of the Design-Build Institute of America, Washington, D.C. 'We have been practicing that for years, but we just didn't put a name on the process,' says Paul Tyler, president of the commercial group at the Haskell Company. 'Doing as many tasks as possible in the building process in-house increases the level of collaboration and provides a more efficient outcome.'"[6] Keep in mind that the form of design-build described here is one in which architects and designers are likely to be employees or consultants to a builder or construction management company, which holds an at-risk contract with an owner. Since the construction company is taking all the risk involved in delivering the project to the client, it will retain most of the power during project execution and reap most of the rewards.

Integrated practice holds forth a different model—that architects and designers are equal partners with builders and construction managers in the project delivery process. It proposes joint venture business arrangements where a new company is formed for the purpose of delivering a particular project. All risk and reward is shared based on the terms of the joint venture agreement. It puts forth a vision of the architect as the leader of a collaborative team that uses BIM to coordinate all information—drawn or specified—into one integrated virtual and intelligent model. This manner of practice is advocated by AIA, and is theoretically applicable to firms and projects of all sizes.

ARCHITECT-LED DESIGN-BUILD

Architect-led design-build is a form of integrated practice in which architects own and direct the design and construction process. Because of the inherent inefficiencies and often higher cost of the traditional "design-bid-build" process, architect-led design-build is being adopted by many small firm leaders. Motivation to do so can come from realizing a competitive advantage in the marketplace, as was described in Chapter 1 by Stan Schachne, AIA. Other architects are motivated by their interest in being involved in both the design and implementation phases of their projects. Many discover that project delivery is easier without any adversarial parties involved and feel that they can offer better value and service to their clients.

In much of the custom residential market, design-bid-build is being replaced by design-estimate/negotiate-build. Contractors regularly give "allowances" for fixtures and finishes in a construction cost estimate, and then decide the final choices (and the final price) with the owner as the project progresses. With this kind of arrangement, the architects' involvement sometimes ends once a building permit is acquired. However, architect-led design-build ensures the architect's involvement continues throughout the entire project. And because the architect's involvement is expanded and construction budgets are considerably larger than design fees, there is potential for higher overall compensation per project. But design-build project delivery can also mean more risk, more potential to lose money through unexpected construction problems, and delays.

CASE STUDY IN ARCHITECT-LED DESIGN-BUILD: GREG GREW, AIA

By his own admission, Greg Grew, AIA, became a general contractor "by accident." His company, Grew Design Incorporated, located in Woodbury, Connecticut, started in 1989 as a home-based practice offering traditional architectural services. Greg describes how he came to expand his services to include construction management and general contracting: "In my practice at the time, I was doing the drawings, getting the permit, and then just handing over the design to the owner. On one job, the lowest bid came in twice as high as expected ($200,000 instead of $100,000). When I looked into 'where we went wrong,' I couldn't see any reason for the price discrepancy. I got some estimates from sub-contractors and determined that I could actually build the project for $75,000. So I offered to build it for the original estimate of $100,000 and the client agreed. We did really well on the job and I never looked back."

To simplify the bookkeeping, taxes, and liability issues, Greg created two different companies: Grew Design Inc. for architectural, consulting, and construction management services; and Grew Construction LLC, for general contracting. Having separate companies, according to Greg, also makes it easier to monitor performance. As the provider of architectural services, Grew Design Inc. follows the same design process, regardless of whether Grew Construction LLC might eventually be chosen as the builder. The process is not unique—initial consultation, schematic design, preliminary cost estimate, approval of design and budget, construction documents, bidding phase, and construction phase services. At the bid phase, the client can request a proposal from Grew Construction LLC, along with other general contractors. If the client chooses Grew Construction to build the project, they are advised as follows: "The critical issue for clients to contemplate is that, when working as the GC [general contractor], Grew Construction has a financial interest in the project and is no longer the independent consultant of the owner. We appreciate the trust and confidence our clients have in us when they ask us to be their construction contractor."[7] If Grew Construction LLC is the general contractor, a construction contract is executed that is completely separate from Grew Design Inc.

Grew Construction LLC and Grew Design Inc. also offer clients a design-build option in which there is a single contract that covers both the design and construction. However, Greg says he will never offer design services as a "loss leader," believing that the quality of the design and the drawings should be consistent, no matter who is building the project. Greg also offers his services as a construction manager through Grew Designs Inc., managing schedule, budget, and subcontractors for homeowners who nominally act as general contractor on their project.

Like Nelson Breech Nave, AIA, (see Chapter 10), Greg Grew is also a licensed building official. This gives him the capability to offer code consulting to other design professionals and to skillfully facilitate the permitting process. Greg's business depends on high productivity and the design firm completes up to 50 projects a year with a staff that has been as large as 10, but was reduced to five by mid-2009. Self-described as a "generalist" practice, the design firm does residential projects that range from "modest" kitchens to 12,000-square-foot homes as well as commercial and institutional work. Greg believes it is important for other architects "not to be afraid to stretch their services and consider how they can become more of a 'master builder' and trusted expert."

LESSONS LEARNED

Greg Grew, AIA, is representative of many small firm practitioners who have expanded the services that they offer to include general contracting. Creating separate companies, separate contracts, and separate processes keeps everything simple and fully disclosed. Nevertheless, design-build is practiced by small firms in a variety of forms and leadership arrangements. Schachne Architects and Builders (see Chapter 1) is a fully integrated firm that builds all the projects that it designs. WT, (see Chapter 6) formed his design-build form by partnering with a construction manager creating, in his case, external unity but internal divisions. Significant risk can accompany the decision to engage in design-build practices. Small firm leaders who are considering this option can get support and resources at the AIA national Design-Build Knowledge Community.[8]

ARCHITECT DEVELOPER

Integrated practice for small firms also includes the notion of architects becoming developers or partnering with developers. The operational concept here is that the architects are not only the designers and builders of the projects, they are also the owners. This is complete integration of all project roles and transforms the "client" into the "buyer." And since developers make many of the important decisions about a project, such as its location and purpose, before an architect is usually on board, being the developer puts more power into the hands of the design professional. As explained by Carolyn Geise, FAIA (see Chapter 6), being the developer allows architects to "go out on a limb a bit and attract others who are willing to do the same."

Creating Pocket Neighborhoods: Ross Chapin, AIA

Ross Chapin, AIA, and Jim Soules, a developer, met at an event hosted by the Northwest Eco-Building Guild in Seattle. They immediately recognized that they had a common interest in creating an alternative to the ubiquitous suburban "McMansion" and the lifeless street-scapes of repeating garage doors. As expressed by Ross, whose firm is located in Langley, Washington, "In response to this soulless sprawl and bland houses on steroids, developer Jim Soules and I came together to demonstrate the [market] demand for an alternative. We sensed that there was a market for smaller houses in a setting that fosters community, and set out to build a new model . . . Our common ground is a passion to create vibrant small houses in great neighborhoods."[9]

Ross goes on to explain what eventually came from this initial meeting. "Our first project on Whidbey Island in 1997 broke fresh ground. The Third Street Cottages was the first cottage housing development in the United States using an innovative code that gave density incentives for limiting the size of the houses. It quickly caught the attention of the national media, including articles in *Metropolitan Home, Sunset Magazine, Fine Homebuilding*, Knight-Ridder Syndicated newspapers, HGTV, and various books including *Solving Sprawl* (NRDC) and *Creating the Not So Big House* by Sarah Susanka. We had, and continue to have, a nearly constant stream of calls and emails from homeowners, community activists, planners, architects, and developers across the country. Our hunch proved to be accurate."[10]

The Cottage Company, formed to develop the Third Street Cottages, was set up as an equal partnership between Ross and Deborah Chapin and Jim Soules and his wife, Linda Pruitt. Ross provided the architectural services and Jim the business know-how required to put together the financing. After the completion of this first project Jim and Linda assumed full ownership of The Cottage Company in order to manage future project planning and construction, and to enable marketing of the finished product. To continue their ground-breaking work, Ross, Deborah, Jim, and Linda formed a new Limited Liability Company (LLC) for each new cottage housing development project.

For each successive development project, Ross Chapin Architects would provide the architectural services, including design, construction documents, permitting, site design, and construction phase consultation. The Cottage Company would provide management of the finances, the construction, and the marketing. When all the units in a development were sold, discounted fees for these services were paid to each of the principal parties, and the remaining profit was split 50/50. Between 1997 and 2008, The Cottage Company and Ross Chapin Architects completed six cottage/small home developments on Whidbey Island and in suburban cities outside of Seattle, totaling over 60 single-family homes. Reflecting the satisfaction that residents feel in their courtyard communities, very few of these homes come on the market as resales.

Costs and Benefits

These development projects represented significant financial risk for Ross. There were no guarantees that the market would accept these small homes organized around landscaped courtyards, and also understand the benefits of the "pocket neighborhood" that is created. It was a very real possibility, if the cottages did not sell, that Ross would be faced with having to contribute cash to service loans and other ongoing maintenance and marketing expenses.

In addition, the development activities created a cash flow strain on Ross' ongoing architectural practice. Staff had to be paid to work on the development projects, but no immediate revenue was created by the effort. The opportunity costs were also significant since Ross and the project architects were often pulled off billable projects to work on the cottage developments, especially during the construction phase. Because Ross' firm had only three to five employees during this time, the impact on overall revenue was significant.

Fortunately, the cottage projects proved to be very popular and the units relatively easy to sell. Although they no longer partner on development projects, both parties enjoy the results of the successful work they did together. The Cottage Company continues its development activities and Ross Chapin, AIA, continues his work with developers as a paid design professional planning cottage housing and new town projects throughout the nation.

In addition to the financial rewards of partnering with a developer, there were benefits to Ross Chapin and his firm that went beyond monetary considerations. The cottage developments were a manifestation of Ross and Jim's sincere passion for an alternative vision of suburban life, one that fosters community and sustainable lifestyles. The developments provide a physical model that helps others imagine the positive aspects of living in well-designed, dense neighborhoods of relatively small houses. Ross Chapin has received considerable recognition for his work in creating these model communities, including national AIA design awards. This has enabled him to attract residential developers from around the nation who are interested in doing something different and has created a booming consulting practice for Ross in residential development site planning.

Ross Chapin Architects also offers cottage and small house designs for sale online as stock plans. According to Ross, "This began as a response to a number of single family homes being published in *Fine Homebuilding* and in numerous Taunton Press books, and as a response to friends who wanted an architect-designed home, but had no budget for one." The inventory of stock plans started small and grew as more cottages and small house models were created for the development work. Now, when Ross works for developers doing the site planning for their projects, they have the option to buy Ross' stock house plans to populate the development. This helps keep costs down for the developer, brings additional revenue into the firm, and assures proven quality of design for the housing units. In addition, Ross' stock plans make good design of small houses affordable to the general public. As a business strategy, the stock plans provide positive cash flow for the modest effort involved in servicing the online orders. This has helped mitigate to some extent, the cash flow drain caused by participation in development projects.

Lessons Learned

Being an equity partner in a development project does give an architect more control of the final product, according to Ross, especially the ability to follow through with the details. However, financial risks bring a sobering reality to decision making. Aesthetic choices are weighed with an eye on the bottom line. It's a balancing act of no small risk. Reflecting on the whole experience, Ross comments, "Being a development partner allowed me to make choices from site planning to planting that contributed to the overall coherence, wholeness and continuity. This opportunity is nearly unheard of for an architect operating in service to a developer."

Ross also points out the difficulty of being a developer while simultaneously running a traditional architectural practice. "I felt like I had two jobs," Ross comments, "and it was hard to meet expenses while delivering projects that went unpaid for months or years." He advises would-be architect/developers to, "keep your eyes open and pay attention to business aspects, including intellectual property, marketing, and sales." Nevertheless, like Carolyn Geise, FAIA (see Chapter 6), Ross believes that architects can use their problem-solving abilities to help heal the planet and our society. He encourages all design professionals to look at global issues and become leaders within their local community.

Green Development: Tony Case, AIA

While Ross Chapin, AIA, became a developer by partnering with one, Tony Case, AIA, grew up in the business. "I was involved as a young person with my father's development company," Tony explains. "I helped renovate buildings and also helped to visualize what they could be. The opportunity to envision and then build projects became very appealing to me."

Not surprisingly, Tony has created an organization, Case Design and Construction Management in Seattle that has competencies in design, construction, and construction management. "We try to hire people who are interested in both design and construction—drafters who are also carpenters and carpenters who are also designers," says Tony as he describes the efficiencies of having diverse skills together under one roof. The firm is primarily focused on the development of sustainable urban residential projects, but also is available to deliver design-build projects for private clients.

Before starting his firm in 1998, Tony worked in the nonprofit sector, managing renovation of housing meant primarily for low-income tenants. He continued to do this work after he established his firm, taking on the nonprofit organizations as clients. This gave Tony a sense of the "social utility of development work" and exposed him to the results of poor building practices over time. "When I would renovate these houses in the south end of Seattle," Tony recalls, "I was shocked by the terrible indoor air quality that resulted from the use of bad materials. And the lack of insulation and the single-paned windows I observed gave me pause about energy consumption and the poor quality of life these houses offered. This experience impacted me and made me determined to build in a different way."

In 2005, Tony developed his first two houses for sale in South Seattle. Designed as green projects, the success of these homes have led to the construction of others and a recent entry into developing green, multi-family, transit-oriented housing. According to the website of Case Design and Construction Management, the "green" aspects of these projects include: "New homes designed with green roof terraces, which not only reduce storm water runoff but also provide outdoor living space; Rainwater harvesting from roofs for other uses, to conserve potable water; Heated concrete slab floors; beautiful, comfortable, and dust-free; Non-toxic interior materials and finishes; Designing our new mixed-use project for Zero-net-energy use."[11]

Business Considerations

Although Tony is committed to environmentally responsible development, he is reflective about his move, over time, from a small idealistic firm to a profit-oriented business offering a competitive product. "It is a challenge to build green efficiently, to give the buyers what they want at a price they can afford. While building green is still important, we've come to understand that the benefits need to be measurable and metrics established to show added value."

Tony advises any architect who is considering becoming a developer to become educated about business. "Consider getting a business degree, or hiring someone who has one," Tony remarks. After years of frustrating on-the-job self-training, Tony hired an experienced financial manager as a full-time employee. Despite the added salary expense, Tony explains that it is money well spent because he is now "free from worry about invoicing, project tracking, and what's going on financially in the company, in general." He appreciates the ability to have forecasts of gross revenue and net income and has mapped out growth plans with revenue milestones in place. As Tony says, "It's time to get real about business."

Tony is representative of the many small firm practitioners who seek to "do good while doing well," meaning that being business-oriented and being environmentally/socially responsible are not adversarial values. This concept will be discussed in more detail in Chapter 13.

Firms of all sizes can be involved in integrated practice and integrated project delivery. Understanding the direction of technological trends and the movement toward integration of design and construction can help firm leaders craft strategy that "swims with the tide," instead of being left behind watching from the shoreline. Chapter 12 looks further into big-picture trends that will surely influence the course of all design firms in the coming decades.

ENDNOTES

1. Laura Lesniewski, AIA, and Eddy Krygiel, AIA, with Bob Berkebile, FAIA, "Roadmap to Integration," *Report on Integrated Practice*, Broshar, Strong, Freidman, eds., American Institute of Architects, Washington, D.C., 2006.

2. Ibid.

3. Lance Kirby, "Introducing BIM into a Small-Firm Work Environment," *Small Project Practitioners Journal*, American Institute of Architects, Washington, D.C., 2006.

4. American Institute of Architects, Integrated Practice and Integrated Project Delivery "Home": **http://aia.org/about/initiatives/AIAS078435?dvid=&recspec=AIAS078435**.

5. American Institute of Architects, AIA Contract Documents: http://aiacontractdocuments. org/ipd/.

6. Gary J. Tulacz, "Is There a Revolution on the Doorstep?" *Engineering News Record*, McGraw-Hill, NY, 2008.

7. Greg Grew, AIA, www.grewdesign.com/construction_services.html.

8. American Institute of Architects, Design-Build Knowledge Community "Home": **www.aia.org/ practicing/groups/kc/AIAS075366**.

9. Ross Chapin, AIA, "The New American Dream: Bigger Is Better or Small Is Beautiful?" *Knowledge by Design Case Study Prize Publication*, Rena M. Klein, FAIA, ed., AIA Seattle, Seattle, WA, 2005.

10. Ibid.

11. Tony Case, AIA, Case Design and Project Management website: **www.case-architects.com/ index.php?itemid=25**.

CHAPTER 12

BIG-PICTURE TRENDS

hapter 7 includes a discussion of the impact of macroeconomic forces on small firm practice. Parts of Chapter 11 focus on technology and its industry-wide impact on project delivery. Other kinds of trends—demographic and sociological—also influence design firms, large and small. As a practical matter, trends are the foundation of strategy. Understanding likely future conditions will help firm leaders make strategic decisions that foster firm sustainability in the long term.

Like it or not, significant demographic changes are on the horizon for the United States. According to a report prepared by the Congressional Research Service of the Library of Congress, the U.S. population is becoming larger, older, and more ethnically diverse.[1] The Pew Research Center echoes these findings in the executive summary of its report on U.S. Population Projections 2005–2050, "If current trends continue, the population of the United States will rise to 438 million in 2050, from 296 million in 2005, and 82% of the increase will be due to immigrants arriving from 2005 to 2050 and their U.S.-born descendants. . . . Among the other key population projections:

- Nearly one in five Americans (19%) will be an immigrant in 2050, compared with one in eight (12%) in 2005.

- The Latino population, already the nation's largest minority group, will triple in size and will account for most of the nation's population growth from 2005 through 2050. Hispanics will make up 29% of the U.S. population in 2050, compared with 14% in 2005.

- The non-Hispanic white population will increase more slowly than other racial and ethnic groups; whites will become a minority (47%) by 2050.

187

■ The nation's elderly population will more than double in size from 2005 through 2050, as the baby-boom generation enters the traditional retirement years. The number of working-age Americans and children will grow more slowly than the elderly population, and will shrink as a share of the total population."[2]

What do these changes mean to the practice of architecture or any business endeavor in the coming decades? Certainly there are strategic marketing directions indicated by these demographic trends, such as elder housing and retirement communities. However, the biggest implication of these trends for the architectural profession is likely to be the move toward a more diverse workforce and a more diverse client base. For a profession in which roughly 92 percent of its members are white, this may represent a significant challenge.[3]

DIVERSITY IN PRACTICE

Even without the demographic shift coming in the twenty-first century, it is well understood that diversity can be good for business. The business case for diversity often centers around two distinct points: (1) it is the right thing to do, and (2) it can provide entry into new markets. The AIA actively supports the first of these traditional approaches to diversity by including a nondiscrimination clause in the AIA Code of Ethics and Professional Conduct. Rule 1.401 requires that "Members shall not discriminate in their professional activities on the basis of race, religion, gender, national origin, age, disability, or sexual orientation."[4] Researchers David Thomas and Robin Ely in their article, "Making Differences Matter," call this the "Fairness and Equality Paradigm." In this approach to diversity, the focus is on compliance with the law (and the ethics code). The idea here is that everyone is treated the same. Often this will also mean that everyone is expected to act the same, which usually means everyone is expected to conform to the majority culture.[5]

The second of these traditional approaches to diversity, in which diverse staff can attract or enable entry into a new market, seems to be a reasonable one for any business, given the demographic trends cited above. While this may be an effective strategy at times, minority employees sometimes feel pigeonholed or even exploited by this approach. The varied perspectives, talents, and world views of these employees are often not fully valued or leveraged to benefit the creative output of the firm.

According to Thomas and Ely, the true benefits of diversity are the increased knowledge, creativity, and innovation that can result from the varied viewpoints and life experiences of a diverse staff. However, in order to take advantage of these benefits, organizations must have a culture that is open to new ideas, new perspectives and to people who may look different than mainstream expectations.[6]

Diversity educators discuss the tendency of all organizations to have a range of normal appearance and behavior styles that is exhibited by the majority of staff. This implicit culture usually mimics the organization's leadership and may be heavily influenced by the legacy and culture of an industry, as is the case with architecture.

Think of "an architect" and notice the image that comes to mind—probably male, white, and young-looking (but not young), with cool glasses. Without intention, many firm leaders will perpetuate this legacy stereotype and narrow the acceptable range by always hiring people who appear to "fit-in."

Firms that want to benefit from differing perspectives and points of view must widen the range of what is considered to be acceptable behavior and appearance. People who look and act differently may also think differently. If they are welcomed and fostered, they will bring new ideas and creative perspectives to an organization. For architectural firms, this capacity is critical.

Small firms have special challenges in relation to diversity. Many are located in parts of the country where the general population is not diverse and it may be difficult to attract minority architects to those environments. Because the number of minority architects is so small—AIA membership in 2008 was only 1 percent African-American, 4 percent Asian, and 3 percent Hispanic—they are sometimes hard to attract away from more lucrative positions in larger firms. Nevertheless, "hiring the familiar" is more common than "hiring the best" in many small firms. This tendency sometimes results in recurring blind spots and a lack of innovation, without different points of view present to literally see things differently.

Having different kinds of people working at a firm is the key to looking at things freshly, stirring the pot, thinking out of the box, and all those other cliché phrases that add up to increased effectiveness, learning, and creativity. Of course, having different kinds of people in the workforce can also be challenging and requires a questioning of the familiar, an attitude of respect, a willingness to learn, and it requires firm leaders to set the example. And, while widening the range of what is acceptable may be challenging, firms that want to succeed in the twenty-first century will have no choice. The next generation of American workers will be significantly more diverse than any who have come before. Having a culture of openness and acceptance will enable firms to attract young talent and retain a diverse staff over the long run.

Even if no other type of diversity exists in a firm, generational differences are likely to be present. It is not uncommon to have three generations working side by side in small design firms. Members of the youngest generation currently entering the workforce have unique capabilities and (sometimes challenging) qualities which some say will be the keys to business success in the twenty-first century.

GENERATION GAPS

The Millennials, also known as Generation Y, are beginning to make their presence felt in the workplace. Born between 1981 and 2000, they are the first generation to grow up with cell phones, instant messaging, and email. These "20-somethings" work differently from other generations and will require different management techniques. They will also expect a different workplace culture.

As described by Morley Safer on the television news magazine, 60-Minutes, the Millennials are causing both consternation and delight in their bosses. Major corporations are hiring consultants to teach managers how to handle these young workers, and to teach the new employees how to behave in a professional environment. While these new workers may eventually conform to traditional workplace standards as have previous generations, experts predict that this may not happen so easily. Because of generational demographics and changing technology, these new workers may have the power to remake the workplace in their own image.[7]

Boomers Out, Millennials In

Generational demographics reveal that there are almost as many Millennials as there are Baby Boomers. Comprised of 75 million individuals in the United States, they loom large behind Generation X (born 1961 to 1980), a cohort that of only 45 million. Their parents (and managers) are both Boomers and Xers since many Boomers had their children late, explaining, to some extent, the smaller size of Generation X. By all accounts, the (middle-class) Millennials were pampered by parents who were extremely focused on and involved with their children's lives. As expressed by Morley Safer, "They were raised by doting parents who told them they are special, played in little leagues with no winners or losers, or all winners. They are laden with trophies just for participating and they think your business-as-usual ethic is for the birds."[8]

In the coming years, as Boomers reach retirement, a huge number of positions in all industries, including architecture, will need to be filled. Between 2005 and 2050, the design fields will be increasingly populated by people over the age of 55 and under the age of 35, while the percentage of staff aged 35 to 55 will actually decrease. This trend will increase competition for the talented and highly capable employees that are critical to design firm success. These conditions, along with the paucity of Gen Xers and the unique competencies of the Millennials, will allow the new generation to have a growing influence on the workplace environment.

As described by Claire Raines in an excerpt from *Connecting Generations: The Sourcebook*, "[The Millennials] are [the] hottest commodity on the job market since Rosie the Riveter. They're sociable, optimistic, talented, well-educated, collaborative, open-minded, influential, and achievement-oriented. They've always felt sought after, needed, indispensable."[9]

Technological Tethering

According to Kathryn Tyler in her article, "The Tethered Generation," marketing researchers report that Millennials spend an average of 72 hours a week connecting with their peers and their parents by cell phone, email, or text messaging.[10] Research shows that many of these young people are in touch with a parent three to five times a day, even after they enter college and the workforce. Parents of Millennials are typically involved in every aspect of their child's life, helping to make all decisions, large and small.

Tyler quotes psychologists and researchers regarding the potential down-sides for individuals who are technologically "tethered" to parents and friends while still developing the capacity to reason, plan, and make decisions. Many believe that Millennials struggle to make independent decisions, engage in critical thinking, and solve problems creatively. Tyler cites a 2006 report that validates these theories, "Roughly three-quarters of executives and HR managers at 400 companies surveyed said that recent four-year college graduates displayed only 'adequate' professionalism and work ethic, creativity and innovation, and critical thinking and problem-solving. Only one-quarter reported an 'excellent' display of those traits in recent college graduates, according to *Are They Really Ready to Work?*, a report by the Society for Human Resource Management, The Conference Board, Corporate Voices for Working Families and the Partnership for 21st Century Skills."[11]

A Mixed Bag

The effects of their upbringing make the Millennials both attractive and challenging for employers. While they are tech-savvy, collaborative, and open-minded, they sometimes lack basic skills in reading, writing, and verbal communication.

Typical strengths of Millennials include:

- Confidence—Can also express as self-doubt or worry.
- Optimistic—Also open to change and experimenting.
- Warm and outgoing—Can also express as sentimental and sensitive.
- Achievement-oriented—Can be highly disciplined and organized when motivated.
- Group-oriented—Teamwork, collaboration, and group decision making come easily.
- Inclusive—Will expect diversity, not just tolerate or accept it.
- Tech-savvy—Comfortable with all aspects of technology and electronic communication.
- Civic minded—Community-oriented values and volunteerism are up among young people.

Typical weaknesses of Millennials include:

- Short attention span – the dark side of multi-tasking and constant stimulation.
- Reading (hardcopy) adverse—If it is not on the Internet, it doesn't exist, coupled with an inability to distinguish between authentic and bogus Internet sources.
- Dismissive of those not as tech-savvy—Not sure there is anything to be learned from their older colleagues.
- Lack of discretion and insensitivity to confidentiality—The "Facebook" effect.
- Lack of independence—They may look to their employers and managers to be like their "over-involved" parents.

■ Unrealistic expectations—They have been told their entire lives how great they are, so they may be unprepared for being challenged in the business environment.

How to Manage Millennials

By all reports, successful management of young workers requires a softer approach that is laced with appreciation and explanation. Coaching which includes both support and direction will be more effective than a purely directive approach. Millennials are used to having constant assistance, assurance, and justification from their parents and may expect their employers to behave in a similar fashion. They don't respond well to harsh criticism and are unashamed about their expectations.

As expressed on *60-Minutes* by Marian Saltzman, an ad agency executive who has been tracking Millennials, "These young people will tell you what time their yoga class is and the day's work will be organized around the fact that they have this commitment. . . . You do have to speak to them a little bit like a therapist on television might speak to a patient. You can't be harsh. You cannot tell them you're disappointed in them. You can't really ask them to live and breathe the company. Because they're living and breathing themselves and that keeps them very busy."[12]

Claire Raines outlines the most frequent requests made by Millennials of their bosses:[13]

1. **You be the leader.** This generation has grown up with structure and supervision, with parents who were role models. The "You be the parent" TV commercials are right on. Millennials are looking for leaders with honesty and integrity. It's not that they don't want to be leaders themselves, they'd just like some great role models first.

2. **Challenge me.** Millennials want learning opportunities. They want to be assigned to projects they can learn from. They're looking for growth, development, a career path.

3. **Let me work with friends.** Millennials say they want to work with people they *click* with. They like being friends with coworkers. Employers who provide for the social aspects of work will find those efforts well rewarded by this newest cohort. Some companies are even interviewing and hiring groups of friends.

4. **Let's have fun.** A little humor, a bit of silliness, even a little irreverence will make your work environment more attractive.

5. **Respect me.** "Treat our ideas respectfully," they ask, "even though we haven't been around a long time."

6. **Be flexible.** The busiest generation ever isn't going to give up its activities just because of jobs. A rigid schedule is a sure-fire way to lose your Millennial employees.

The bottom line is that employers cannot expect their "20-something" workers to give up texting and listening to their iPod simply because they are at work. The good news is that they can likely do the work they are given much faster than previous generations of workers. The bad news is that the work may not be as thorough or complete.

While Boomer and Gen X employers and managers are quick to complain about the younger generation, experts advise that the ability to recruit and retain Millennials is critical to competitive success in the coming decades. As explained by Sommer Kehrli and Trudy Sopp, "Put an end to your pain and don't get caught up in the power struggle. They know you are in charge. They don't care. You can accomplish more for your organization when you make nice with Generation Y, an enormously optimistic, educated, energetic and compassionate generation."[14]

WOMEN IN DESIGN FIRM LEADERSHIP

Sit around a table with a group of women architects and before long the conversation will turn to the challenges faced in their career paths. Although it is rare to hear stories of overt discrimination, it is not uncommon to hear of sacrifices made to pursue the beloved occupation of architecture. "Many of my female colleagues in their thirties are choosing not to have children," says one woman architect. Another one recounts the common wisdom among professional women, "You can only have two of the following three things: a satisfying career; a good marriage; or a family with children. Two, but not all three, you have to choose."

While complaints about low pay and pigeonholing are voiced, the women architects around the table are clearly driven by a passion for their work. As told by one woman architect, "I was offered a high-paying managerial position by a prestigious corporation, but I turned it down. I just couldn't leave architecture." Despite this passion and perseverance, the conversation turns to how very few women are in senior leadership at architectural firms. "Ten years ago, I was the first woman hired by the large firm I work for—now there are more of us, but still no woman among the partners." A woman architect who works in government then speaks up, "That's why I pursued an alternative career path. My boss is a woman and so is hers."

While few women architects will say they have personally experienced sexism in their careers, statistics show that there is a systemic problem. In March 2008, the American Institute of Architects (AIA) reported that women make up 14 percent of AIA regular members and that 16 percent of firm principals and partners are women, up from 12 percent in 1999. Anecdotally, it is known that most of these female principals and partners are solo practitioners or owners of small firms.

Research studies of managerial demographics in the United States show that while women occupy 40 percent of all managerial positions, only six percent of the most highly paid executive positions are held by women. In her book, *Designing for Diversity,*[15] Kathryn Anthony reports that the wage gap between men and women in architecture widens dramatically with experience. A male architect with more than 15 years experience can expect to earn around 25 percent more than his female counterpart.

"Brain Drain" Revealed

One explanation for this phenomenon is that fewer women reach the more highly paid positions in the industry. It may also indicate that women are less successful or less interested than men in using the traditional routes of career advancement. Anecdotal evidence supports the existence of a female "brain-drain" occurring in architectural firms of all sizes, as smart and capable women leave for more promising alternatives.

With support from industry, the Center for Work Life Policy has conducted research on the female "brain-drain" in science, engineering, and technology. An executive summary of their report states the following: "Our research findings show that on the lower rungs of corporate career ladders, fully 41% of highly qualified scientists, engineers, and technologists are women. But the dropout rates are huge: over time 52% of these talented women quit their jobs. Most strikingly, this female exodus is not a steady trickle. Rather, there seems to be a key moment in women's lives—in their mid to late thirties—when most head for the door."[16] Although there is no statistical evidence to prove a similar situation in architecture—over 50 percent of women in their mid- to late 30s quitting their firms—it seems reasonable to assume the situation would be consistent with the findings for science, engineering, and technology.

Many women in architecture appear to leave their employment to start their own firms rather than to leave the profession completely. They do this in search of more flexibility, more opportunity, and more control of their work schedules. As expressed by one woman architect, "Simply put, there was just no growth potential for me in the firm I worked for. I was great at my job as a project manager, had opportunities to run large and interesting projects, but I could see no clear path to becoming a partner." Another explains, "They tracked me toward technical project support. I was not given 'designer-like tasks,' and I know I am a good designer. I left the firm and started my own in order to have the opportunity to design." A third woman architect represents many when she described her reason for going out on her own: "In the culture of my old firm, overtime was expected and part-time or flex-time seen as impractical. With a toddler at home, I just needed more flexibility in my work schedule. I started my own firm so I could work from home and determine my own work commitments."

While leaving to start one's own firm is not the same as leaving the profession, the loss of skilled and experienced women from established firms, large and small, represents a loss of intelligence, training, and most importantly, potential leadership for the firm. As expressed by the researchers on women in science, "Stop for a moment and let these statistics sink in. Can you imagine the dustup in the boardroom if 50% of a company's most promising products were abandoned midstream? And yet companies routinely invest large sums of money in developing female talent, only to see half of that talent walk out. The scale of the loss is enormous."[17] In Chapter 6, Carolyn Geise, FAIA, remarked that one of her motivations to start her own firm in the early 1970s was to gain respect as a woman architect from clients and colleagues. Over 30 years later, it seems that many women architects feel that little has changed.

In small design firms, this loss of talented and experienced women employees can be a significant problem. Considering the demographic shifts facing design firms noted previously, retaining workers over the age of 35—the age in which 50 percent of women in technical fields leave their jobs—will be extremely important to the success and longevity of a firm. Without realizing it, small firm leaders who fail to recognize the leadership potential of their women employees, or are unwilling to establish family-friendly workplace policies, may forfeit more than the obvious loss of competency, creativity, and new perspectives.

Labyrinth to the Top

For those women who do remain employed in established firms and seek to advance to principal or partner, there appears to be numerous barriers, and even if they do achieve promotion there are no guarantees. As explained by one woman architect, "I became a partner in a large prestigious firm, the only woman partner in the company. Before long I began to suffer the effects of tokenism and was marginalized, despite the support of important mentors. Eventually, just as I was beginning to have some successes in my new position, I was asked to step down to Associate 'for the good of the firm.' I resigned and began my own small firm."

In their article, "Women and the Labyrinth of Leadership,"[18] researchers Alice H. Eagly and Linda L. Carli discuss the barriers women face as they aspire toward professional leadership and make practical suggestions for how organizations can support and retain women leaders. This is important information for women architects and for architectural firms that seek to retain their best and brightest female employees.

The phrase "glass ceiling" became popular in the 1980s as a metaphor for gender discrimination in business leadership. It describes a goal that can be seen clearly, but is not attainable. It suggests a situation that occurs once in a career, when a woman reaches an absolute barrier at a specific high level in an organization. Eagly and Carli propose a new metaphor for what women confront in their professional endeavors—the labyrinth. "For women who aspire to top leadership, routes exist but are full of twists and turns, both unexpected and expected. Because all labyrinths have a viable route to the center, it is understood that goals are attainable. The metaphor acknowledges obstacles but is not ultimately discouraging."[19]

No Easy Path

The article reports numerous findings about the barriers faced by professional women. Although the studies cited don't specifically discuss women architects, there is no doubt that they face similar hurdles. The first of these challenges is the demands that family life makes on women. Although men have begun to contribute more to child care and household chores, the majority of these tasks still fall to women. This can cause women to miss work and put less time in at the office overall. This is clearly a detriment to advancement in an industry that traditionally values long hours at the office as an indicator of commitment. Anecdotally, it seems as if most women who do achieve leadership positions in established design firms either don't have children or have active support from their partner and/or an extended family system.

In addition to the demands of family life, women who seek to become leaders in their firms and profession must confront what Eagly and Carli call "vestiges of prejudice." They cite studies that show white men to be statistically advantaged over all other groups, at entry and through all career stages, and their advantage grows as they advance. Even in fields dominated by women such as nursing and interior design, men rise to management positions faster and in greater number.[20]

Actions that Work

To counter these forces and to foster the success of female professional staff, there are steps that small firm leaders can take. First of these is to recognize the potential that women staffers offer to the firm. Take care not to unconsciously pigeonhole or track women into areas such as project management or residential work. Recognize that talented and well-organized women employees may excel in areas traditionally dominated by men, such as design and project leadership.

Actions to Prevent Female "Brain Drain"

How to Retain and Promote Valued Women Employees

- Recognize potential contributions
- Challenge with stretch assignments
- Re-think assumptions about long hours and face-time
- Institute flex-time, part-time, and teleworking options
- Actively support and mentor
- Aspire to gender equity
- Welcome women back

Prepare women that have potential for leadership by giving them challenging assignments that stretch their capacity. This will engender commitment and engagement, as well as provide important experience.

Re-think industry norms that emphasize time spent in the office and perhaps exaggerate the importance of working long hours in the same physical place. Hours in the office do not necessarily correlate with more productivity, especially with the remote technology available today. Question measures of productivity that are based solely on hours worked, and rewards such as bonuses, that are based solely on total annual hours. Consider factoring in project profitability, client satisfaction, and other metrics to evaluate an employee's contribution.

Many firms have instituted flex-time, part-time, and teleworking arrangements and find that there is no reduction of productivity or quality. This will be discussed more fully in the section to follow, on twenty-first-century workplaces.

Firm principals can support their valuable women employees with personal mentoring that includes connection to their business-related social network. Because of family demands, women often have less time for social networking, so the guidance of an influential mentor is often a significant boost.

Although women are only about 20 percent of the architectural workforce, women make up about 50 percent of the students in the nation's architecture schools, and have for decades. This persistent circumstance is caused to some extent by the exit of experienced women in their late 30s from the profession. Firms can avoid the blind spots that lack of diversity brings by acting to retain these women and aspiring to gender equity at all levels of the firm structure.

Even if a valued woman employee has to leave the firm, much can be gained from staying connected and welcoming her back to the firm when that is possible.

Awareness of barriers that women face in their professional careers, and strategies designed to retain and promote talented women can help stem the "brain drain" from the architectural profession. For small firms, keeping experienced and savvy women employees may actually become a key competitive advantage.

TWENTY-FIRST-CENTURY WORKPLACE

A picture begins to emerge from technological, demographic, and sociological trends of a future workplace with big differences from the norms of the first decade of the new century. Firms headed by Gen Xers and Millennials are likely to be more family and technology friendly. Around 2025, the Millennials will be in their late 30s and perhaps changes in the workplace will prevent the exodus of this generation of women from established firms, large and small. The workplace is likely to be populated by people with many different appearances and behavior styles as the result of the immigrant population and the decades of global exposure and mixing.

Technology already enables many kinds of work to be completed from locations remote from the office setting. The need for members of a firm to gather daily for many hours in one physical place may come to seem less important in years to come. Technology already offers professional workers many effective options for interaction and collaboration that no longer require 40 or more hours per week at the office. Arguments over whether flex-time and family-friendly policies are practical in architectural firms may become a thing of the past.

The Teleworking Option

The high cost of commuting, both economic and environmental, and the perceived benefit to work-life balance are causing firms to consider teleworking, also known as telecommuting. In her article, "Works Well with Others," appearing in *Mother Jones Magazine*, Kiera Butler discusses trends and practices in teleworking. Butler notes that it is now possible to work anywhere and the advantages of doing so are many. Time spent commuting, up to four hours a day in some cases, could be spent in many more productive ways. The environmental benefits are equally attractive—a workforce that doesn't commute doesn't use as much fuel, puts less carbon into the atmosphere, and places less strain on existing transportation infrastructures.[21] For architectural firms, teleworking may also offer the promise of better balance between work and family life for employees and principals alike.

The Telework Coalition is an advocacy group for teleworking and telecommuting. According to their 2006 Benchmarking Study, many organizations see teleworking as an integral part of their everyday operations. Participating companies report many advantages including, "greater flexibility for employees to relocate to other parts of the country, greater ability to maintain business continuity in response to natural or man-made disasters, lower turn-over rates and better performance for teleworking employees, access to a larger number of qualified applicants, and fewer layoffs for teleworkers than their office-based counterparts."[22]

Importance of Social Interaction

Despite these benefits, teleworking has yet to really catch on. With the exception of virtual call-centers and other "work-from-home" enterprises, acceptance of telecommuting has fallen short of expectations. According to Butler, people who work at home are often troubled by distractions and are subject to feeling lonely and unmotivated. In her article, she cites the work of Stephen Humphrey, professor of management at Florida State University. Through analysis of 40 years of research, Humphrey found a strong reinforcing correlation between the level of social interaction in a workplace and the level of job satisfaction and productivity among the workers.[23]

Since productivity is critical to profitability in architectural firms, this connection between social interaction and productivity is significant. In many cases, social interaction will prove essential to the successful completion of work, especially complex and nonroutine projects. Face-to-face get-togethers allow for informal information exchange, stimulating conversations, and creative encounters. Social interaction often builds familiarity and caring among coworkers which can inspire commitment and mutuality.

While social interaction is important, other forces also impact job satisfaction and productivity. Balancing work and family life has become a critical issue in employee retention, especially with more mothers in the workforce and fathers increasingly involved in care-giving. Teleworking is a family-friendly option that firms can consider along with other flexible arrangements. In addition, other studies challenge Humphrey's assertion of a reinforcing relationship between social interaction and productivity.

In an article by Kurt Cagle called "Is Telework the New Face of an Agile Workforce?," he cites a study that found, "one of the biggest incentives for telework is that it provides a way to cut down on the non-essential interactions of work—the coworker who wants to come in and kibbitz about their trip, the noisy distractions from a loud telephone call in the next cubicle, meetings called by anxious managers who themselves had been in back-to-back meetings. Indeed, one result of this survey was to call into question whether the concept that such physical rapport at work is in fact necessary at all. Indeed, there's some evidence that these particular social bonding efforts create 'background noise' that makes it harder for workers to actually work."[24]

An AIA Best Practices document called "Teleworking Considerations" outlines sample policies for firms when initiating a teleworking program. This document warns of the need for clarity in purpose, eligibility, work schedule, and communication protocols. Keys to successfully combining teamwork with teleworking include: adequate structure, both social and technological; frequent communication between all parties; transparent decision-making processes; explicit expectations in terms of schedule and deliverables; and at least one face-to-face meeting per week.[25]

The Coworking Option

For all the perceived benefits of teleworking, there remains evidence that some people do not enjoy working by themselves at home. According to Professor Humphrey, as related by Butler in the *Mother Jones Magazine* article, "the office has become a refuge of sorts ... we suddenly start to realize, we miss socializing—and we need it."[26] Anecdotal evidence shows that some architects who leave established firms to work on their own experience similar misgivings.

Across the nation, teleworking entrepreneurs have devised a solution to this problem. Known as "coworking spaces," freelance and independent teleworkers rent desks in an office fitted with business amenities. Butler cites an example in San Francisco—a coworking space called the Hat Factory. Here independent workers can have, "a desk and standard office amenities, and access to a shared kitchen, private meeting room, and lounge. And something else—social interactions and networking." Many of these facilities operate on a model similar to a gym membership—workers are not assigned to specific desks, making coworking cheaper than most subleasing arrangements.

Although coworking spaces have been used mostly by independent teleworkers, they can provide a solution for solo practitioners who miss the collegiality of an office atmosphere. The coworking concept can also solve problems facing architectural firms located outside of an urban center. A small firm located 90 minutes away from Seattle, provides an example. All six professional employees of CA Architects live in Seattle and until recently, most commuted daily from Seattle to the firm's office, mostly in their own cars, expending considerable time and expense. Rising gas prices and environmental concerns prompted CA to establish a coworking space for her employees located in Seattle, close to their homes. Firm employees each spend two days a week in this space, which can accommodate four of them at a time, telecommunicating with their boss and coworkers at the distant office. This coworking space is not a branch office—clients will never come there and CA rarely goes there in person. Instead, it is meant to provide opportunity for professional collaboration among the staff without the long commute. Through this arrangement CA Architects achieves social interaction, effective work processes, and significant savings in time, expense, energy, and carbon footprint.

While CA Architects may seem unique, many firms are located some distance from where most of their staff resides. This may be true of a New York City firm with staff that live in the suburbs; or a rural architecture firm, located hours from the nearest urban center. Firms in this kind of situation sometimes find it difficult to recruit and retain qualified staff. Setting up a coworking/teleworking space close to the residences of current staff (and potential staff) may be part of the solution for these firms. Firms with individual telecommuters might consider renting a desk in an existing coworking space for their employee. Even a new mother, who might take her sleeping infant with her, needs professional and social interaction. For those who find working alone at home isolating or distracting, and for firms where commuting is impractical or undesirable, coworking may provide a viable option.

Teleworking is one strategy that architectural firms can use to provide employees with flexible and sustainable workplace alternatives. The technology is improving rapidly and is already enabling individuals to communicate more effectively—closer to face-to-face exchange than previously possible. With improvements to file sharing capabilities that enable large drawing files to be exchanged electronically and Internet portals that allow for simultaneous collaboration, many of the technological barriers to teleworking have been lifted.

The capacity for teleworking has many implications for the future of the architectural workplace. The expense involved with increasing the size of the physical workplace as a firm grows will be significantly diminished; the opportunities to employ a skilled but geographically diverse workforce will significantly increase; and the ability to offer greater work-life balance to valuable employees will be simplified. Although the management and mentoring of teleworkers may be challenging and may require new approaches, the benefits clearly indicate that it will be worth the effort.

As summed up by Cagle, "Telework promises to get cars off the road, to make working with increasingly far-flung staff and contractors easier, to cut overall corporate and governmental energy costs, to reduce demand on expensive and limited commercial real estate and give to workers considerable more ability to structure their work times to fit their needs rather than the needs of running a company's physical power plant. It provides corporate security by insuring that a disaster or power outage does not significantly disrupt a company's operations, and it provides a valuable tool in recruiting and retaining technical, creative and managerial talent regardless of where they may be located."[27]

ENDNOTES

1. Laura B. Shrestha, "Report for Congress: The Changing Demographic Profile of the United States," Congressional Research Service of The Library of Congress, Washington, D.C., 2006: www.fas.org/sgp/crs/misc/RL32701.pdf.

2. Jeffrey S. Passel and D'Vera Cohn, "U.S. Population Projections: 2005–2050," Pew Research Center, Washington, D.C., 2008: http://pewhispanic.org/files/reports/85.pdf.

3. American Institute of Architects, "Diversity Within the AIA," www.aia.org/about/initiatives/AIAS076703.

4. American Institute of Architects, "The AIA Code of Ethics and Professional Conduct" **www.aia.org/SiteObjects/files/bookmark_ethics_final.pdf**.

5. David Thomas and Robin Ely, "Making Differences Matter: A New Paradigm for Managing Diversity," *Harvard Business Review*, Harvard Business School Publishing Corp., Cambridge, MA, 1998.

6. Ibid.

7. CBS 60 Minutes Report: "The 'Millennials' Are Coming," **www.cbsnews.com/stories/2007/ 11/08/60minutes/main3475200.shtml**.

8. Ibid.

9. Clair Raines, *Connecting Generations: The Sourcebook*, Crisp Publications, Menlo Park, CA, 2003.

10. Kathryn Tyler, "The Tethered Generation," *HR Magazine,* Society for Human Resource Management, Alexandria, VA, 2007.

11. Ibid.

12. CBS 60 Minutes Report: "The 'Millennials' Are Coming," **www.cbsnews.com/stories/2007/ 11/08/60minutes/main3475200.shtml**.

13. Clair Raines, Generations at Work, **www.generationsatwork.com/articles/millenials.htm**.

14. Sommer Kehrli and Trudy Sopp, "Managing Generation Y," *HR Magazine*, Society for Human Resource Management, Alexandria, VA, 2006.

15. Kathryn Anthony, *Designing for Diversity*, University of Illinois Press, Urbana, IL, 2001.

16. Sylvia Ann Hewlett, Carolyn Buck Luce, and Lisa J. Servon, "Stopping the Exodus of Women in Science," *Harvard Business Review*, Harvard Business School Publishing Corp., Cambridge, MA, 2008.

17. Ibid.

18. Alice H. Eagly and Linda L. Carli, "Women and the Labyrinth of Leadership," *Harvard Business Review*, Harvard Business School Publishing Corp., Cambridge, MA, 2007.

19. Ibid.

20. Ibid.

21. Kiera Butler, "Works Well with Others," *Mother Jones Magazine*, San Francisco, CA, 2008.

22. The Telework Coalition, **www.telcoa.org/**.

23. Kiera Butler, "Works Well with Others," *Mother Jones Magazine*, San Francisco, CA, 2008.

24. Kurt Cagle, "Is Teleworking the New Face of the Agile Workforce?" O'reilly®, **http://news.oreilly.com/2008/08/is-telework-the-face-of-the-ag.html**.

25. AIA Best Practices on Teleworking: **www.aia.org/aiaucmp/groups/ek_members/documents/ pdf/aiap016519.pdf**.

26. Kiera Butler, "Works Well with Others," *Mother Jones Magazine*, San Francisco, CA, 2008.

27. Kurt Cagle, "Is Teleworking the New Face of the Agile Workforce?" O'reilly®, **http://news. oreilly.com/2008/08/is-telework-the-face-of-the-ag.html**.

CHAPTER 13

SUSTAINABLE ECONOMICS

While the discourse among designers has shifted to sustainable design and construction materials and methods, little attention has been paid to the sustainability of design firm practice. Sustainable practice is the business equivalent of sustainable building design and construction. It involves making decisions based on long-term considerations as well as immediate effect. Beyond that, going to a deeper level, it involves a shift in world view and a turn toward values-based decisions.

Understanding the principles of sustainable economics can give firm leaders a new way of thinking about the future of their firms. It can help them craft business strategies that work well with changing global circumstances and big-picture trends. Like sustainable design, sustainable economics provides a business case for looking beyond short-term expense.

In conventional economic theory, the primary factors limiting productivity and growth are the availability of labor, energy, machinery, technical ability to extract resources, and financial capital. Because of the low (short-term) cost of resources and energy and the relatively high cost of labor, industry has continually sought to replace labor with automated processes that use increasing amounts of cheap (in the short-term) material resources and energy.

Sustainable economics, also known as Natural Capitalism,[1] puts forth the notion that it is the availability of natural capital—mineral resources, energy resources, and ecosystem services—that is now becoming the primary limiting factor to growth.

The proponents of natural capitalism suggest:

- Increasing the productivity of natural resources through conservation, reuse, and reduction of waste;
- Shifting to biologically inspired models, known as biomimicry or "cradle to cradle"[2] thinking;
- Investing in the health of ecosystems, as is done in building development projects that use regenerative design principles; and
- Recognition of the scarcity shift—people are now plentiful and natural capital is not.[3]

TRIPLE BOTTOM LINE

To participate in creating a better society, architectural firms can do more than just design the built environment. They can join with other socially responsible businesses in using the "triple bottom line" (TBL). This way of measuring business success includes ecological and social metrics in addition to the usual focus on economic outcomes.

The term *triple bottom line* was popularized by Andrew Savitz and Karl Weber with the publication of their book, *The Triple Bottom Line: How Today's Best-run Companies Are Achieving Economic, Social and Environmental Success.*[4] Sometimes referred to with the shorthand phrase "People, Planet, and Profit," the triple bottom line has become synonymous with socially and environmentally responsible business practices.

TBL recognizes that there are other sorts of capital, besides man-made capital, that are invested in any business enterprise. There is natural capital, as discussed earlier in this chapter and there is human capital in the form of people's voluntary effort, creativity, and intelligence. Return on investment (ROI) in human capital is manifest as enthusiasm, commitment, and loyalty. ROI from natural capital is the continued sustainability of human life.

Triple bottom line metrics include consideration of:
- Social (People)
  - Health and well-being of workforce
  - Contributions to local community
  - Fairness to suppliers and customers
- Ecological (Planet)
  - Health of resource base (natural capital)
  - Investment in regenerative practices
  - Mitigation of harmful practices

■ Economic (Profit)
  ■ Profitability
  ■ Return on monetary investment
  ■ Accumulation of man-made capital

For architects who are AIA members, the 2007 Code of Ethics and Professional Conduct encourages members to aspire to both ecological and socially beneficial practices. While these "Ethical Standards" are not mandatory requirements, as are the Rules of Conduct, they represent a collective agreement on desirability of these actions.

From the AIA 2007 Code of Ethics and Professional Conduct[5]

Ethical Standard 2.2 Public Interest Services: Members should render public interest professional services, including pro bono services, and encourage their employees to render such services. Pro bono services are those rendered without expecting compensation, including those rendered for indigent persons, after disasters, or in other emergencies.

Canon VI Obligations to the Environment: Members should promote sustainable design and development principles in their professional activities.

Ethical Standard 6.1: Sustainable Design: In performing design work, members should be environmentally responsible and advocate sustainable building and site design.

Ethical Standard 6.2: Sustainable Development: In performing professional services, members should advocate the design, construction, and operation of sustainable buildings and communities.

Ethical Standard 6.3: Sustainable Practices: Members should use sustainable practices within their firms and professional organizations, and they should encourage their clients to do the same.

Ethical practice for architects therefore already includes triple bottom line thinking. AIA member architects must consider including both environmentally responsible activities and contributions to their community as part of their everyday practice.

According to proponents of TBL, investments in human and natural capital bring tangible returns in business development, professional success, and profitability. The TBL approach applies quantitative and qualitative tools to measure the positive business impact of these activities. Sustainability of a small design firm may be enhanced and may actually depend on the firm's participation in positive social and environmental actions.

SUSTAINABLE DESIGN FIRM PRACTICE

Sustainability for a small design firm also involves minimizing risk. The following are examples of actions small firm leaders can take to manage risks:

- Don't "overfish"—notice overbuilding trends in primary market and make moves to diversify project types.
- Purchase "Errors and Omissions" insurance, even if it is not required by the state—there are policies tailored to small firm practice.
- Arrange for offsite Internet backup of all data on office server(s) and periodically check that it is actually working.
- Be scrupulous about paying all taxes on time.
- Be scrupulously legal in employment practices, especially in using contract labor.
- Be scrupulously honest with all clients and consultants—communicate often, take responsibility for mistakes and correct them quickly and as best as possible—even if it costs money, it is likely to be less costly and stressful than legal action.
- Be scrupulously honest with employees—have fair and legal employment policies written down and distributed to all employees.
- Be generous and appreciative to employees—it is a myth that running a successful business means looking only at bottom-line considerations; happy and committed staff is key to small design firm sustainability.
- Institute teleworking systems that enable continued operations in the event of a natural disaster, flu pandemic, or terrorist act.
- Create strategic alliances with like-minded design professionals, contractors, artists, and consultants of all kinds.
- Contribute to the local community through pro-bono work, professional organizations, forward thinking development projects, and through civic involvement.

GREENING THE WORKPLACE

Sustainability of a design practice also depends on staying current with trends. This includes learning about green design practices, as is now required for all AIA members. It may also include pursuit of other credentials such as LEED Accreditation or becoming a Certified Sustainable Building Advisor. In the coming years, the requirements for carbon-neutral buildings will likely require a renewed focus on building science and local site context.

Having a sustainable design practice will involve an ability to connect the dots between a firm's workplace practices and its professional output. Clients cannot be expected to consider sustainable practices in their building projects unless they also see this behavior modeled in the design firms they encounter. Happily, as is the case for many green building methods, the switch to environmentally responsible workplace practices will also save money.

Top Environmentally Responsible Practices in the Workplace

- Encouraging employees to work in a more environmentally friendly way (two-sided copies; turning off computers when not in use; using energy efficient bulbs in desk lamps . . .)
- Promoting walking, biking, carpooling, taking public transit
- Using energy efficient lighting systems and equipment
- Offering recycling programs for office products and personal items such as cell phones
- Buying or leasing refurbished goods (toner cartridges, copiers, printers . . .)
- Partnering with environmentally friendly suppliers/companies (recycled paper, ink cartridge refills)
- Minimizing water consumption by installing water saving plumbing fixtures
- Installing automatic shut-off for equipment
- Donating used office furniture or excess supplies to charities or to employees, rather than throw them away
- Sponsoring or participating in projects and events in the community that improve the environment
- Using recycled and other green materials in the construction and furnishing of the workplace

Source: Society of Human Resource Management[6]

According to a survey conducted by the Society of Human Resource Management, the source of the sidebar list, there are numerous beneficial outcomes of environmentally responsible programs. The most significant of these is an improvement in employee morale. This was especially true in smaller companies, where these programs can serve as a unifying cause. Other benefits include stronger public image, reductions in the cost of operations, increased employee loyalty and retention, and increased workforce productivity. For designers, environmentally friendly workplaces reinforce and validate both the profession's leadership and a small firm's initiative toward sustainable building design.

VALUES-BASED PRACTICE

Common wisdom about the future of architectural practice deems that the profession will need to become more businesslike to compete in the global marketplace and to meet, as equals, with business-oriented clients. While being more business oriented is likely to be a positive direction for many small firms, does this also imply a shift in the espoused values of the profession? In her *DesignIntelligence* article "Red Business Blue Business," Barbara Golter Heller suggests that architectural firms need to emulate their commercial and institutional clients by being more interested in the profit motive. Without this shift, she warns, architects will fail to gain leadership in the developing practices of integrated project delivery.[7]

Heller uses the red/blue metaphor in its 2008 popular culture context—as shorthand for conservative or liberal political views and social values. Although Heller admits that using the red/blue divide to separate human activities is imprecise, she suggests that it accurately describes differences in business models and approach. "Red business success is defined by profit margins, revenue growth, productivity, stock valuation, and other financial metrics. Blue businesses have a service imperative that dominates their activities, and they tend to measure success by human, social, and cultural accomplishments in addition to money."[8]

Heller generalizes that in the construction industry, owners are red, whether they are university administrators or private developers. Architects, engineers, and surprisingly, building contractors are classified by Heller as blue. She describes the decentralization and local control of the construction industry, which she calls an "immense aggregation of cottage industries," and contrasts that to the centralized management of corporate entities. Heller contends that architects are failing to adjust to a new business reality in which owners are demanding more efficient performance. "In the blue world of architectural practice, normalization or standardization is anathema. Efficiency, while desirable, is not essential, nor is it measured."[9]

Another Point of View

While it may be true that there are cultural differences between owners and architects, some would argue that work processes are not red or blue. Most businesses, red, blue, or purple, would say that they want efficient work processes and cost consciousness. Most architectural firms are extremely concerned with the effectiveness of their operations. Differences in values create different definitions of what is efficient and effective, and what constitutes achievement.

Standardization and central control, the corporate model, can result in efficiency to be sure, but there is a risk of losing sensitivity to critical regionalism. Local control of the building process exists because of the differences in local climate, materials, construction methods, and community values. Designs that respond to local considerations generally work best for the users, the community, and the environment and, as a result, often contribute more to financial returns over time. Thinking only of short-term profitability can result in blind spots to other factors that play a role in the long-term health of an enterprise.

Sustainable Economics Applied

Owners who do not shift their thinking risk ending up like the whaling industry of nineteenth-century New England as described by Andrew Savitz and Karl Weber in their book, *The Triple Bottom Line.*[10] After aggressively killing whales for decades and reaping steady profits from the efficiency of their work, the natural capital the whalers depended upon (the whale) was wholly depleted. The whaling industry ceased to be viable as a result. Owners who ignore the health of the community and the environment in which they build may be heading in the same direction.

No one denies that return on investment is important and critical to both those who employ architects and to architects themselves. However, an argument that places financial considerations above human, social, and cultural considerations frames the world as if these were somehow adversarial concepts. Sustainable economics shows that "red and blue" goals are actually compatible, especially if you consider long-term returns and include the cost of natural capital in the calculation. All businesses depend on natural capital, yet many use the natural environment as if it is an infinite supplier of resources and a limitless place to dump waste. Focusing on short-term profitability merely puts off the long-term costs of natural capital, adding a high level of risk to future financial success.

Construction Industry Impact

The impact that the construction industry has on the Gross Domestic Product is substantial but is no more significant than other impacts of this $1.2 trillion industry. Thomas Fisher outlines these other impacts in his book *Architectural Design and Ethics: Tools for Survival*, "[The construction industry consumes] sixteen percent of the available fresh water annually, forty percent of the world's total energy use, about one third of the emissions of heat-trapping carbon dioxide from fossil fuel burning, two-fifths of the acid rain causing sulphur-dioxide and nitrogen-oxides, and forty percent of the total materials flow in the global economy. At the same time, construction waste constitutes between one quarter and one third of all U.S. landfills."[11]

Given these conditions, all stakeholders in the construction industry, including owners, must see beyond short-term gain. The efficiencies realized through the use of Building Information Modeling (BIM) and Integrated Project Delivery can provide time and money to improve design solutions, sustainable building performance, and project delivery processes. This dividend of integrated technology is critical to a future of zero-emissions buildings that are in themselves energy independent.

Turn Red Business Blue

While architects may need to take on leadership in IPD, it is important not to confuse leadership and management, which involve similar but different skill sets. Leaders set direction, managers plan budgets and schedules; leaders motivate and inspire, managers control and problem-solve. While management is an important subset within the skills of most architects, leadership is a core competency. Creative, visionary, and integrative thinking is nurtured in architecture school and at all levels of practice. Management is learned on the job and is often a secondary interest. While many would agree that architects could benefit from more training in management, and more attention to work processes, it is unlikely that managing the business processes of design and construction would leverage the strengths of the profession.

Instead of the blue design and construction industry turning red, what if the owners turned blue? If architects do assume the lead as integrated practice develops, it will likely be because the economic bottom line is seen in a much wider context, including the ability of economies to be sustained. The contributions of architects in reshaping the construction industry will be about assuming leadership in doing what is right for people and the planet, along with the usual concern for economic outcomes.

As explained by Thomas Fisher, "The challenge that designers face, when engaging in a value-creating process, is dealing with clients, communities, and consumers who sometimes do not understand this way of working and who see creative exploration as a waste of time and money. But here is where the ethical turn in design can reposition the field in eyes of many people. . . . [The old tension] between the client who just wants something that works and the designer who also wants something that inspires takes on a new twist when what most inspires us is also what works best for the greatest number of those affected by it. . . . Both [client and designer] want to accomplish the most with the least, and achieve the greatest benefit at the lowest cost. The ethical turn in design provides one way of linking what has, for too long, been viewed as opposing positions."[12]

FINAL WORDS

For owners of small design firms, the opportunity to create a practice that reflects personal values, preferences, and passions is unlimited, as are the opportunities to contribute to local communities and to the built environment around the world. Understanding trends and patterns at a global, organizational, and personal level will give small firm leaders insight into how to craft meaningful strategy. Strategic thinking and action, which sometimes involves profound change, can help firm leaders to achieve their professional goals, large and small. Understanding trends and patterns, both macro and micro, is the key to success in the unpredictable and chaotic environments in which small design firms operate.

Small design firm practitioners have enormous potential to positively influence the quality of their own lives, the lives of their employees, and the quality of life for people in their communities, and around the globe. The tools, case studies, and knowledge compiled in this book are an invitation to participate in these affirmative efforts.

ENDNOTES

1. Amory Lovins, Hunter Lovins, and Paul Hawkins, "A Road Map for Natural Capitalism," *Harvard Business Review*, Harvard Business School Publishing, Cambridge, MA, 2007.
2. William McDonough and Michael Braungart, *Cradle to Cradle*, North Point Press, NY, 2002.

3. Amory Lovins, Hunter Lovins, and Paul Hawkins, "A Road Map for Natural Capitalism," *Harvard Business Review*, Harvard Business School Publishing, Cambridge, MA, 2007.

4. Andrew Savitz and Karl Weber, *The Triple Bottom Line: How Today's Best-Run Companies Are Achieving Economic, Social, and Environmental Success*, John Wiley & Sons, Inc., Hoboken, NJ, 2006.

5. American Institute of Architects, "The AIA Code of Ethics and Professional Conduct" **www.aia.org/SiteObjects/files/bookmark_ethics_final.pdf.**

6. Society of Human Resource Management: **http://shrm.org.**

7. Barbara Golter Heller, "Red Business Blue Business," *DesignIntelligence*, Greenway Communications, Norcross, GA, 2008.

8. Ibid.

9. Ibid.

10. Andrew Savitz and Karl Weber, *The Triple Bottom Line: How Today's Best-Run Companies Are Achieving Economic, Social, and Environmental Success*, John Wiley & Sons, Inc., Hoboken, NJ, 2006.

11. Thomas Fisher, *Architectural Design and Ethics: Tools for Survival*, Architectural Press, Burlington, MA, 2008.

12. Ibid.

INDEX